HARCOURT SCIENCE
ASSESSMENT GUIDE

Harcourt School Publishers

Orlando • Boston • Dallas • Chicago • San Diego

www.harcourtschool.com

Copyright © by Harcourt, Inc.

All rights reserved. No part of this publication may be reproduced or transmitted in any form or by any means, electronic or mechanical, including photocopy, recording, or any information storage and retrieval system, without permission in writing from the publisher.

Permission is hereby granted to individual teachers using the corresponding student's textbook or kit as the major vehicle for regular classroom instruction to photocopy Copying Masters from this publication in classroom quantities for instructional use and not for resale. Requests for information on other matters regarding duplication of this work should be addressed to School Permissions and Copyrights, Harcourt, Inc., 6277 Sea Harbor Drive, Orlando, Florida 32887-6777. Fax: 407-345-2418.

HARCOURT and the Harcourt Logo are trademarks of Harcourt, Inc., registered in the United States of America and/or other jurisdictions.

Printed in the United States of America

ISBN 0-15-323709-0

2 3 4 5 6 7 8 9 10 054 2004 2003 2002

Contents

Overview	AGv
Assessment Components	AGvi
Formal Assessment	AGvii
Test-Taking Tips	AGviii
Performance Assessment	AGix
Scoring a Performance Task	AGxi
Classroom Observation	AGxii
Observation Checklist	AGxiv
Using Student Self-Assessment	AGxv
Self-Assessment—Investigate	AGxvi
Self-Assessment—Learn About	AGxvii
Experiment/Project Evaluation Checklist	AGxviii
Experiment/Project Summary Sheet	AGxix
Portfolio Assessment	AGxx
Science Experiences Record	AGxxii
Guide to My Science Portfolio	AGxxiii
Portfolio Evaluation Checklist	AGxxiv

UNIT A — Processes of Living Things

Chapter 1—From Single Cells to Body Systems	AG1
Performance Task	AG6
Chapter 2—Classifying Living Things	AG8
Performance Task	AG13
Chapter 3—Animal Growth and Heredity	AG15
Performance Task	AG20
Chapter 4—Plants and Their Adaptations	AG22
Performance Task	AG27
Unit A Test	AG29

UNIT B — Systems and Interactions in Nature

Chapter 1—Cycles in Nature	AG33
Performance Task	AG38
Chapter 2—Living Things Interact	AG40
Performance Task	AG45
Chapter 3—Biomes	AG47
Performance Task	AG52
Chapter 4—Protecting and Preserving Ecosystems	AG54
Performance Task	AG59
Unit B Test	AG61

UNIT C — Processes That Change the Earth

Chapter 1—Changes to Earth's Surface AG65
Performance Task AG70
Chapter 2—Rocks and Minerals AG72
Performance Task AG76
Chapter 3—Weather and Climate AG78
Performance Task AG83
Chapter 4—Exploring the Oceans AG85
Performance Task AG90
Unit C Test AG92

UNIT D — The Solar System and Beyond

Chapter 1—Earth, Moon, and Beyond AG96
Performance Task AG101
Chapter 2—The Sun and Other Stars AG103
Performance Task AG108
Unit D Test AG110

UNIT E — Building Blocks of Matter

Chapter 1—Matter and Its Properties AG114
Performance Task AG119
Chapter 2—Atoms and Elements AG121
Performance Task AG126
Unit E Test AG128

UNIT F — Motion and Energy

Chapter 1—Forces AG132
Performance Task AG137
Chapter 2—Motion AG139
Performance Task AG144
Chapter 3—Forms of Energy AG146
Performance Task AG151
Chapter 4—How People Use Energy AG153
Performance Task AG158
Unit F Test AG160

Answer Key AG164–AG195

Overview

In *Harcourt Science,* the Assessment Program, like the instruction, is student-centered. By allowing all learners to show what they know and can do, the program provides you with ongoing information about each student's understanding of science. Equally important, the Assessment Program involves the student in self-evaluation, offering you strategies for helping students evaluate their own growth.

The *Harcourt Science* Assessment Program is based on the Assessment Model in the chart below. The model's framework shows the multidimensional aspect of the program, with five kinds of assessment, supported by both teacher-based and student-based assessment tools.

The teacher-based strand, the left column in the model, involves assessments in which the teacher evaluates a student product as evidence of the student's understanding of chapter content and of his or her ability to think critically about it. The teacher-based strand consists of two components: Formal Assessment and Performance Assessment.

The student-based strand, the right column in the model, involves assessments that invite the student to become a partner in the assessment process. These student-based assessments encourage students to reflect on and evaluate their own efforts. The student-based strand also consists of two components: Student Self-Assessment and Portfolio Assessment.

There is a fifth component in the *Harcourt Science* assessment program—Ongoing Assessment, which involves classroom observation and informal evaluation of students' growth in science knowledge and process skills. This essential component is listed in the center of the Assessment Model because it is the "glue" that binds together all the other types of assessment.

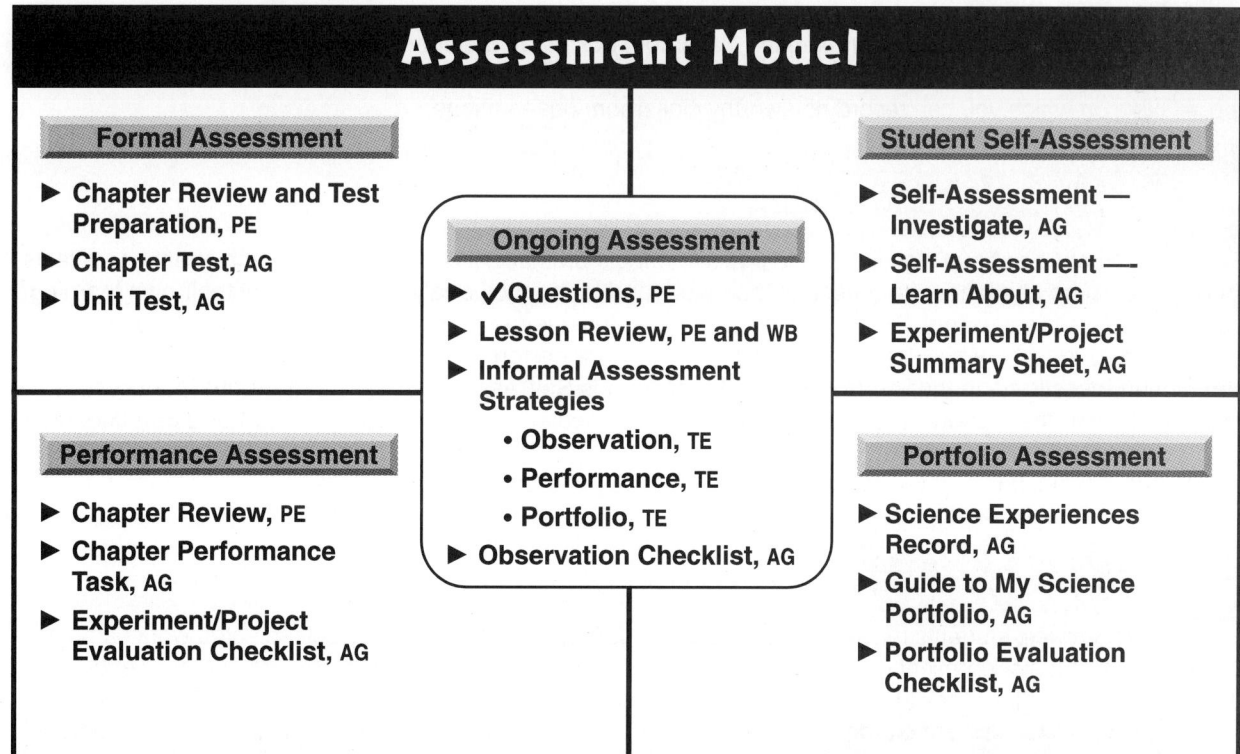

(**Key:** PE=Pupil Edition; TE=Teacher's Edition; AG=Assessment Guide; WB=Workbook)

Assessment Components

Formal Assessment

Research into the learning process has shown the positive effects of periodic review. To help you reinforce and assess mastery of chapter objectives, *Harcourt Science* includes both reviews and tests. You will find the Chapter Review and Test Preparation in the pupil book and the Chapter Test and Unit Test in this **Assessment Guide.** Answers to all assessments, including sample responses to open-ended items, are provided.

Performance Assessment

Science literacy involves not only what students know but also how they think and how they do things. Performance tasks provide evidence of students' ability to use science process skills and critical thinking skills to complete an authentic problem-solving task. A performance task is included in each chapter review. Another follows each Chapter Test in this **Assessment Guide**. Each includes teacher directions and a scoring rubric. Also in this booklet, you will find the Experiment/Project Evaluation Checklist (p. AGxviii), for evaluating unit experiments and projects.

Ongoing Assessment

Opportunities abound for observing and evaluating student growth during regular classroom instruction in science. *Harcourt Science* supports this informal, ongoing assessment in several ways: Within each lesson in the **Pupil Edition** (grades 3–6), there are boldface ✔ questions at the end of sections to help you assess students' immediate recall of information. Then, at the end of each lesson, there is a Lesson Review to help you evaluate how well students grasped the concepts taught. The Lesson Review also includes a multiple-choice "test prep" question. In grades 1 and 2, caption questions and Think About It after every lesson are tools for ongoing assessment. Additional material for reviewing the lesson is provided in the **Workbook.**

    The **Teacher's Edition** offers Informal Assessment Strategies. These strategies, which appear at point of use within chapters, give ideas for integrating classroom observation, performance assessment, and portfolio assessment with instruction. Located in this **Assessment Guide** is yet another tool, the Observation Checklist (pp. AGxiv), on which you can record noteworthy classroom observations.

Student Self-Assessment

Self-assessment can have significant and positive effects on student achievement. To achieve these effects, students must be challenged to reflect on their work and to monitor, analyze, and control their own learning. Located in this **Assessment Guide** are two checklists designed to do just that. One is Self-Assessment—Investigate (p. AGxvi), which leads students to assess their performance and growth in science skills after completing Investigate in the **Pupil Edition.** The second is Self-Assessment— Learn About (p. AGxvii), a checklist to help the student reflect on instruction in a particular lesson or chapter in *Harcourt Science*. Also in this booklet, following the checklists, you will find the Experiment/Project Summary Sheet (p. AGxix), on which students describe and evaluate their own science projects and experiments.

Portfolio Assessment

In *Harcourt Science*, students may create their own portfolios. The portfolio holds self-selected work samples that the student feels represent gains in his or her understanding of science concepts and use of science processes. The portfolio may also contain a few required or teacher-selected papers. Support materials are included in this **Assessment Guide** (pp. AGxx–AGxxiv) to assist you and your students in developing portfolios and in using them to evaluate growth in science skills.

Formal Assessment

Formal assessment is an essential part of any comprehensive assessment program because it provides an objective measure of student achievement. This traditional form of assessment typically consists of reviews and tests that assess how well students understand, communicate, and apply what they have learned. This is the type of assessment that is typically used in state and local standardized tests in science.

Formal Assessment in *Harcourt Science*

Formal assessment in the *Harcourt Science* program includes the following measures: Chapter Review in **Pupil Edition** grades 1 and 2; Chapter Review and Test Preparation in **Pupil Edition** grades 3–6; and Chapter and Unit Assessments in this **Assessment Guide.** The purpose of the review is to assess and reinforce not only chapter concepts and science skills but also students' test-taking skills. The purpose of the Chapter and Unit Assessments is, as with other formal assessments, to provide an objective measure of student performance. Answers to chapter reviews, including sample responses to open-ended items, are located in the Teacher's Edition, while answers to chapter and unit tests are located in the Answer Key in this booklet.

Types of Review and Test Items

Students can be overwhelmed by the amount of information on a test and uneasy about how to answer different types of test questions about this information. The Chapter Review and Test Preparation is designed to help familiarize students with the various item formats they may encounter: *multiple-choice items* (with a question stem; sentence fragment; graph, table, map, model, or picture; or using negatives such as *not, least,* and so on), *open-ended items* (which require the student to write a short answer, to record data, or to order items), and *scenarios,* in which the student is asked to respond to several items in either a multiple-choice or open-ended format.

Test-Taking Tips

Harcourt Science offers test-taking tips—aimed at improving student performance on formal assessment—in the Teacher's Edition. The section titled Test Prep—Test-Taking Tips spells out what students can do to analyze and interpret multiple-choice or open-ended types of questions. Each tip suggests a strategy that students can use to help them come up with the correct answer to an item. Included in the strategies are tips to help students

- focus on the question.
- understand unfamiliar words.
- identify key information.
- analyze and interpret graphs, charts, and tables.
- eliminate incorrect answer choices.
- find the correct answer.
- mark the correct answer.

The tips include the following suggestions:

- Scan the entire test first before answering any questions.
- Read the directions slowly and carefully before you begin a section.
- Begin with the easiest questions or most familiar material.
- Read the question and *all* answer options before selecting an answer.
- Watch out for key words such as *not, least,* and so on.
- Double-check answers to catch and correct errors.
- Erase all mistakes completely and write corrections neatly.

Test Preparation

Students perform better on formal assessments when they are well prepared for the testing situation. Here are some things you can do before a test to help your students do their best work.

- Explain the nature of the test to students.
- Suggest that they review the questions at the end of the lessons and the chapter.
- Remind students to get a good night's sleep before the test.
- Discuss why they should eat a balanced meal beforehand.
- Encourage students to relax while they take the test.

Performance Assessment

Teachers today have come to realize that the multiple-choice format of traditional tests, while useful and efficient, cannot provide a complete picture of students' growth in science. Standardized tests may show what students know, but they are not designed to show how they *think and do things*—an essential aspect of science literacy. Performance assessment, along with other types of assessments, can supply the missing information and help balance your assessment program.

An important feature of performance assessment is that it involves a hands-on activity to solve a situational problem. An advantage of this type of assessment is that students often find it more enjoyable than the traditional paper-and-pencil test. Another advantage is that it models good instruction: students are assessed as they learn and learn as they are assessed.

Performance Assessment in *Harcourt Science*

The performance task, science project, unit experiment, and other hands-on science activities provide good opportunities for performance assessment. The performance task is particularly useful because it provides insights into the student's ability to apply key science process skills and concepts taught in the chapter.

At grades 3–6, *Harcourt Science* provides performance assessment in the Chapter Review and Test Preparation feature in the pupil book and in the Chapter Test in this **Assessment Guide**. In the review at grades 1 and 2, the performance assessment is the last item of the Chapter Review; in the test, it is a performance task. The Experiment/Project Evaluation Checklist (p. AGxviii) is a measure you can use to evaluate unit experiments and projects.

Administering Performance Tasks

Unlike traditional assessment tools, performance assessment does not provide standardized directions for its administration or impose specific time limits on students, although a time frame is suggested as a guideline. The suggestions that follow may help you define your role in this assessment.

▶ *Be prepared.*

A few days before students begin the task, read the Teacher's Directions and gather the materials needed.

▶ *Be clear.*

Explain the directions for the task; rephrase them as needed. Also, explain how students' performance will be evaluated. Present the rubric you plan to use and explain the performance indicators in language your students understand.

▶ *Be encouraging.*

Your role in administering the assessments should be that of a coach—motivating, guiding, and encouraging students to produce their best work.

▶ *Be supportive.*

You may assist students who need help. The amount of assistance needed will depend on the needs and abilities of individual students.

▶ *Be flexible.*

All students need not proceed through the performance task at the same rate and in the same manner. Allow them adequate time to do their best work.

▶ *Involve students in evaluation.*

Invite students to join you as partners in the evaluation process, particularly in development or modification of the rubric.

Rubrics for Assessing Performance

A well-written rubric can help you score students' work accurately and fairly. Moreover, it gives students a better idea of what qualities their work should exhibit *before* they begin a task.

Each performance task in the program has its own rubric. The rubric lists performance indicators, which are brief statements of what to look for in assessing the skills and understandings that the task addresses. A sample rubric follows.

Scoring Rubric

Performance Indicators

_____ Assembles the kite successfully.

_____ Carries out the experiment daily.

_____ Records results accurately.

_____ Makes an accurate chart and uses it to report the strength of wind observed each day.

Performance Indicators

| 3 | 2 | 1 | 0 |

Scoring a Performance Task

The scoring system used for program performance tasks is a 4-point scale (3-2-1-0) that is compatible with those used by many state assessment programs. You may wish to modify the rubrics as a 3- or 5-point scale, as your individual needs and circumstances require. To determine a student's score on a performance task, review the indicators checked on the rubric and then select the score that best represents the student's overall performance on the task.

4-Point Scale			
Excellent Achievement	Adequate Achievement	Limited Achievement	Little or No Achievement
3	2	1	0

How to Convert a Rubric Score into a Grade

If, for grading purposes, you want to record a letter or numerical grade rather than a holistic score for the student's performance on a task, you can use the following conversion table:

Holistic Score	Letter Grade	Numerical Grade
3	A	90–100
2	B	80–89
1	C	70–79
0	D–F	69 or below

Developing Your Own Rubric

From time to time, you may want to either develop your own rubric or work together with your students to create one. Research has shown that significantly improved performance can result from student participation in the construction of rubrics.

Developing a rubric for a performance task involves three basic steps: (1) Identify the process skills taught in the chapter that students must perform to complete the task successfully and identify what understanding of content is also required. (2) Determine which skill/understanding is involved in each step. (3) Decide what you will look for to confirm that the student has acquired each skill and understanding you identified.

Classroom Observation

"Kid watching" is a natural part of teaching and an important part of evaluation. The purpose of classroom observation in assessment is to gather and record information that can lead to improved instruction. In this booklet, you will find an Observation Checklist (p. AGxiv) on which you can record noteworthy observations of students' ability to use science process skills.

Using the Observation Checklist

▶ *Identify the skills you will observe.*
Find out which science process skills are introduced and reinforced in the chapter.

▶ *Focus on only a few students at a time.*
You will find this more effective than trying to observe the entire class at once.

▶ *Look for a pattern.*
It is important to observe the student's strengths and weaknesses over a period of time to determine whether a pattern exists.

▶ *Plan how and when to record observations.*
Decide whether to
- record observations immediately on the checklist as you move about the room or
- make jottings or mental notes of observations and record them later.

▶ *Don't agonize over the ratings.*
Students who stand out as particularly strong will clearly merit a rating of 3 ("Outstanding"). Others may clearly earn a rating of 1 ("Needs Improvement"). This doesn't mean, however, that a 2 ("Satisfactory") is automatically the appropriate rating for the rest of the class. For example, you may not have had sufficient opportunity to observe a student demonstrate certain skills. The checklist cells for these skills should remain blank under the student's name until you have observed him or her perform the skills.

▶ *Review your checklist periodically and ask yourself questions such as:*

What are the student's strongest/weakest attributes?

In what ways has the student shown growth?

In what areas does the class as a whole show strength/weakness?

What kinds of activities would encourage growth?

Do I need to allot more time to classroom observation?

▶ **Use the data you collect.**

Refer to your classroom observation checklists when you plan lessons, form groups, assign grades, and confer with students and family members.

Date _____

Observation Checklist

Rating Scale

- **3** Outstanding
- **2** Satisfactory
- **1** Needs Improvement
- ☐ Not Enough Opportunity to Observe

Names of Students

Science Process Skills										
Observe										
Compare										
Classify/Order										
Gather, Record, Display, or Interpret Data										
Use Numbers										
Communicate										
Plan and Conduct Simple Investigations										
Measure										
Predict										
Infer										
Draw Conclusions										
Use Time/Space Relationships										
Hypothesize										
Formulate or Use Models										
Identify and Control Variables										
Experiment										

Using Student Self-Assessment

Researchers have evidence that self-evaluation and the reflection it involves can have positive effects on students' learning. To achieve these effects, students must be challenged to reflect on their work and to monitor, analyze, and control their own learning—beginning in the earliest grades.

Frequent opportunities for students to evaluate their performance builds the skills and confidence they need for effective self-assessment. A trusting relationship between the student and the teacher is also essential. Students must be assured that honest responses can have only a positive effect on the teacher's view of them, and that they will not be used to determine grades.

Student Self-Assessment in *Harcourt Science*

The assessment program offers three self-assessment measures, which are located in this booklet. The first one is Self-Assessment—Investigate: a form that invites students to reflect on how they felt about, and what they learned from, Investigate, a hands-on investigation at the beginning of each lesson. The second measure is Self-Assessment—Learn About: a form that leads students to reflect on and evaluate what they learned from reading and instruction in Learn About at either the lesson or chapter level. The third is the Experiment/Project Summary Sheet—a form to help students describe and evaluate their unit experiments and projects.

Using Self-Assessment Forms

▶ *Explain the directions.*
Discuss the forms and how to complete them.

▶ *Encourage honest responses.*
Be sure to tell students that there are no "right" responses to the items.

▶ *Model the process.*
One way to foster candid responses is to model the process yourself, including at least one response that is not positive. Discuss reasons for your responses.

▶ *Be open to variations in students' responses.*
Negative responses should not be viewed as indicating weaknesses. Rather they confirm that you did a good job of communicating the importance of honesty in self-assessment.

▶ *Discuss responses with students.*
You may wish to clarify students' responses in conferences with them and in family conferences. Invite both students and family members to help you plan activities for school and home that will motivate and support their growth in science.

Name _____
Date _____
Investigate _____

Self-Assessment— Investigate

Think It Over

Decide whether you agree or disagree with each statement below. Circle the word that tells what you think. If you are not sure, circle the question mark.

1. I followed the directions for Investigate. Agree ? Disagree

2. I used materials and tools correctly. Agree ? Disagree

3. I followed science safety rules. Agree ? Disagree

4. I recorded data accurately. Agree ? Disagree

5. I solved problems without the teacher's help. Agree ? Disagree

6. I completed the investigation. Agree ? Disagree

Complete each sentence.

7. The science process skill that I learned or practiced in Investigate was _____.

8. I used this skill in the investigation to _____.

9. I also used these science skills: _____

10. This is what I learned from the investigation: _____

AG xvi **Assessment Guide**   Grade 5

Name _____
Date _____
Lesson or Chapter _____

Self-Assessment—Learn About

My Thoughts Exactly!

Decide whether you agree or disagree with each statement below. Circle the word that tells what you think. If you are not sure, circle the question mark.

1. The pictures and captions in the book helped me understand what I was reading.　　Agree　?　Disagree

2. When I didn't understand, I asked questions.　　Agree　?　Disagree

3. I learned a lot from class discussions.　　Agree　?　Disagree

4. I used the ✓ questions and the review questions to test my understanding.　　Agree　?　Disagree

5. I understand the new science words.　　Agree　?　Disagree

6. I have a good understanding of the topic.　　Agree　?　Disagree

7. I think I am doing well in science.　　Agree　?　Disagree

Think about what you learned. Then complete the sentence.

8. Three things I learned about the topic are _____
_____
_____ .

9. I learned these new science words: _____
_____
_____

Name _____
Date _____

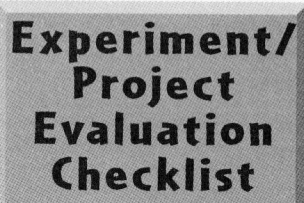
Experiment/Project Evaluation Checklist

Experiment/Project Evaluation

Aspects of Science Literacy	Evidence of Growth
1. **Understands science concepts** *(Animals, Plants; Earth's Land, Air, Water, Space; Weather; Matter, Motion, Energy)*	_____ _____ _____
2. **Uses science process skills** *(observes, compares, classifies, gathers/interprets data, communicates, measures, experiments, infers, predicts, draws conclusions)*	_____ _____ _____ _____ _____
3. **Thinks critically** *(analyzes, synthesizes, evaluates, applies ideas effectively, solves problems)*	_____ _____ _____
4. **Displays traits/attitudes of a scientist** *(is curious, questioning, persistent, precise, creative, enthusiastic; uses science materials carefully; is concerned for environment)*	_____ _____ _____ _____ _____

Summary Evaluation/Teacher Comments: _____
_____
_____
_____
_____

AG xviii Assessment Guide   Grade 5

Name _____

Date _____

Experiment/ Project Summary Sheet

You can tell about your science project or experiment by completing the following sentences.

My Unit Experiment/Project

1. My experiment/project was about _____
_____
_____.

2. I worked on this experiment/project with _____
_____
_____.

3. I gathered information from these sources: _____
_____
_____.

4. The most important thing I learned from doing this experiment/project is _____
_____
_____.

5. I think I did a (an) _____ job on my experiment/project because
_____
_____.

6. I'd also like to tell you _____
_____
_____
_____
_____.

Grade 5

Assessment Guide AG xix

Portfolio Assessment

A portfolio is a showcase for student work, a place where many types of assignments, projects, reports, and writings can be collected. The work samples in the collection provide "snapshots" of the student's efforts over time, and taken together they reveal the student's growth, attitudes, and understanding better than any other type of assessment. However, portfolios are not ends in themselves. Their value comes from creating them, discussing them, and using them to improve learning.

The purpose of using portfolios in science is threefold:

▶ *To give the student a voice in the assessment process.*

▶ *To foster reflection, self-monitoring, and self-evaluation.*

▶ *To provide a comprehensive picture of a student's progress.*

Portfolio Assessment in *Harcourt Science*

In *Harcourt Science,* students create portfolio collections of their work. The collection may include a few required papers, such as the Chapter Test, Chapter Performance Task, and Experiment/Project Evaluation.

From time to time, consider including other measures (Science Experiences Record, Experiment/Project Summary Sheet, and Student Self-Assessment Checklists). The Science Experiences Record, for example, can reveal insights about student interests, ideas, and out-of-school experiences (museum visits, nature walks, outside readings, and so on) that otherwise you might not know about. Materials to help you and your students build portfolios and use them for evaluation are included in the pages that follow.

Using Portfolio Assessment

▶ *Explain the portfolio and its use.*
Describe how people in many fields use portfolios to present samples of their work when they are applying for a job. Tell students that they can create their own portfolio to show what they have learned, what skills they have acquired, and how they think they are doing in science.

▶ *Decide what standard pieces should be included.*
Engage students in identifying a few standard, or "required," work samples that each student should include in his or her portfolio, and discuss reasons for including them. The student's recording sheet for the Chapter Performance Task, for example, might be a standard sample in the portfolios because it shows students' ability to use science process skills and critical thinking skills to solve a problem. Together with your class, decide on the required work samples that everyone's portfolio will include.

▶ *Discuss student-selected work samples.*
Point out that the best work to select is not necessarily the longest or the neatest. Rather, it is work the student believes will best demonstrate his or her growth in science understanding and skills.

▶ *Establish a basic plan.*
Decide about how many work samples will be included in the portfolio and when they should be selected. Ask students to list on Guide to My Science Portfolio (p. AG xxiii) each sample they select and to explain why they selected it.

▶ *Tell students how you will evaluate their portfolios.*
Use a blank Portfolio Evaluation sheet to explain how you will evaluate the contents of a portfolio.

▶ *Use the portfolio.*
Use the portfolio as a handy reference tool in determining students' science grades and in holding conferences with them and family members. You may wish to send the portfolio home for family members to review.

Name _____ Date _____

Science Experiences Record

Date	What I Did	What I Thought or Learned

GUIDE TO MY Science Portfolio

Name _____ Date _____

What Is in My Portfolio	Why I Chose It
1.	
2.	
3.	
4.	
5.	
6.	
7.	

I organized my Science Portfolio this way because _____
_____
_____
_____
_____

Grade 5

Assessment Guide AG xxiii

Student's Name _____

Date _____

Portfolio Evaluation Checklist

Portfolio Evaluation

Aspects of Science Literacy	Evidence of Growth
1. **Understands science concepts** *(Animals, Plants; Earth's Land, Air, Water, Space; Weather; Matter, Motion, Energy)*	_____ _____ _____ _____
2. **Uses science process skills** *(observes, compares, classifies, gathers/interprets data, communicates, measures, experiments, infers, predicts, draws conclusions)*	_____ _____ _____ _____ _____
3. **Thinks critically** *(analyzes, synthesizes, evaluates, applies ideas effectively, solves problems)*	_____ _____ _____ _____
4. **Displays traits/attitudes of a scientist** *(is curious, questioning, persistent, precise, creative, enthusiastic; uses science materials carefully; is concerned for environment)*	_____ _____ _____ _____ _____

Summary of Portfolio Assessment

For This Review			Since Last Review		
Excellent	Good	Fair	Improving	About the Same	Not as Good

AG xxiv **Assessment Guide**

Grade 5

Name _____
Date _____

From Single Cells to Body Systems

Part 1 Vocabulary

Match each term in Column B with its meaning in Column A.

Column A

____ 1. Thin cell covering that holds the parts of the cell together

____ 2. Movement of water and dissolved materials through the cell membrane

____ 3. Tissues that work together

____ 4. Organelle that controls a cell's activities

____ 5. Jellylike substance that contains many chemicals to keep a cell functioning

____ 6. Organs that work together to perform a function

____ 7. Cells that work together to perform a specific function

____ 8. Process by which particles of a substance move from an area where there are many particles of the substance to an area where there are fewer particles of the substance

____ 9. Basic unit of structure and function of all living things

Column B

A cell

B cell membrane

C nucleus

D cytoplasm

E diffusion

F osmosis

G tissue

H organ

I system

Unit A • Chapter 1   (page 1 of 5)   Assessment Guide   AG 1

Name _____

Use the letters of the terms in the Word Bank to complete the sentences.

A alveoli	C receptors	E bone marrow	G neurons	I capillaries
B ligaments	D tendons	F nephrons	H joints	J villi

The circulatory system transports blood through various-sized tubes called arteries, veins, and **10.** ___. The smallest of these tubes are blood vessels so tiny that blood cells have to move through them in single file. In the respiratory system, air travels into and out of the lungs through tubes. The smallest tubes end in tiny sacs called **11.** ___, which are surrounded by capillaries. Nutrients move from the digestive system into the blood by traveling through **12.** ___, tiny tubes sticking out of the wall of the small intestine. In the body's excretory system, urea and water travel from the blood into the kidneys and diffuse into **13.** ___. Bones have a hard outer membrane and a soft center that contains **14.** ___. This soft material is connective tissue that produces red and white blood cells. Bones are attached to each other in places called **15.** ___. Tough bands of tissue called **16.** ___ attach bones to muscles. Other bands of tissue called **17.** ___ attach bones to each other. To move, a muscle must receive a signal from the nervous system. Specialized cells called **18.** ___ transmit and receive nervous-system signals. Some kinds of nerve cells, called **19.** ___, detect conditions in the body's environment.

Part II   Science Concepts and Understanding

Write the letter of the best choice.

___ 20. Which of the following allows water to flow into the roots of plants?
   A cytoplasm
   B mitochondria
   C osmosis
   D vacuoles

Name _____

____ 21. Osmosis is one kind of —
     F active transport   H carrier
     G organelle   J diffusion

____ 22. Plants and animals grow when cells —
     A reproduce   C get rid of wastes
     B release energy   D repair themselves

____ 23. An animal's skin is an example of —
     F connective tissue
     G muscle tissue
     H epithelial tissue
     J nervous tissue

____ 24. Oxygen enters the body through the —
     A digestive system
     B respiratory system
     C circulatory system
     D excretory system

____ 25. Oxygen travels to every cell in the body through the —
     F respiratory system
     G circulatory system
     H digestive system
     J excretory system

____ 26. Which system breaks down food into nutrients?
     A respiratory   C circulatory
     B digestive   D excretory

____ 27. The heart is a —
     F muscle   H cartilage
     G nerve   J synapse

____ 28. Which of the following is a ball-and-socket joint?
     A knee   C hip
     B elbow   D toe

____ 29. The nervous system carries ____ to and from the brain.
     F nutrients   H signals
     G blood   J oxygen

Unit A • Chapter 1   (page 3 of 5)   Assessment Guide   AG 3

Name _____

Use the terms in the Word Bank to label the following diagram.

| nucleus | chromosomes | cell membrane | cell wall |
| chloroplast | vacuole | mitochondria | cytoplasm |

30. _____
31. _____
32. _____
33. _____
34. _____
35. _____
36. _____
37. _____

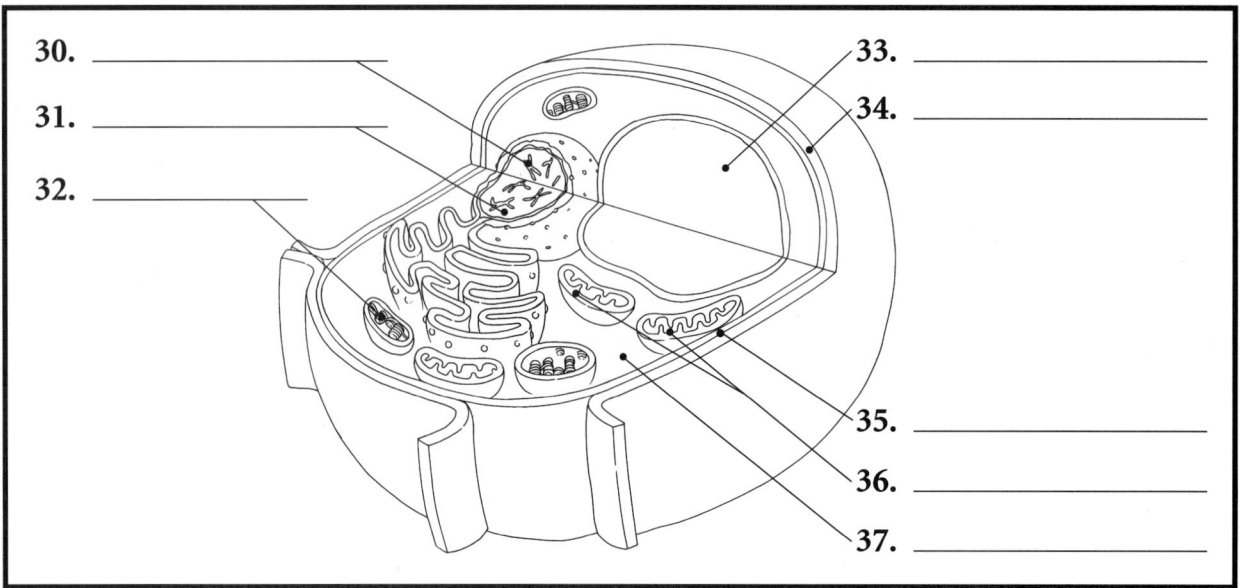

Use the terms in the Word Bank to label the following diagram.

| esophagus | stomach | small intestine | liver | large intestine | pancreas |

38. _____
39. _____
40. _____
41. _____
42. _____
43. _____

Name _____

Part III Critical Thinking

44. Would you expect to find muscle tissue in a plant? Why or why not?

_____

_____

45. What kinds of things does the blood transport? Why are these things important to cells in the body?

_____

_____

46. You can contract your voluntary muscles on purpose. Can you contract your smooth muscles and cardiac muscles on purpose? Why or why not?

_____

_____

Part IV Process Skills Application

47. Compare the organelles in a cell to organs in a human body. How are organelles similar to organs?

_____

_____

48. Hypothesize how your body's receptors keep you safe.

_____

_____

49. If you are observing cells under a microscope, what would lead you to **infer** that the cells are **NOT** animal cells?

_____

_____

Name _____ Date _____

Range of Motion

Materials

paper   pencil

Suppose you are a physical trainer. Your job is to study the movements that a joint makes. Work with a partner to observe the movements of a particular joint.

1. Select a joint to investigate. Find out what movements the joint allows you to make. Record your observations in the following table.

Joint Name	Moves in One Direction	Moves in More Than One Direction	Moves in a Circular Motion	Moves Back and Forth

2. Choose three more joints and repeat Step 1.

3. Compare the results. Look for similarities and differences among the joint movements.

4. Brainstorm some ways in which your life would be different if you could not move the bones in a particular joint.

5. Write a hypothesis about the effect this loss of movement would have on your everyday life. Share your findings with the class.

Teacher's Directions

Range of Motion

Materials paper, pencil, skeleton model (optional)

Time 30 minutes

Suggested Grouping pairs

Science Processes observe, compare, hypothesize

Preparation Hints Have a model or diagram of a skeleton available if possible.

Introduce the Task Ask students to share what they know about the joints in their hands. Ask them to think about how they would use their hands if there were no joints in them. Ask them to pick up a piece of paper or a pen while keeping the joints in their fingers stiff. Tell them they will study and record movements that certain joints make.

Promote Discussion Have students share and compare their findings about different joints with the class. If you have a diagram or model of a skeleton in your classroom, ask students to point out how the bones are attached at the joints. Discuss students' hypotheses about the effects that loss of movement in a joint would have on everyday life.

Scoring Rubric

Performance Indicators

_____ Observes the movements of various joints.

_____ Records observations in a table.

_____ Compares the movements of joints by stating similarities and differences.

_____ Writes a hypothesis about the effects of loss of movement in a particular joint.

Observations and Rubric Score

3　　2　　1　　0

Name _____
Date _____

Classifying Living Things

Part I Vocabulary

Use the letters of the terms in the Word Banks to complete the sentences.

A genus	C classification	E kingdoms	G fungi
B protists	D species	F monerans	

1. ____ is the act of grouping things by using a set of rules. All living things belong to one of five groups called 2. ____ . Living things that have many cells and get food from other living things are 3. ____ . Living things that have one cell with a nucleus are 4. ____ . Those with no nucleus are 5. ____ . A kingdom is the largest group in which living things are classified, a 6. ____ is the smallest, and a 7. ____ is the second smallest.

H birds	K invertebrates	N vascular
I nonvascular	L amphibians	O vertebrates
J reptiles	M fish	P mammals

Within the animal kingdom, there are two main groups. One group, animals that have a backbone, is called 8. ____ . It is divided into several smaller groups. These are 9. ____ , or animals that have hair; 10. ____ , or animals with dry, scaly skin; 11. ____ , or animals that have moist skin with no scales; 12. ____ , or animals with feathers; and 13. ____ , or animals that have hard scales and live in water. 14. ____ are the animals without a backbone. Within the plant kingdom, there are two large groups. Plants that have tubes in their roots, stems, and leaves are 15. ____ . 16. ____ plants do not have tubes and pass water and nutrients directly from cell to cell.

AG 8   Assessment Guide   (page 1 of 5)   Unit A • Chapter 2

Name _____

Part II Science Concepts and Understanding

Use the pictures to answer Questions 17–19. Write *reptile* if the picture shows an example of a reptile and *amphibian* if it shows an example of an amphibian.

17. _____ 18. _____ 19. _____

Use the pictures to answer Questions 20–22. Write *vascular* if the picture shows an example of a vascular plant and *nonvascular* if it shows an example of a nonvascular plant.

20. _____ 21. _____ 22. _____

Write the letter of the best choice.

_____ 23. Which is an example of a mollusk?
   A spider   C snail
   B bear   D lizard

_____ 24. All of the following are fungi EXCEPT —
   F mushrooms   H yeasts
   G algae   J molds

Unit A • Chapter 2   (page 2 of 5)   Assessment Guide   AG 9

Name _____

_____ 25. Where would nonvascular plants most likely be found?
   A under a cactus
   B along a riverbed
   C on the sea floor
   D on a sunny prairie

_____ 26. Which of the following are one-celled organisms with no nucleus?
   F monerans
   G fungi
   H protists
   J mollusks

_____ 27. In what living things are sharp senses and large brains usually found?
   A invertebrates
   B vascular plants
   C nonvascular plants
   D vertebrates

_____ 28. Which are examples of monerans?
   F mushrooms
   G algae
   H ferns
   J bacteria

_____ 29. Which of these are nonvascular plants?
   A flowers   C mosses
   B grasses   D trees

_____ 30. Which animal species are **NOT** vertebrates?
   F spiders   H whales
   G zebras   J lizards

_____ 31. Which is an invertebrate?
   A shark   C monkey
   B turtle   D clam

Name _____

_____ 32. Any plant that has flowers or cones is a —
   F hardwood   H vascular plant
   G protist   J nonvascular plant

_____ 33. Which animal is an amphibian?
   A frog   C fish
   B sea gull   D whale

Part III   Critical Thinking

34. How would understanding the science of living things be more difficult if they weren't classified?

_____

_____

_____

35. Why are vascular plants generally taller than nonvascular plants?

_____

_____

_____

36. What would scientists do if they found an animal that didn't fit into any kingdom?

_____

_____

37. Why might a break in the main stem of a plant cause it to die?

_____

_____

_____

_____

Name _____

Part IV Process Skills Application

Use the pictures to answer Question 38. Then give the reason for your choice.

     Giraffe   **Zebra**   **Koala**   **Panther**

38. Which animal do you **infer** is best at hunting? What do you **observe** about this animal that leads you to infer that?

   _____

   _____

   _____

39. Which would make a better **model** for the protective covering of a beetle—a peanut shell or a bottle cap? Why?

   _____

   _____

   _____

40. **Classify** a monkey by naming the kingdom and two other groups to which it belongs.

   Kingdom: _____

   Other groups: _____

41. **Compare** a snake and a worm. How are they alike? How are they different?

   Alike: _____

   Different: _____

   _____

Name _____ Date _____

Animal Kingdom Picture Game

PERFORMANCE TASK

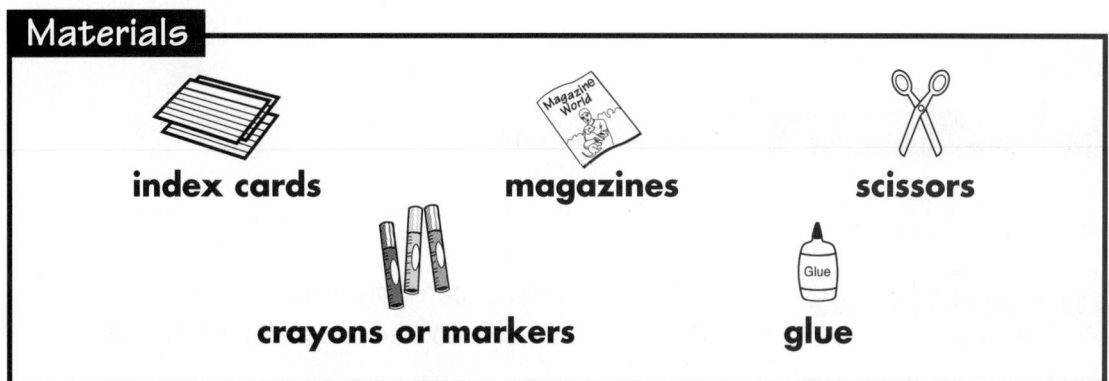

Materials
- index cards
- magazines
- scissors
- crayons or markers
- glue

Invent a game in which players classify living things into five kingdoms. You will need to make picture cards and a set of directions for playing the game. Test your game by playing it with a partner.

Mammals
Clues:
- has fur
- born live
- drinks milk from mother

Reptiles
Clues:
-
-

Amphibians
Clues:
-
-
-

Unit A • Chapter 2

Assessment Guide   AG 13

Teacher's Directions

Animal Kingdom Picture Game

PERFORMANCE TASK

Materials — Performance Task sheets, index cards, magazines, scissors, crayons or markers, glue

Time — 30 minutes

Suggested Grouping — individuals or pairs

Science Processes — communicate, compare, infer, make models

Preparation Hints — Count out 20 index cards for each student ahead of time. You may wish to cut construction paper to use as cards for the game.

Introduce the Task — Review different characteristics of groups of animals. Explain to students that they will be inventing games they can use to classify animals into kingdoms. Tell them they will prepare pictures and corresponding clues. You may wish to suggest matching, trivia, or other types of games.

Promote Discussion — Have students play one another's games. Ask them to compare their games. Encourage them to give details when they describe how their games are different or similar.

Scoring Rubric

Performance Indicators

____ Makes more than one picture card for each of the five kingdoms (animals, plants, fungi, protists, monerans).

____ Writes more than one clue card for each of the five kingdoms, listing important characteristics.

____ Writes clear game directions for others to follow.

____ Tests game by playing it at least one time with a partner.

Observations and Rubric Score

| 3 | 2 | 1 | 0 |

Name _____
Date _____

Animal Growth and Heredity

Part 1   Vocabulary

Use the letters of the terms in the Word Banks to complete the sentences.

| A mitosis | C asexual reproduction | E life cycle | G sexual reproduction |
| B chromosomes | D direct development | F meiosis | H metamorphosis |

Many primitive organisms require only one parent to produce offspring. This is known as **1.** ____. Yeast is an example. It produces offspring by budding. More complex organisms produce offspring through **2.** ____. In this process, two parents are required. A zygote is formed from the joining of the parents' reproductive cells. The reproductive cells form through **3.** ____. In this process, the cell divides twice. After the first division, the nucleus of each new cell has the same number of **4.** ____ as the nucleus of the parent cell. After the second division, the nucleus of each new cell has only half as many as the nucleus of the parent cell.

As organisms grow and mature, some go through distinct stages. A caterpillar, for example, goes through four stages to become a butterfly. This process of development is called **5.** ____. Other animals go through a different kind of development. Young animals that have the same shape as their parents go through **6.** ____ to become adults. Each species has its own **7.** ____, a process in which an animal is born unable to reproduce and grows to become a reproducing adult. All animals grow through **8.** ____, a process in which cells make exact copies of themselves.

| I inherited trait | J genes | K dominant trait | L recessive trait |

Eye color is an **9.** ____ that parents pass on to their offspring. If one parent has a **10.** ____, such as blue eyes, it may be masked by the stronger **11.** ____ of brown eyes. All these characteristics are located on the DNA, which is contained in the **12.** ____. When the offspring become adults, they will pass their characteristics on to their young, continuing the family's unique attributes.

Unit A • Chapter 3   (page 1 of 5)   Assessment Guide AG 15

Name _____

Part II   Science Concepts and Understanding

Write the letter of the best choice.

____ 13. Cells going through mitosis produce —
   A half as many chromosomes
   B six new male and female cells
   C identical copies of the original cell
   D offspring by budding

____ 14. What does rapid mitosis allow a lizard to do if its tail is cut off?
   F divide a new tail   H fuse a new tail
   G spindle a new tail   J regenerate a new tail

____ 15. Through the process of metamorphosis, an insect —
   A changes the form of its body as it grows
   B molts the outer covering of its skeleton
   C becomes a hopping, wingless insect
   D hatches from an egg in late summer

____ 16. What are the three stages of incomplete metamorphosis?
   F egg, pupa, chrysalis
   G larva, pupa, cocoon
   H egg, nymph, adult
   J nymph, larva, adult

____ 17. Which of the following is required in sexual reproduction?
   A siblings   C two parents
   B budding   D one parent

____ 18. How does the nucleus of a cell prepare for mitosis?
   F It divides cells into exact copies.
   G It makes exact copies of chromosomes.
   H It pinches the cell membrane at the middle.
   J Its chromosomes pull apart the DNA coding.

____ 19. In sexual reproduction, two cells combine to form a one-cell —
   A gamete   C egg
   B pupa   D zygote

Name _____

____ 20. Genes found on chromosomes contain the DNA codes for —
    F hypothesized factors
    G second-generation offspring
    H Mendel's factors
    J inherited traits

____ 21. In direct development, offspring —
    A go through incomplete metamorphosis
    B have the same shape as adults
    C go through complete metamorphosis
    D become nymphs

____ 22. One human trait that is **NOT** inherited is —
    F tongue curling   H balance
    G attached earlobes   J hair color

____ 23. An example of incomplete metamorphosis is the life cycle of the —
    A butterfly   C grasshopper
    B rabbit   D frog

Use the following pictures to answer Question 24.

24. Write *1*, *2*, *3*, or *4* to indicate the correct order of development.

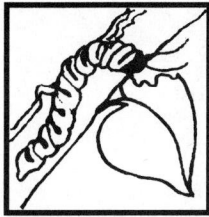   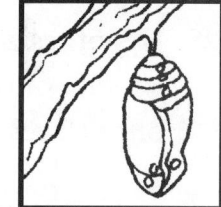

Use the following pictures to answer Question 25.

25. Write *1*, *2*, *3*, or *4* to indicate the correct order of mitosis.

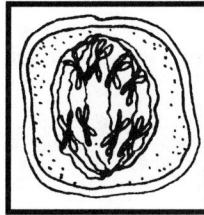 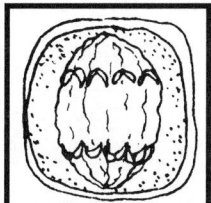 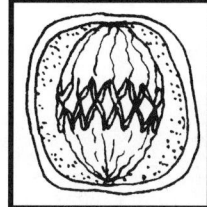 

Name _____

Part III Critical Thinking

26. Why is it **NOT** a good idea to try to get rid of ocean sponges by chopping them up?

_____

_____

27. Why do the cells of an adult continue to divide after the adult has stopped growing?

_____

_____

Part IV Process Skills Application

28. Compare mitosis with meiosis.

_____

_____

_____

29. Hypothesize what might happen to an insect larva placed in a glass jar with only grass to eat. What would happen if the insect was in the pupa stage?

_____

_____

_____

30. If a body cell has 22 chromosomes, what would be the chromosome count for the reproductive cells? **Use numbers** to explain your answer.

_____

_____

_____

Name _____

Observe the following diagram to answer Questions 31–32.

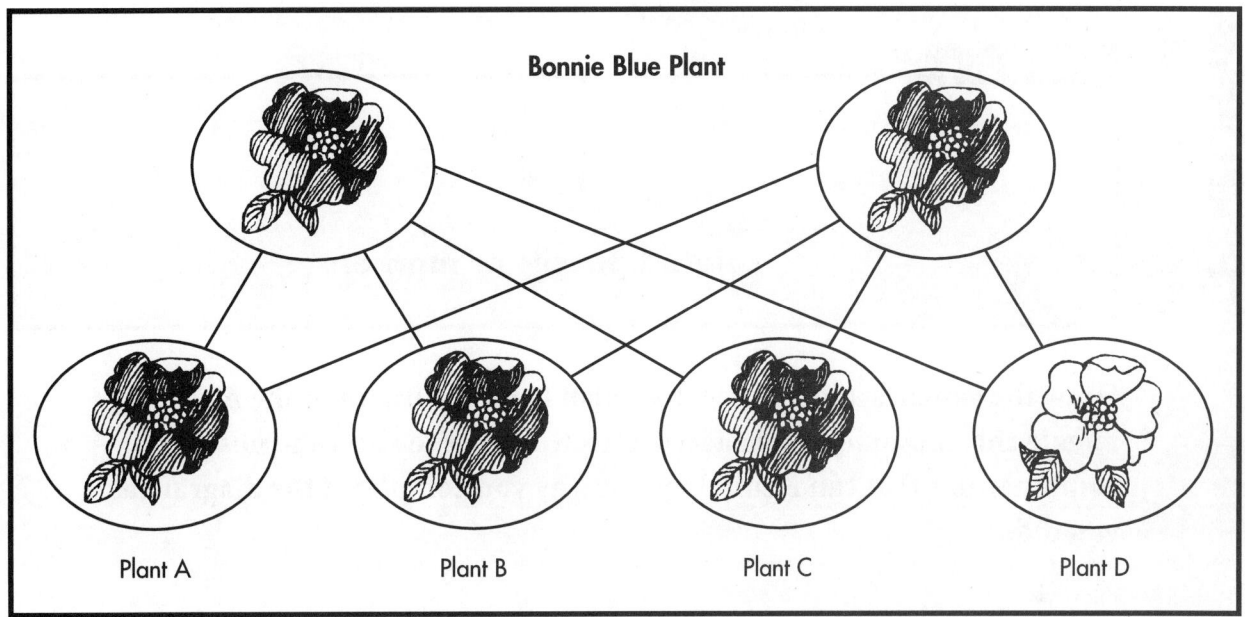

31. What can you **infer** about the recessive trait of the Bonnie Blue parent plant?

   _____

   _____

   _____

32. What did Plant D inherit from both its parents?

   _____

   _____

   _____

33. When you get a small cut on your finger, the skin copies itself exactly as the cut heals. **Hypothesize** why it is important for the cells to duplicate themselves exactly.

   _____

   _____

   _____

Unit A • Chapter 3   (page 5 of 5)   Assessment Guide   AG 19

Name _____ Date _____

Modeling Meiosis

Materials

colored pencils or markers

Draw the gametes and zygotes that form from the union of the male and female chromosomes. Then add connecting lines to show the possible combinations that can result. Explain why you completed the diagram as you did.

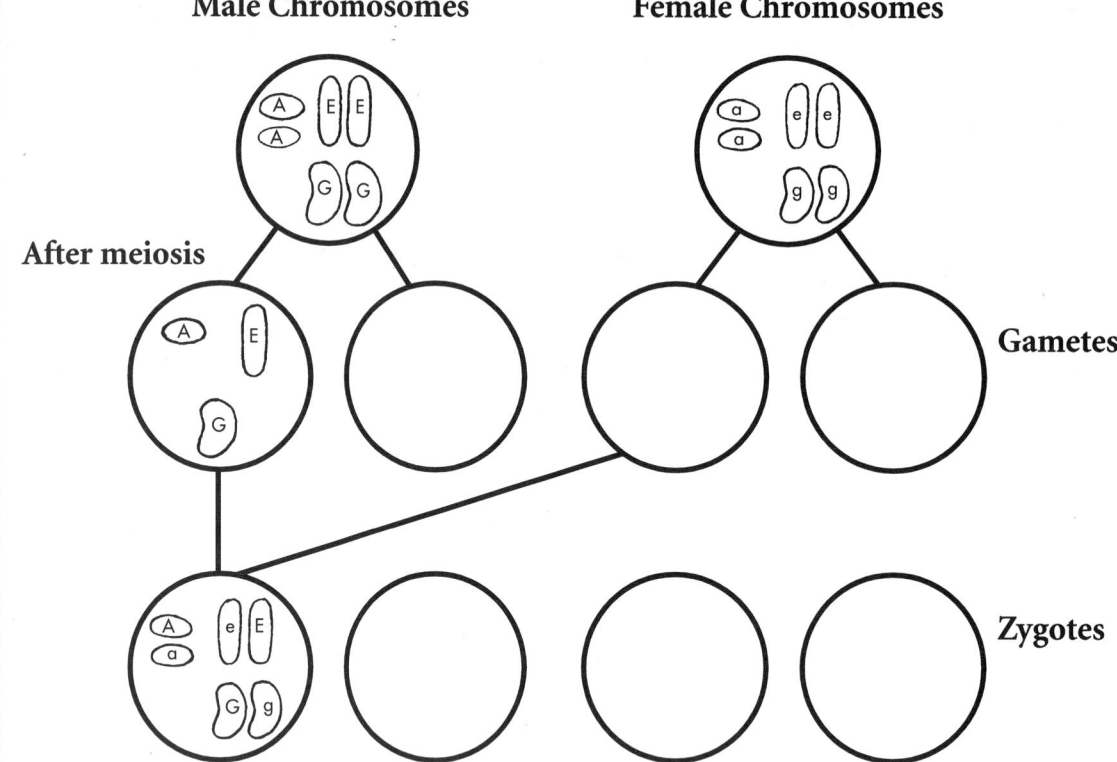

Teacher's Directions

Modeling Meiosis

Materials Performance Task sheet, colored pencils or markers

Time 10–20 minutes

Suggested Grouping individuals or pairs

Science Processes infer, compare, hypothesize

Preparation Hints Review the math lesson on possible outcomes and recording outcomes and explain how this can be used in the task.

Introduce the Task Ask students to recall what they know about meiosis. Make sure they understand why it is necessary that this process reduce the number of chromosomes in reproductive cells. Tell them they are going to diagram the gametes and then the zygotes that form from the union of male and female gametes.

Promote Discussion Ask students to compare answers and discuss differences. If a diagram is incorrectly filled out, have other students explain why it is not correct. Ask students why chromosomes always occur in even numbers.

Scoring Rubric

Performance Indicators

_____ Draws combinations of gametes that show the union of the male and female chromosomes.

_____ Draws combinations of zygotes that are possible results of the chromosomes reproducing.

_____ Draws lines to connect gametes and zygotes correctly.

_____ Clearly explains why the combinations of chromosomes drawn are correct.

Observations and Rubric Score

| 3 | 2 | 1 | 0 |

Name _____
Date _____

Plants and Their Adaptations

Part 1 Vocabulary

Match each term in Column B with its meaning in Column A.

Column A

____ 1. Process by which plants use light energy to produce sugar

____ 2. Plant material that can be separated into thread

____ 3. Flower structures that contain the male reproductive cells

____ 4. Helps plants use light energy to make food

____ 5. Single reproductive cell that grows into a new plant

____ 6. Tubes in plants that carry water and nutrients

____ 7. Flowering, fruit-producing plant

____ 8. Tubes in plants that carry food

____ 9. Plant with unprotected seeds

____ 10. What a seed does when conditions are right for growth

____ 11. The seeds of certain grasses from which cereals are made

Column B

A angiosperm

B chlorophyll

C gymnosperm

D photosynthesis

E phloem

F grain

G spore

H germinates

I xylem

J fiber

K pollen

AG 22 Assessment Guide   (page 1 of 5)   Unit A • Chapter 4

Name _____

Part II   Science Concepts and Understanding

Write the letter of the best choice.

____ 12. Quinine and digitalis are examples of —
   A medicines made from plants
   B xylem and phloem
   C plants used for making clothing
   D foods made from the leaves of plants

____ 13. Which of the following is **NOT** a way that a fruit helps the seed inside it?
   F The fruit protects the seed from cold weather.
   G The fruit keeps the seed from being eaten.
   H The fruit provides extra nutrition for the new plant.
   J The fruit helps the seed transfer pollen.

____ 14. Root hairs —
   A anchor the plant to the ground
   B take in nutrients and water
   C store food
   D take water directly from the air

____ 15. All organisms release _____ as they turn food into energy.
   F oxygen   H nitrogen
   G helium   J carbon dioxide

____ 16. More spores are produced from a spore-producing plant than seeds from a seed-producing plant because —
   A spores have less of a chance of growing than seeds
   B there are more spore-producing plants
   C spores don't fall far from the plant that produced them
   D spores are larger than most seeds

____ 17. Prop roots —
   F anchor the plant to the soil
   G keep plants from blowing over
   H reach water deep in the ground
   J help make food

Unit A • Chapter 4   (page 2 of 5)   **Assessment Guide AG 23**

Name _____

Use the diagrams below to answer Questions 18–21.

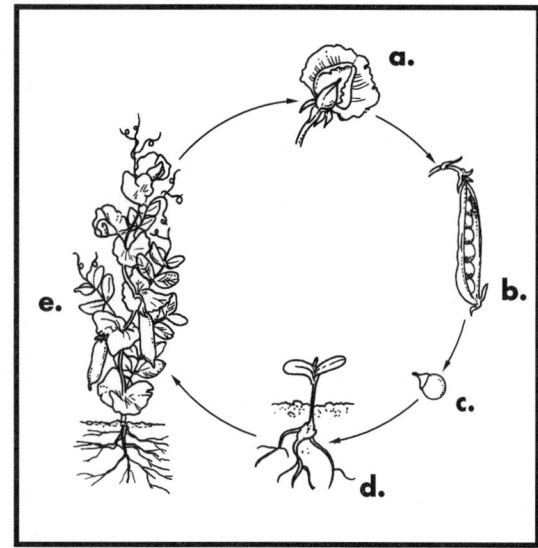

I

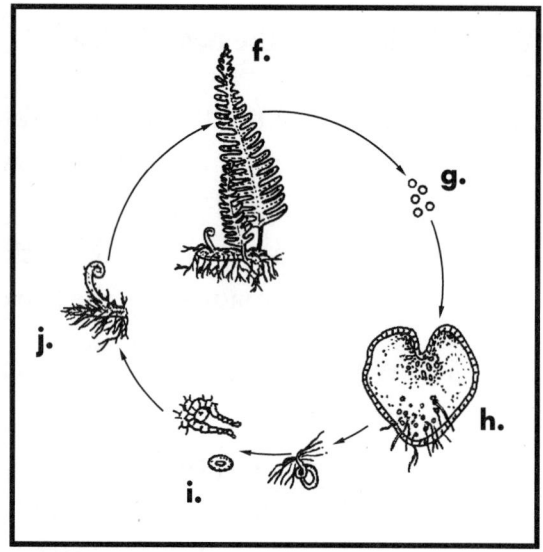

II

____ 18. A plant life cycle is shown by —
   A I   C both I and II
   B II   D neither I nor II

____ 19. Diagram I represents —
   F a gymnosperm   H a nonvascular plant
   G a moss   J an angiosperm

____ 20. In Diagram II, *g* represents —
   A spores   C a flower
   B seeds   D a leaf

____ 21. In Diagram I, *b* represents —
   F spores   H a fruit
   G seeds   J a flower

Write the letter of the best choice.

____ 22. Xylem and phloem are found only in —
   A vascular plants   C woody plants
   B nonvascular plants   D leaves of large trees

Name _____

____ 23. Which of the following is **NOT** a reason why plants store food?
    F Plants may not get enough water to make food during dry periods.
    G Most plants cannot make food during the winter.
    H Some plants store food to survive brief temperature changes.
    J Plants must store some food to survive in a flood.

____ 24. Carrots, sweet potatoes, turnips, and beets are all —
    A storage leaves   C storage roots
    B root hairs   D storage stems

____ 25. The leaves of plants take in ____ to use in photosynthesis.
    F oxygen   H chlorophyll
    G carbon dioxide   J bacteria

____ 26. The material in old ____ hardens to become the "wood" of a tree.
    A phloem   B branches   C bark   D xylem

____ 27. Fibers are —
    F like root hairs in taproots
    G materials that can be separated into thread
    H the xylem "strings" of celery
    J phloem in leaves

Part III   Critical Thinking

28. Would you expect a plant with large, flat leaves to live in a desert? Why or why not?

_____
_____
_____

29. Could a vascular plant live without its roots? Explain.

_____
_____
_____

NMU LIBRARY

Name _____

30. Think of all the things you use in a day that are plant parts or plant products. How would your life be different if there were no plants?

_____

_____

_____

Part IV   Process Skills Application

31. Infer why a plant from one island begins to grow on a distant island where that kind of plant had never grown before.

_____

_____

_____

Interpret the circle graph to answer 32–33.

32. Observe the circle graph. What is the total percentage of foods from plants that should be part of a healthful diet?

_____

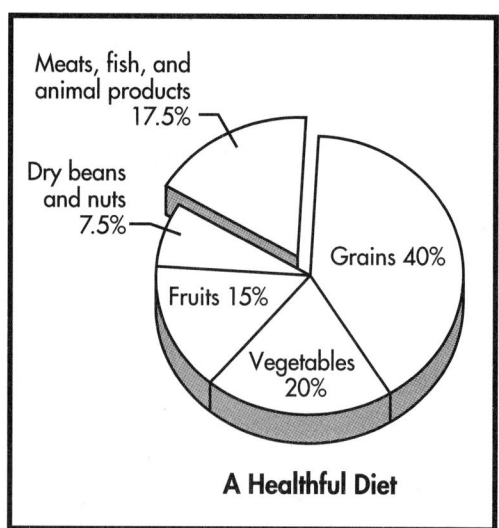

33. Infer why a pyramid is a good way to indicate the amounts of each food group you should eat.

_____

_____

_____

_____

_____

Name _____ Date _____

Observing Stems

Materials

- collection of stems from several different plants
- hand lens
- pen or pencil
- kitchen knife
- paper

1. Select samples of stems from several different kinds of plants. Carefully observe each stem. Are there attached leaves? If so, how are they attached—at the ends of the stems or on the sides?

2. What color is each stem? Is it hard or soft? Is it covered with bark? Are there any branches?

3. Cut across each stem. **Be careful when using the knife.** Use a hand lens to look at the cut end. What can you observe?

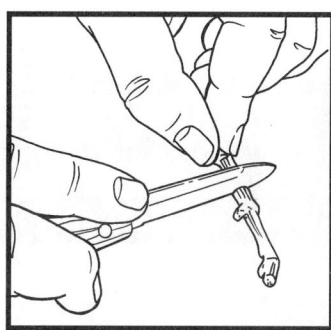

4. Cut down the length of each stem. Be especially careful with the knife when cutting a thin stem. Use a hand lens to observe the inside of the stem. What parts can you see? What can you infer about the function of these parts?

5. Make a chart to record all of your observations. Include the name of each plant if you know it.

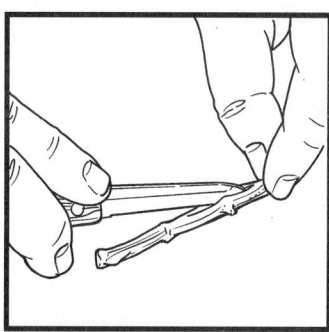

6. Set up a classification key to classify the stems in your collection. When you finish, see whether one of your classmates can correctly classify your stems by using your key.

PERFORMANCE TASK

Unit A • Chapter 4

PERFORMANCE TASK

Teacher's Directions

Observing Stems

Materials   Performance Task sheet, collection of stems from several different plants, hand lens, pen or pencil, kitchen knife, paper

Time   30 minutes

Suggested Grouping   individuals or pairs

Science Processes   observe, infer, communicate

Preparation Hints   Gather enough stems for each student or pair of students to have five or six different kinds of stems. If time, weather, and local restrictions allow, have students go outdoors to gather their own collections. Caution them about which plants are not acceptable for collection. As another alternative, ask students to bring stems from home.

You may want to make the cross section and longitudinal cuts for the students. On the cross section of an angiosperm, especially a dicot, students may be able to distinguish one or more annual rings. On the longitudinal section, they may be able to detect vascular tubes.

Introduce the Task   Remind students about the functions of stems (to support the plant and carry water and food to all parts of the plant). Tell students they will look for evidence of these functions in the stems they observe.

Promote Discussion   Have volunteers share their chart or classification system.

Scoring Rubric

Performance Indicators

_____ Develops a chart that clearly lists physical characteristics such as color, bark, leaves, and so on, of each stem in the collection.

_____ Sets up a usable classification key.

_____ Observes the presence of vascular tissue within the stems.

_____ Infers the function of vascular tissue as the carrier of food and water to all parts of the plant.

Observations and Rubric Score

3	2	1	0

AG 28 Assessment Guide   Unit A • Chapter 4

Name _____
Date _____

Living Systems

Write the letter of the best choice.

_____ 1. Which organelles are found only in a plant cell?
A cytoplasm and cell wall
B chromosomes and chloroplasts
C chloroplasts and cell wall
D cell wall and cell membrane

_____ 2. The passage of water and dissolved materials through a cell membrane is known as —
F digestion   H hydration
G osmosis   J diffusion

_____ 3. Which organelle is correctly matched with its function?
A mitochondria – controls all cell activities
B cytoplasm – separates the cell from its surroundings
C vacuoles – store food, wastes, or water
D chloroplasts – release energy from food

_____ 4. The smallest blood vessels are called —
F arteries   H alveoli
G veins   J capillaries

_____ 5. What takes place in the alveoli?
A transportation of blood to cells
B exchange of oxygen and carbon dioxide
C excretion of bodily fluids
D digestion of your food

_____ 6. How does the body obtain nutrients from food?
F The stomach absorbs food particles.
G Nutrients diffuse through the villi in the small intestine.
H Nutrients are absorbed as they pass through the pancreas.
J Digested food diffuses through the large intestines.

_____ 7. The kidney is an organ of which system?
A digestive   C circulatory
B excretory   D respiratory

_____ 8. Ligaments —
F produce red blood cells
G detect conditions in the body
H hold the skeleton together
J connect muscle to bone

Unit A   (page 1 of 4)   Assessment Guide AG 29

Name _____

_____ 9. Your body uses receptors and produces a reflex when you —
   A listen to soft music
   B lie down and go to sleep
   C touch a hot plate of food
   D jump rope

_____ 10. Which of the following is NOT one of the five kingdoms?
   F protist   H fungi
   G genus   J moneran

_____ 11. Scientists use classification to —
   A make animals easier to find
   B make it easier to categorize living things and to talk about them
   C help protect the environment
   D create an organized environment for plants and animals

_____ 12. Which group contains only invertebrates?
   F birds   H amphibians
   G mammals   J arthropods

_____ 13. Frogs are —
   A amphibians   C monerans
   B invertebrates D reptiles

_____ 14. What is the difference between a vascular plant and a nonvascular plant?
   F A vascular plant has transport tubes.
   G A vascular plant loses its leaves in the winter.
   H A vascular plant needs water.
   J A vascular plant needs light.

_____ 15. Moss is an example of —
   A a vascular plant
   B a protist
   C a nonvascular plant
   D an invertebrate

_____ 16. Mitosis —
   F occurs only in sexual reproduction
   G occurs during regeneration
   H reduces the number of chromosomes
   J divides one cell into four cells

_____ 17. Asexual reproduction requires how many parents?
   A none   C two
   B one   D three

_____ 18. What process forms reproductive cells for sexual reproduction?
   F mitosis   H regeneration
   G meiosis   J photosynthesis

Name _____

_____ 19. Which of the following grow through complete metamorphosis?
A scorpions   C grasshoppers
B spiders   D frogs

_____ 20. If both parent flowers are red but their offspring is white, what does this tell you about flower color?
F Flower color is not an inherited trait.
G Red color is a weak trait.
H White color is a recessive trait.
J There is no gene for flower color.

_____ 21. If a cat has white hair when both of its parents have brown hair, how many white-haired genes must it have inherited?
A one   C twenty-three
B two   D forty-six

_____ 22. Which tubes in a vascular plant transport food?
F phloem   H taproots
G xylem   J prop roots

_____ 23. Male reproductive cells in gymnosperms are in —
A pollen   C apples
B spores   D flowers

_____ 24. What gives plants and leaves their green color?
F stomata   H chlorophyll
G pollen   J photosynthesis

_____ 25. Reproductive cells in nonvascular plants are —
A seeds   C pollen
B spores   D flowers

_____ 26. What makes angiosperms different from other vascular plants?
F roots   H leaves
G bark   J flowers

_____ 27. Which of the following is made from the fibers of cotton?
A perfumes   C paper
B blue jeans D shampoo

_____ 28. Most breakfast cereals are made of —
F grains   H stems
G leaves   J flowers

Name _____

Answer in complete sentences.

29. A loud noise startles you from behind. Explain how the nervous system, the muscular system, and the skeletal system work together to make you jump.

_____
_____
_____
_____
_____
_____

30. A new organism is found that is multicellular, does not have a backbone, and has six legs. While studying the organism, you notice that it develops somewhat like a grasshopper. Explain how you would classify this organism, and discuss the stages of its development.

_____
_____
_____
_____
_____
_____

31. (3.3) Explain how a child can have blue eyes when both parents have brown eyes.

_____
_____
_____
_____
_____
_____

Name _____
Date _____

Cycles in Nature

Part I   Vocabulary

Match each term in Column B with its meaning in Column A.

Column A

____ 1. Cycle in which plants turn gas in air into oxygen

____ 2. Water falling from clouds

____ 3. Water turning into water vapor

____ 4. Cycle in which a gas in the air is fixed into a form that plants can use

____ 5. Water vapor turning into water

____ 6. Plants losing water through their stomata

____ 7. Cycle in which water moves through the environment

____ 8. Process of releasing energy from food

Column B

A nitrogen cycle

B evaporation

C water cycle

D condensation

E carbon-oxygen cycle

F respiration

G transpiration

H precipitation

Part II   Science Concepts and Understanding

Write the letter of the best choice.

____ 9. ____ provides energy for plants to grow.
  A natural gas   C respiration
  B sunlight   D carbon dioxide

____ 10. Plants release ____ into the atmosphere as a byproduct of photosynthesis.
  F carbon dioxide   H nitrogen
  G oxygen   J helium

Name _____

_____ 11. Plants and animals release _____ as a product of respiration.
 A oxygen C nitrogen
 B helium D carbon dioxide

_____ 12. During _____, plants use sunlight, water, and carbon dioxide to make their own food.
 F photosynthesis H decay
 G respiration J transformation

_____ 13. Which of the following does NOT produce carbon dioxide?
 A people burning fuels
 B people breathing
 C plants using sunlight
 D animals breathing

_____ 14. Which of the following return to the soil in animal waste?
 F nitrates and oxygen H ammonia and oxygen
 G ammonia and nitrates J oxygen and bacteria

_____ 15. Plants make proteins from —
 A water in the soil C nitrogen in the air
 B nitrates in the soil D oxygen

_____ 16. In what process do bacteria and fungi break down a dead organism's tissues and use some of the carbon as food?
 F decay H water cycle
 G photosynthesis J carbon dioxide–water cycle

_____ 17. Petroleum is made from —
 A coal and oil
 B bacteria and fungi
 C plants releasing oxygen
 D decayed organisms

_____ 18. Burning fuels in cars and factories —
 F puts oxygen into the air
 G puts nitrogen into the air
 H upsets the balance of the nitrogen cycle
 J upsets the balance of the carbon-oxygen cycle

Name _____

Use the following pictures to answer Questions 19–21.

_____ 19. Which picture represents condensation?

_____ 20. Which picture represents evaporation?

_____ 21. Which picture represents precipitation?

Write the letter of the best choice.

_____ 22. Water falls to Earth as rain after water vapor _____ into clouds.
     A evaporates
     B warms
     C becomes heavy
     D condenses

_____ 23. Chemicals and pesticides get into groundwater supplies through —
     F rain   H transpiration
     G evaporation   J water vapor

_____ 24. Plants return water to the environment through —
     A photosynthesis   C transpiration
     B respiration   D evaporation

Name _____

____ 25. Which of the following describes a part of the nitrogen cycle?
    F Plants use nitrogen gas and return it to soil.
    G Lightning turns fixed nitrogen into nitrogen gas.
    H Bacteria in the soil fix nitrogen for plants.
    J Animals turn fixed nitrogen into nitrogen gas.

____ 26. Which of the following is **NOT** a part of a natural cycle?
    A Water evaporates into water vapor and condenses as clouds.
    B Natural gas burns to produce energy, carbon dioxide, and water.
    C Carbon dioxide is used in photosynthesis.
    D Animals eat fixed nitrogen when they eat plants.

____ 27. Cold air causes water vapor to ____ and form ____.
    F precipitate; puddles   **H** be fixed; lightning
    G evaporate; water vapor   **J** condense; clouds

____ 28. Ammonia is a usable form of ____ that bacteria use in the ____.
    A carbon dioxide; carbon-oxygen cycle
    B nitrogen; nitrogen cycle
    C water vapor; water cycle
    D protein; nitrogen cycle

Part III   Critical Thinking

Answer the following on a separate sheet of paper.

29. If plants and animals lived forever, what would happen to the nitrates in Earth's soil?

30. What are three ways to help keep the carbon-oxygen cycle in balance?

31. Do rain puddles disappear more quickly on a cloudy day or on a clear day? Why?

32. What would happen if the air in the upper atmosphere were warmer than water vapor in the air?

Name _____

Part IV Process Skills Application

33. Rabbits eat lots of green, leafy plants and rarely drink any water. What could you **infer** from this behavior?

_____
_____
_____

34. What did scientists **observe** that made them infer that burning fuels is bad for the air?

_____
_____
_____

Observe and *interpret* the following circle graphs to answer Questions 35–38.

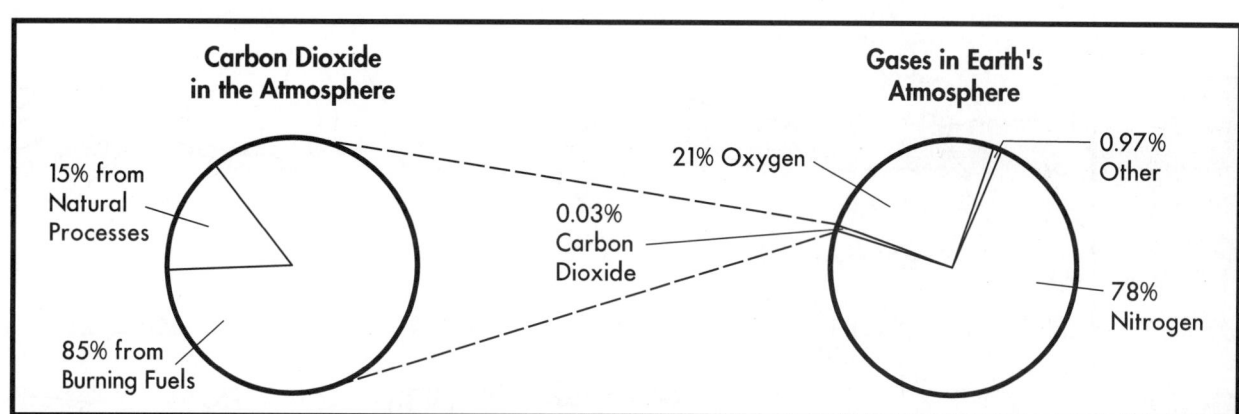

35. Which gas makes up most of Earth's atmosphere? _____

36. What percentage of Earth's atmosphere is oxygen? _____

37. What percentage of Earth's carbon dioxide is produced by natural processes? _____

38. What gas do you **infer** would be most affected if human activity increased the burning of fuels?

_____

Name _____ Date _____

Which Cycle Is Which?

PERFORMANCE TASK

Materials: red pencil, blue pencil, green pencil

On the diagram below, draw blue arrows to show the water cycle, red arrows to show the nitrogen cycle, and green arrows to show the carbon-oxygen cycle. Add labels for each cycle.

Choose one of the cycles. Explain how life on Earth is involved in this cycle.

AG 38 Assessment Guide

Unit B • Chapter 1

Teacher's Directions

Which Cycle Is Which?

Materials Performance Task sheets; red, blue, and green pencils

Time 30 minutes

Suggested Grouping individuals

Science Processes infer, observe, communicate

Preparation Hints Review the water cycle, nitrogen cycle, and carbon dioxide–oxygen cycle with students before assigning the task.

Introduce the Task Ask students to tell what they know about the water, nitrogen, and carbon–oxygen cycles in nature. Explain to students that they will be adding arrows to a picture to demonstrate how the water cycle works. Blue arrows on the diagram will show the water cycle, red arrows will show the nitrogen cycle, and green arrows will show the carbon–oxygen cycle. Students also need to label each cycle. Then they are to choose one of the cycles and write a short explanation of how life on Earth is involved in it.

Promote Discussion Lead a discussion about how life on Earth would be different if any one of these cycles were changed in any way. If the water cycle were disrupted, would it affect animals or plants first? What about the nitrogen or carbon–oxygen cycle? When would people be affected by any change in these cycles?

Scoring Rubric

Performance Indicators

_____ Draws blue arrows to show evaporation, condensation, and precipitation in the water cycle.

_____ Draws red arrows to show how nitrogen gas is changed to ammonia and nitrates for plants to use.

_____ Draws green arrows to show how carbon and oxygen move among plants, animals, and the environment.

_____ Gives a clear explanation of the cycle chosen, and tells how life is involved in the cycle.

Observations and Rubric Score

| 3 | 2 | 1 | 0 |

Unit B • Chapter 1

Name _____

Date _____

Living Things Interact

Part 1   Vocabulary

Use the letters of the terms in the Word Banks to complete the sentences.

| A individual | C niche | E habitat |
| B ecosystem | D population | F community |

An environment includes all living and nonliving things in an area. A single organism in an environment is called an **1.** ____. Organisms of the same kind living in the same environment make up a **2.** ____. All the populations of organisms living together in an environment make up a **3.** ____. This part of the environment and its physical factors make up an **4.** ____. Every population lives in a certain part of an ecosystem, known as its **5.** ____. Within this part of the ecosystem, each population has a certain role, or **6.** ____.

| G producers | I food chain | K decomposers |
| H energy pyramid | J food web | L consumers |

The sun provides the energy for almost every ecosystem on Earth. All life in an ecosystem depends on **7.** ____ to capture the energy of the sun, change it into living tissue, and pass it on to other organisms. All other organisms in an ecosystem community must eat to get the energy they need. So the animals in a community are **8.** ____. A **9.** ____ shows how consumers in an ecosystem are connected to one another according to what they eat. Plants are usually at the base. First-level consumers, or herbivores, eat the plants. Second-level consumers, or carnivores, eat the herbivores. **10.** ____, such as mushrooms and bacteria, break down the tissues of dead organisms. A **11.** ____ shows the relationships between many food chains within a single ecosystem. An **12.** ____ shows the amount of energy available to pass from one level of a food chain to the next.

Name _____

| M symbiosis | O competition | Q extinct | S instinct |
| N threatened | P endangered | R learned behavior | T exotic |

Because most ecosystems don't have unlimited resources, there may be
13. ____ for these resources among organisms. Organisms also share
resources, however. In some cases, different organisms live together for
most or all of their lives. A long relationship between different kinds of
organisms is called 14. ____. Animals behave in certain ways to survive in
their communities. An inherited behavior is called an 15. ____. A behavior
that is developed over time is called a 16. ____. A population of organisms
can survive only if enough individuals produce healthy offspring. A population
that begins to decline is listed as 17. ____. A population that is likely
to die out unless steps are taken to save it is listed as 18. ____. A decline
in population may result from the importing of 19. ____, or nonnative,
plants, or animals into the community. When the last individual of a population
dies, that kind of organism becomes. 20. ____.

Part II   Science Concepts and Understanding

Write the letter of the best choice.

____ 21. In a healthy ecosystem, populations of living things are —
   F independent   H interdependent
   G enemies   J large

____ 22. The types and number of animals in an ecosystem are determined
   by the —
   A types and number of plants   C types and number of individuals
   B types and number of communities D population density

____ 23. What do the producers in a community do?
   F hunt prey   H eat other organisms
   G decompose organisms   J make food

Name _____

____ 24. In a food chain, each level of consumer eats organisms —
  A from the level above it   C in the same niche
  B from the level below it   D in the same population

____ 25. What percentage of energy at any level of a food chain is passed on to the next higher level?
  F about 10 percent   H It depends on the population.
  G about 90 percent   J It depends on the community.

____ 26. Different organisms can share the same resource, such as a tree, because they have different —
  A populations   C communities
  B niches   D ecosystems

____ 27. A cleaner fish picks bits of food from between a shark's teeth. This relationship is an example of —
  F independence   H mutualism
  G competition   J camouflage

____ 28. Behaviors for building shelters, finding mates, and hunting are usually —
  A learned   C competitive
  B symbiotic   D instinctive

Use the following diagram to answer Questions 29–33. Write the letter of the organism that belongs at each level of the food chain.

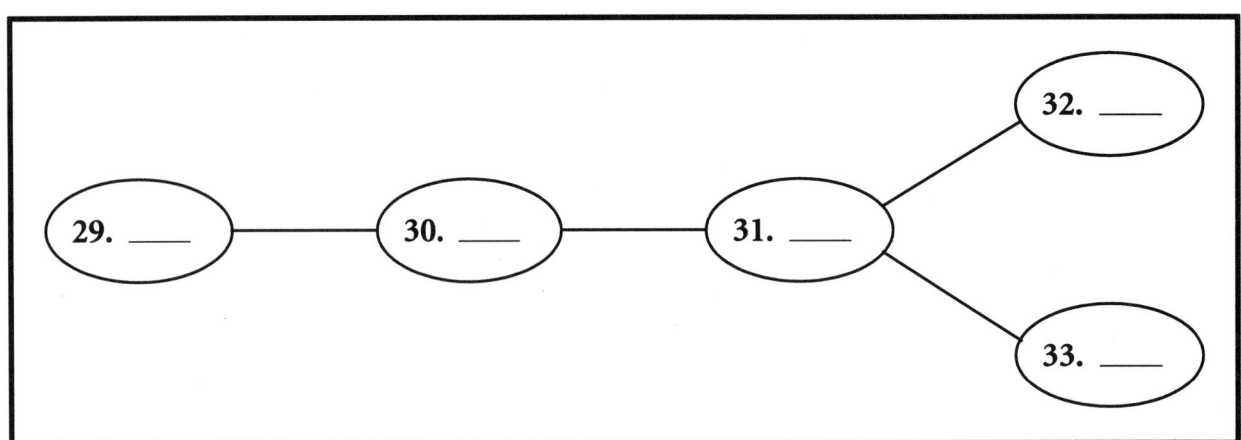

| A coyote | B green plant | C vulture | D mushroom | E rabbit |

AG 42 Assessment Guide   (page 3 of 5)   Unit B • Chapter 1

Name _____

Write the letter of the best choice.

____ 34. Which of the following is **NOT** a natural cause for a population decline?
F drought
G pesticides
H floods
J hurricanes

____ 35. Most declines in populations of organisms today are caused by —
A human activity   C disease
B natural disasters D old age

Part III   Critical Thinking

Answer the following on a separate sheet of paper.

36. The environment determines an area's ecosystem. What might happen if an area has a dramatic decrease in rainfall?

37. Giraffes, antelopes, and rhinos all eat from the same trees. What would happen if these animals were all the same size?

38. What difference does it make if an organism becomes extinct?

Part IV   Process Skills Application

39. How could you **gather data** about the number of red-tailed hawks that live in your state?

_____

_____

_____

Name _____

40. What characteristics would you use to **classify** birds?

_____
_____
_____
_____

41. The larger the population in an area, the greater the competition for food. **Predict** what would happen if the population of a species in an area doubled.

_____
_____
_____
_____

42. Suppose an area that normally receives five inches of rain in May receives only one inch in May. **Draw a conclusion** about what will happen to the producers and first-level consumers in the area.

_____
_____
_____
_____

43. Domestic horses often become uneasy when they are away from other horses. From this fact, what can you **infer** about the behavior of wild horses?

_____
_____
_____
_____

Name _____ Date _____

Design a Community

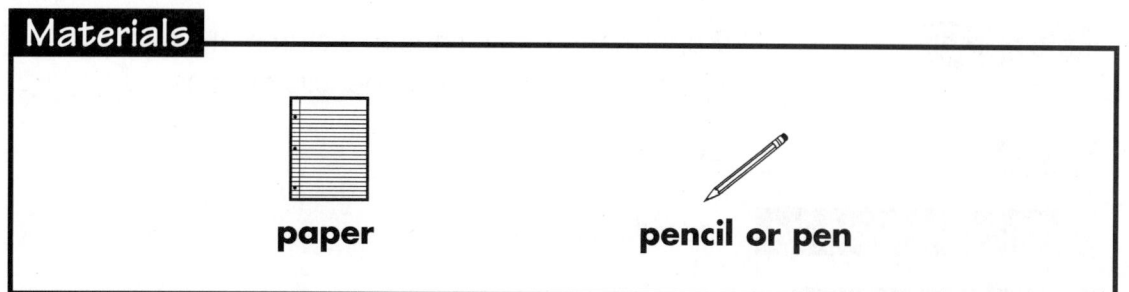

Choose a small habitat, such as a tree or bush, and design a community that shares this habitat. Have at least four populations in your community. At least two of the populations should interact with one another.

1. What are the four populations in your community, and what is the niche of each?

   _____

   _____

2. How many individuals are in each population?

   _____

   _____

3. In what ways do the populations in your community interact?

   _____

   _____

4. Draw a picture of your habitat, and show some individuals in each population.

5. Present your community to the class. Explain how the populations interact.

   _____

   _____

Unit B • Chapter 2   Assessment Guide   AG 45

PERFORMANCE TASK

Teacher's Directions

Design a Community

Materials — Performance Task sheets, pictures of different habitats, paper, pencils or pens

Time — 20–25 minutes

Suggested Grouping — individuals or pairs

Science Processes — classify, predict, infer

Preparation Hints — Place pictures of different habitats around the room.

Introduce the Task — Ask students to look at the pictures around the room. What kinds of communities exist in these habitats? Tell students they are going to design a community, although the organisms they choose for their habitats don't need to be real. Emphasize the importance of designing a community in which populations can survive and interact. Tell them that they will be sharing their ideas with the class.

Promote Discussion — When students finish, ask for volunteers to share their communities. Encourage the class to ask questions. Ask students about their communities and populations. For example, what difficulties did students have in deciding what the different organisms would eat?

Scoring Rubric

Performance Indicators

_____ Chooses at least four populations and explains each one's niche.

_____ Demonstrates an understanding of an ecosystem.

_____ Demonstrates an understanding of a population.

_____ Provides a sensible explanation of how the populations interact.

Observations and Rubric Score

| 3 | 2 | 1 | 0 |

Name _____
Date _____

Biomes

Part I Vocabulary

Match each term in Column B with its meaning in Column A.

Column A

____ 1. Region where annual patterns of rainfall, temperature, and sunlight are similar throughout

____ 2. Area of deep water where most animal and plant organisms live at the surface

____ 3. Area of calm water, constant temperature, and much algae growth

____ 4. Place where a freshwater river empties into the ocean

____ 5. Large-scale ecosystem defined by the plants and animals adapted to live in its climate

____ 6. Area where waves and tides reach the shore

Column B

A open-ocean zone

B biome

C estuary

D intertidal zone

E climate zone

F near-shore zone

Part II Science Concepts and Understanding

Write the letter of the best choice.

____ 7. Desert biomes have all of the following EXCEPT —
   A hot and sunny days
   B usually cold night temperatures
   C very dry soil and air
   D animals active in the daytime

Name _____

____ 8. The taiga has —
   F grasses with long, slender leaves
   G frozen soil with few plants
   H pine, fir, and spruce trees
   J oak, maple, and hickory trees

____ 9. The floor of the rain forest has little plant life because —
   A the vines and ferns choke off the other plants
   B the rain forest gets too much sunlight
   C very little sunlight gets through the canopy
   D toads and salamanders eat the plants on the forest floor

____ 10. Evergreens are adapted to life in the taiga because they —
   F shed needles that form a thick mat on the forest floor
   G have a waxy covering over their needles
   H grow taller than most deciduous trees
   J have roots that spread out near the surface

____ 11. What is the correct order of the ocean zones from shallowest to deepest?
   A intertidal zone, near-shore zone, open-ocean zone
   B near-shore zone, open-ocean zone, intertidal zone
   C near-shore zone, intertidal zone, open-ocean zone
   D intertidal zone, open-ocean zone, near-shore zone

____ 12. Freshwater ecosystems occur in —
   F swamps and marshes
   G oceans and seas
   H estuaries
   J the intertidal zone

____ 13. Permafrost is found in the ____ biome.
   A grassland
   B taiga
   C tundra
   D desert

Name _____

_____ 14. The biome with the greatest diversity of life is the —
   F taiga   H deciduous forest
   G grassland   J tropical rain forest

_____ 15. Which is **NOT** true of estuaries?
   A Their waters are calm and still.
   B They have the fewest number of species of any biome.
   C They help prevent coastal flooding and erosion.
   D They are the most productive ecosystems on Earth.

_____ 16. In an ocean ecosystem, the deeper the water the —
   F greater the number of animals
   G warmer the temperature
   H less the amount of sunlight
   J greater the number of plants

Part III   Critical Thinking

17. Why do large herbivores such as bison and elephants live in grasslands rather than in tropical rain forests?

   _____
   _____
   _____
   _____
   _____

18. Why do plants of the tundra grow low to the ground and have a thick mat of shallow roots?

   _____
   _____
   _____
   _____
   _____

Name _____

19. Justin made a freshwater pond in his back yard and stocked it with goldfish. He might want to add some water lilies and cattails to make the pond beautiful. Give other reasons why Justin might add these plants.

_____
_____
_____

20. At night, the temperature in the desert drops a lot, sometimes causing dew to form on some plants. Explain how dew helps preserve life in the desert.

_____
_____
_____

Part IV   Process Skills Application

Observe these two hares.

21. Compare the physical features of the two animals. What can you **infer** about how each hare is adapted to its environment?

_____
_____
_____

Name _____

22. Fill in the blanks in the chart below to compare the six biomes.

Biome	Plant Example	Animal Example	Rainfall (high, moderate, or low)
Tropical Rain Forest			very high
Deciduous Forest		rabbits, skunks, deer, chipmunks	
Grassland	grasses, grains		
	cactus, mesquite, creosote		very low
Taiga			moderate to low
	mosses, lichens, dwarf willow		low

Unit B • Chapter 3

Name _____ Date _____

Biome Mobile

PERFORMANCE TASK

Materials

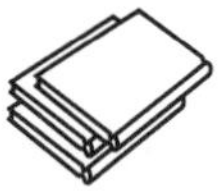

- books about biomes
- wire hanger 
- construction paper
- scissors 
- hole punch 
- paper clips 
- cotton string 
- colored pencils 
- ruler 
- crayons or markers 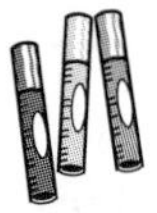

Choose and model a biome.

1. Choose a biome described in the chapter. Write a description of its vegetation and animal life.

2. Draw and color pictures of the plants and animals in the biome you chose. Cut them out. Lay out the pictures to show how you would group them.

3. Make a biome mobile by hanging your pictures on the hanger in groups. Add the name of the biome and some key words that describe the characteristics of the biome's climate zone.

4. Share your biome mobile with the class. Be prepared to discuss the animals, plants, and climate zone represented in your mobile.

Teacher's Directions

Biome Mobile

Materials Performance Task sheet, books about biomes, wire hangers, construction paper, scissors, hole punch, paper clips, cotton string, colored pencils, ruler, crayons, markers

Time 20–30 minutes

Suggested Grouping pairs

Science Processes observe, classify, compare

Preparation Hints Ask students to bring a wire coat hanger from home. Instead of drawing pictures, students may wish to cut out pictures from old magazines.

Introduce the Task Ask students to recall characteristics of certain biomes. Tell them they are going to choose a biome and research it. They will write a description of the biome and draw or cut out pictures of plants and animals that inhabit the biome. This will provide a plan for their mobile.

Promote Discussion Have student pairs display their mobiles, explaining which biomes they chose, their climate zones, and the plants and animals found there. Compare the mobiles after all student pairs have made their presentations.

Scoring Rubric

Performance Indicators

_____ Researches a biome.
_____ Writes an accurate description of the biome.
_____ Groups plants and animals that inhabit the biome.
_____ Shows understanding of the characteristics of the biome.

Observations and Rubric Score

| 3 | 2 | 1 | 0 |

Name _____
Date _____

Protecting and Preserving Ecosystems

Part 1 Vocabulary

Match each term in Column B with its meaning in Column A.

Column A

____ 1. Waste products that damage an ecosystem

____ 2. Saving resources

____ 3. Last stage of primary succession

____ 4. To keep items that can be used again

____ 5. Water ecosystems, such as saltwater marshes, mangrove swamps, and mud flats

____ 6. Gradual natural change in an ecosystem

____ 7. To cut down on the use of resources

____ 8. To recover a resource from an item and use it to make a new item

____ 9. Process of restoring a damaged ecosystem

____ 10. Nitric and sulfuric acid condensing into clouds and falling to Earth

____ 11. First plants to invade a bare area

Column B

A succession

B pioneer plants

C climax community

D pollution

E acid rain

F conserving

G reduce

H reuse

I recycle

J reclamation

K wetlands

Name _____

Part II Science Concepts and Understanding

Write the letter of the best choice.

____ 12. At which stage of primary succession do lichens start to grow on exposed rocks?
    A pioneer-plant stage   C grassy stage
    B mossy stage   D climax-community stage

____ 13. During the second stage of primary succession, —
    F lichens grow on rocks   H alders and willows grow
    G wildfires often occur   J mosses take over

____ 14. Secondary succession might happen after —
    A primary succession   C a forest fire
    B a harsh winter   D glaciers melt

____ 15. Air pollution is caused by —
    F cutting trees   H burning fossil fuels
    G building roads   J strip mining

____ 16. Which of the following is an example of reusing?
    A riding a bicycle   C recovering aluminum from cans
    B using solar heat   D cloth diapers

____ 17. Which of the following human activities helps protect ecosystems?
    F using less water
    G using chemical fertilizers
    H strip mining
    J building shopping malls

____ 18. Why are landfills **NOT** a perfect solution for disposing of solid wastes?
    A They use energy.   C They cause acid rain.
    B They use scarce land.   D They pollute the air.

____ 19. Why are wetlands important ecosystems?
    F They purify water.
    G They attract endangered animals.
    H They have been polluted.
    J They speed up succession.

Name _____

_____ 20. Two examples of climax-community plants are —
   A lichens and mosses   C hemlock and spruce
   B grasses and wildflowers   D willows and aspens

_____ 21. Which of the following is NOT an example of reclamation?
   F constructing an artificial wetland
   G growing prairie grasses for lawns
   H cleaning up a polluted river
   J conserving electricity

_____ 22. What is the first step in the process of reclamation?
   A researching the problem   C building a small pond
   B attracting wildlife to the area D planting native plants

_____ 23. How can planting native plants help restore an ecosystem?
   F The plants provide food for people.
   G The plants attract wildlife to the area.
   H The plants add water to the habitat.
   J The plants attract builders to the area.

_____ 24. Which of the following does NOT describe wetlands?
   A They act as water filters.   C They are hard to restore.
   B They are homes for animals.   D They only contain fresh water.

_____ 25. How are forest fires helpful in an ecosystem?
   F They speed up secondary succession.
   G They draw nutrients from the soil.
   H They destroy unwanted plants and animals.
   J They add oxygen to the atmosphere.

_____ 26. The three *Rs* of conserving resources are —
   A reduce, reuse, and remind   C refuse, reduce, and release
   B reward, reuse, and recycle   D reduce, reuse, and recycle

_____ 27. The causes of acid rain include —
   F runoff from roads   H waste water from factories
   G exhaust from cars   J organic fertilizers

_____ 28. The fireweed is an example of —
   A an endangered plant   C a pioneer plant
   B a deciduous-forest plant   D a climax-community plant

Name _____

Use the letters of the terms in the Word Bank to label the stages of **primary succession**.

| A climax community | B pioneer-plant stage | C mossy stage | D grassy stage |

29. ____   30. ____   31. ____   32. ____

Part III   Critical Thinking

33. If people did not change climax communities, would they stay the same forever? Why?

    _____

    _____

34. What are some ways people benefit from healthy ecosystems?

    _____

35. Suppose the people in Town A conserve resources and avoid burning fossil fuels. The people in Town B to the northwest burn lots of fossil fuels and dump wastes into the river. How might the people in Town A be affected by the actions of the people in Town B?

    _____

    _____

36. Compare the process of reclamation with that of secondary succession.

    _____

    _____

Name _____

Part IV   Process Skills Application

37. Design an experiment that will determine what kind of window covering will keep sunny classrooms the warmest in cool weather. What tools would you need to use? **Identify the variables** you might need to **control.**

_____
_____
_____

38. The following table shows how much water people use in various everyday activities. **Interpret** the data, and **infer** how people could conserve water.

Activity	Liters of Water Used
Drinking water	2 (per day)
Showering	19 (per minute)
Flushing toilet	23 (per flush)
Watering lawn	38 (per minute)
Bathing	135 (per day)
Leaking faucet	180–910 (per day)

_____
_____
_____

39. Describe how you could **make a model** of secondary succession.

_____
_____

Name _____ Date _____

Cleaning Up Oil

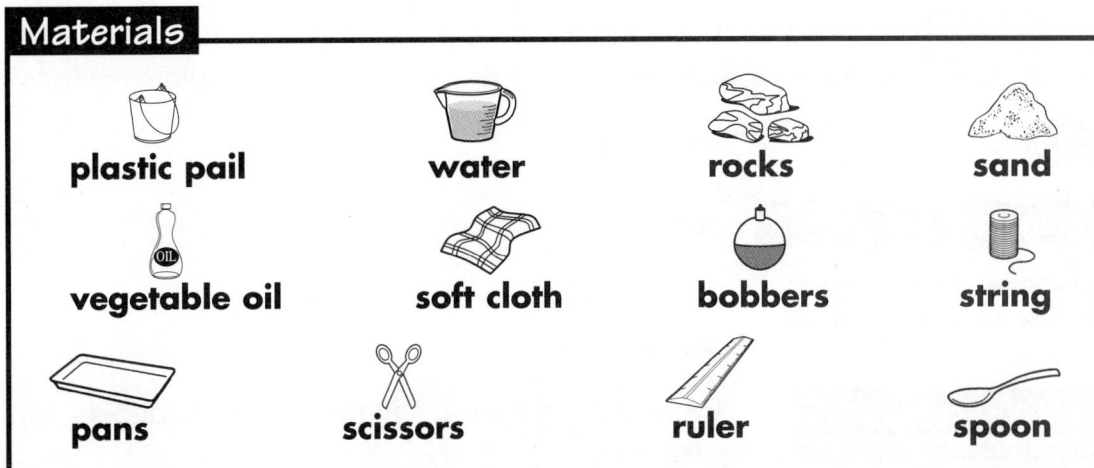

Materials: plastic pail, water, rocks, sand, vegetable oil, soft cloth, bobbers, string, pans, scissors, ruler, spoon

You are the mayor of a small seaside town. An oil spill has occurred on your town's beach. You want to find the best way to remove the oil from the water, the rocks, and the sand.

1. Use the materials provided to make a model of a beach. Use the oil to model an oil spill at sea.

2. Describe how the oil reacted with the different materials (water, sand, and rock).

   _____

   _____

3. Describe how you cleaned up the water, the sand, and the rocks.

   _____

   _____

   _____

4. What problems might you face if your method was used to clean up a real oil spill?

   _____

   _____

Unit B • Chapter 4   **Assessment Guide** AG 59

Teacher's Directions

Cleaning Up Oil

PERFORMANCE TASK

Materials Performance Task sheet, plastic pails, water, rocks, sand, pans, vegetable oil, soft cloths, bobbers, string, scissors, rulers, spoons

Time 30 minutes

Suggested Grouping pairs

Science Processes observe, make models, experiment, draw conclusions

Preparation Hints Provide a work area, covered with newspapers, for working with water and vegetable oil.

Introduce the Task Discuss how oil spills, which occur when oil tankers have accidents, are a form of water pollution. Explain to students that they will make a model of an oil spill and experiment to find the best way to clean it up. Remind them that the methods used to clean up an oil spill must be safe for the environment. Point out some of the materials provided, and ask students to discuss some possible uses for these materials.

Promote Discussion Ask students how oil that is spilled in the ocean spreads to cover large areas. (Wind and ocean currents carry the oil far from where it was originally spilled.) Encourage them to consider the effort and time involved in cleaning up a spill that covers thousands of miles of coastline. Encourage them also to consider the effects of oil spills on coastal wildlife.

Scoring Rubric

Performance Indicators

_____ Makes models of a beach and an oil spill.
_____ Observes that oil floats on water, clings to rocks, and makes sand lumpy.
_____ Uses materials to experiment with ways to remove oil.
_____ Explains difficulties inherent in cleaning up oil spills.

Observations and Rubric Score

3	2	1	0

AG 60 Assessment Guide — Unit B • Chapter 4

Name _____
Date _____

Systems and Interactions in Nature

Write the letter of the best choice.

_____ 1. How does nitrogen move through an ecosystem?
  A plants → soil → animals
  B lightning → soil → animals
  C soil → plants → animals
  D animals → plants → soil

_____ 2. What process releases oxygen to the air?
  F respiration   H evaporation
  G photosynthesis J condensation

_____ 3. Which is the correct path of water in the water cycle?
  A evaporation → condensation → precipitation
  B precipitation → condensation → evaporation
  C condensation → evaporation → precipitation
  D precipitation → condensation → transpiration

_____ 4. Plants return water to the environment through —
  F photosynthesis
  G condensation
  H evaporation
  J transpiration

_____ 5. Why is only 1 percent of Earth's fresh water usable?
  A Groundwater cannot be used.
  B Most is frozen in glaciers.
  C Fresh water evaporates instantly.
  D Most is found in plants.

_____ 6. An ecosystem is made up of —
  F the living things in a community
  G air, water, and land
  H species of plants and animals
  J a community and its physical environment

_____ 7. Two different consumers exist in the same environment and eat the same food. One hunts at night and the other hunts during the day. These animals have different —
  A habitats   C ecosystems
  B communities   D niches

_____ 8. What does NOT determine the types of plants in an ecosystem?
  F temperature range
  G soil conditions
  H number of animals
  J amount of precipitation

Unit B   (page 1 of 4)   Assessment Guide AG 61

Name _____

___ 9. Which shows a possible food chain?
   A sun → consumer → producer → decomposer
   B herbivore → plant → decomposer → carnivore
   C sun → mushroom → grass → snake → grasshopper
   D plant → herbivore → snake → third-level consumer

___ 10. How does available energy change as it is passed from one level to the next in a food chain?
   F Each level receives more energy than the level before.
   G The same amount of energy is passed from one level to the next.
   H About 10 percent of the energy is passed from one level to the next.
   J No energy is passed from one level to the next.

___ 11. Which two organisms would you expect to compete with each other?
   A hyenas and cheetahs
   B deer and fish
   C fish and trees
   D flowers and rabbits

___ 12. Which two organisms have a symbiotic relationship?
   F cheetahs and zebras
   G bees and flowers
   H raccoons and sea turtles
   J warblers and insects

___ 13. A behavior that an organism is born with is —
   A a learned behavior
   B a competition
   C an instinct
   D a symbiotic behavior

___ 14. Which is **NOT** a result of human development in an ecosystem?
   F endangered species
   G competition for food
   H destruction of animal habitat
   J an increase in a population

___ 15. What happens when a natural event kills the producers in a food chain?
   A The consumer population increases.
   B The consumer population decreases.
   C The producer population increases.
   D There is no effect.

___ 16. If a species becomes endangered, it —
   F will definitely disappear
   G may become extinct
   H is increasing in population
   J has lost its instincts

___ 17. A biome includes _____, but a climate zone does not.
   A temperature
   B rainfall
   C animals
   D amount of sunlight

Name _____

_____ 18. Why are there few plants on the floor of the rain forest?
F not enough sunlight
G too many herbivores
H lack of water
J too little space

_____ 19. Which plant is NOT matched with its biome?
A oak tree – deciduous forest
B mesquite – desert
C grass – grasslands
D palm tree – tundra

_____ 20. Which is NOT a saltwater ecosystem?
F lake zone
G near-shore zone
H intertidal zone
J open-ocean zone

_____ 21. Areas where fresh and salt water mix at the mouth of a river are called —
A springs
B ports
C vents
D estuaries

_____ 22. Which is an example of primary succession?
F land uncovered by a melting glacier
G sprouting and growth of pioneer plants
H land covered by a volcanic eruption
J an earthquake damaging land

_____ 23. Secondary succession occurs after —
A an increase in native species
B an ecosystem has been heavily damaged
C a short growing season
D a long, cold winter

_____ 24. Which are two types of waste produced by human activity?
F energy and acid rain
G energy and air pollution
H oxygen and air pollution
J acid rain and air pollution

_____ 25. A change from which an ecosystem cannot recover is called a —
A catastrophic change
B primary change
C secondary succession
D new beginning

_____ 26. The process of restoring damaged ecosystems is called —
F recycling
G rural development
H reclamation
J rebirth

_____ 27. Which is an example of conserving our resources?
A throwing away newspapers
B reusing old clothes
C running a half-full dishwasher
D using disposable paper plates

Name _____

Answer in complete sentences.

28. Describe the carbon–oxygen cycle.

29. Do you think Jerome, Alabama, should fill in its remaining wetlands with more housing developments? Explain your answer.

30. When you are using resources wisely, what are the three Rs to remember, and how can you put them to use?

Name _____
Date _____

Changes to Earth's Surface

Part 1   Vocabulary

Match the terms in Column B with the meanings in Column A.

Column A

___ 1. Remains or traces of past life found in the crust

___ 2. Theory of how continents move over Earth's surface

___ 3. Shaking of ground from energy release in the crust

___ 4. Hot, soft rock from the lower mantle

___ 5. Physical feature on Earth's surface

___ 6. Place where pieces of the crust move

___ 7. "Supercontinent" on Earth millions of years ago

___ 8. Opening in the crust through which lava flows

___ 9. Rigid block of crust and upper-mantle rock

___ 10. Downhill shifting of rock and soil because of gravity

___ 11. Process in which soil, sand, and sediment are formed

___ 12. Process of moving sediment from one place to another

___ 13. Process of dropping sediment in a new location

___ 14. Outer, very thin layer of Earth

___ 15. Center and hottest layer of Earth

___ 16. Middle layer of Earth

Column B

A   continental drift

B   mantle

C   fault

D   fossils

E   erosion

F   magma

G   mass movement

H   deposition

I   plate

J   volcano

K   core

L   crust

M   Pangea

N   landform

O   earthquake

P   weathering

Unit C • Chapter 1   (page 1 of 5)   Assessment Guide AG 65

Name _____

Part II Science Concepts and Understanding

For Questions 17–19, describe how water is weathering rock in each of the pictures.

17. _____

18. _____

19. _____

Use the following pictures to answer Questions 20–22.

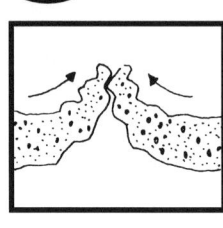 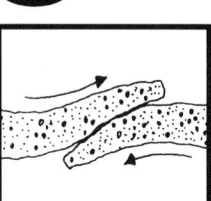 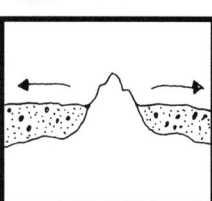  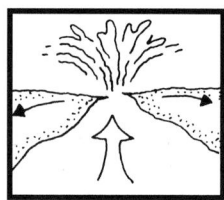

20. Which picture or pictures show how mountains are formed?

    _____

21. In what other way can a mountain form that is **NOT** pictured above? Name a famous mountain range of this type.

    _____

    _____

22. Which picture shows how most of the highest mountains are formed? Name a famous mountain range of this type.

    _____

AG 66 Assessment Guide   (page 2 of 5)   **Unit C • Chapter 1**

Name _____

Write the letter of the best choice.

____ 23. Why would footprints made on the moon last for hundreds of years?
    A There is no weathering on the moon.
    B There is no wind or water to erode the footprints.
    C The footprints on the moon are very deep because of the Apollo astronauts' shoes.
    D The Apollo astronauts on the moon made shoe deposits with space-age materials.

____ 24. If the center of Earth is its hottest part, why is it solid?
    F because the core is made of metal
    G because that is where rocks come from, and rocks are solid
    H because the hotter things are, the more solid they are
    J because of the great pressure at the center of Earth

____ 25. What does it mean to say that Earth's plates "float"?
    A The plates float on the soft rock of the lower mantle, which has currents like water.
    B The plates float on the oceans, which is why there is water underground.
    C The plates never become liquid rock or sink, so they float.
    D The plates only sometimes become liquid rock, so they float.

____ 26. What does it mean to say that "the Atlantic Ocean is getting wider, pushing Europe and North America apart"?
    F The ocean is eroding more of the beaches on the coasts of North America and Europe.
    G The ocean deposits heavy sediment on both coasts, pushing them apart.
    H The North American and European plates are moving away from each other.
    J The North American and European plates are moving closer to each other.

Name _____

Part III Critical Thinking

27. How do fossils help scientists learn about plants and animals of the past?

   _____
   _____
   _____

28. Would you expect many earthquakes to occur along the Ring of Fire? Why or why not?

   _____
   _____
   _____
   _____

29. What would the surface of Earth eventually look like if Earth's plates stopped moving? Why?

   _____
   _____
   _____
   _____

30. How is it possible that rock from some of the highest mountains has fossils?

   _____
   _____
   _____

31. In 1963 a new island formed off the coast of Iceland. This island, named Surtsey, is part of the Mid-Atlantic Ridge. What forces do you think are building Surtsey? Why?

   _____
   _____
   _____
   _____

Name _____

Part IV Process Skills Application

Look at the picture below. For Question 32, name a place where you *observe* that water weathering has occurred. For Question 33, name a place where you *observe* that wind weathering has occurred.

32. _____   33. _____

For Questions 34–35, respond and explain your answer in complete sentences.

34. Which would be a better **model** of Earth's plates—a tile floor or a stack of dishes? Why?

   _____
   _____
   _____

35. Which would be a better **model** of Earth's layers—an orange or a peach? Why?

   _____
   _____
   _____

Name _____ Date _____

PERFORMANCE TASK

Design a Planet

Materials

- one-half of a 6-in. solid Styrofoam ball
- crayons
- white paper
- glue

Design your own planet by drawing lines on the flat part of the Styrofoam ball to show the relative thickness of each of the planet's layers. Color each layer with crayons. Then use the paper and glue to add drawings of various landforms to the curved side of the ball.

Answer the questions on a separate sheet of paper.

1. List the layers of your planet from the thickest to the thinnest. How is your planet similar to and different from Earth?

2. Compare the temperature of your planet's core with the temperature of its other layers.

3. Describe the landforms on your planet.

4. What do you think would happen if you soaked your model planet in water and then put it into a freezer? Explain your answer.

5. If you use your fingernail to scratch the curved surface of your planet model, what process are you modeling—erosion, deposition, weathering, earthquakes, or volcanic eruptions? Why?

AG 70 Assessment Guide   **Unit C • Chapter 1**

Teacher's Directions

Design a Planet

Materials Performance Task sheet, 6-in. solid Styrofoam balls (cut in half), crayons, white paper, glue

Time 20–30 minutes

Suggested Grouping pairs or small groups

Science Processes make models, observe, infer, communicate

Preparation Hints Cut each Styrofoam ball in half before you begin the activity.

Introduce the Task Explain to students that they will be making a model of a planet. Review building of landforms on Earth.

Promote Discussion When students finish, ask volunteers to share their models and responses with the class. Have students suggest other models that would illustrate continental drift, erosion, weathering, earthquakes, and volcanic eruptions.

Scoring Rubric

Performance Indicators

_____ Describes the characteristics of the model's layers and the similarities and differences between the model planet and the Earth.

_____ Identifies layers in the model, such as a crust (with continents), a core (made solid by pressure), and possibly some layer between the crust and core.

_____ Demonstrates an understanding that freezing the soaked model would cause the ice to expand and cause the model to break or form cracks.

_____ Compares fingernail scratches to weathering because they will deform the surface of the ball by causing bits of Styrofoam to come off.

Observations and Rubric Score

3	2	1	0

Unit C • Chapter 1

Name _____

Date _____

Rocks and Minerals

Part 1   Vocabulary

Use the letters of the terms in the Word Bank to complete the sentences.

A mineral	D streak	G rock cycle
B rock	E igneous rock	H metamorphic rock
C sedimentary rock	F hardness	I luster

____ 1. Rock that forms when melted rock hardens is called ____.

____ 2. A mineral's ____ describes how its surface looks when light reflects from it.

____ 3. Earth's ____ is the pattern of slow changes in rocks from one kind to another.

____ 4. ____ forms when rock pieces deposited over time are squeezed and stuck together.

____ 5. When you rub a mineral against a white tile, its ____ is the color of the powder left behind.

____ 6. Material made up of one or more minerals is called ____.

____ 7. A rock that has been changed by high heat and great pressure is ____.

____ 8. A natural solid that has its particles arranged in a crystal pattern is called a ____.

____ 9. A mineral's ____ is its ability to resist being scratched.

Name _____

Part II   Science Concepts and Understanding

For Questions 10–13, use the following chart. Choose the best answer.

MOHS' HARDNESS SCALE 1 is softest. 10 is hardest.									
1 Talc	2 Gypsum	3 Calcite	4 Fluorite	5 Apatite	6 Orthoclase	7 Quartz	8 Topaz	9 Corundum	10 Diamond

____ 10. Which of the following minerals is the hardest?
   A gypsum   C topaz
   B talc   D calcite

____ 11. Which of the following minerals can fluorite scratch?
   F quartz   H orthoclase
   G apatite   J calcite

____ 12. Which of the following minerals can scratch corundum?
   A gypsum   C quartz
   B diamond   D topaz

____ 13. Scientists sometimes use a copper penny with a hardness of 3 or a glass with a hardness of 6 to test a mineral's hardness. Which of the following minerals could be scratched by a glass but **NOT** by a penny?
   F quartz   H orthoclase
   G gypsum   J apatite

For Questions 14–16, choose the best answer.

____ 14. You find a rock with pieces of seashells in it. Which kind of rock is it?
   A metamorphic   C sedimentary
   B volcanic   D igneous

Unit C • Chapter 2   (page 2 of 4)   Assessment Guide AG 73

Name _____

___ 15. Which of the following is **NOT** a characteristic scientists use to classify minerals?
    F hardness   H luster
    G volume   J streak

___ 16. Halite is another term for —
    A water   C table salt
    B pepper   D copper

Part III   Critical Thinking

17. Why is a piece of pumice lighter than a piece of obsidian of equal size?

_____

_____

18. How is a rock different from a mineral?

_____

_____

19. Why aren't you likely to find a fossil in metamorphic rock or igneous rock?

_____

_____

Part IV   Process Skills Application

20. Which would be a better **model** of how an igneous rock changes into a sedimentary rock — an eraser rubbed on paper, or crushed graham crackers that are mixed with melted butter and pressed into a pie pan to make a crust? Explain your answer.

_____

_____

_____

Name _____

21. Which would be a better **model** of how metamorphic rocks form — chocolate chip cookie dough that is flattened and then baked into cookies, or chocolate chips and milk melted together in a pan and then cooled to make fudge? Explain your answer.

_____
_____
_____
_____

Use the following *classification* chart for Questions 22–23.

Mineral	Color	Color of Streak	Hardness
Talc	light green	white	1
Fluorite	light purple	white	4
Feldspar	white, salmon pink	white	5
Quartz	clear, milky white, rose, violet, smoky gray	none	7

_____ 22. A mineral sample has a white streak and is so soft that it can be scratched by your fingernail. Which mineral is it?
    A talc   C fluorite
    B quartz   D feldspar

_____ 23. A mineral sample is purple, has a white streak, and cannot be scratched by a penny. Which mineral is it?
    F talc   H fluorite
    G quartz   J feldspar

Name _____ Date _____

PERFORMANCE TASK

The Rock Cycle Story

Materials

crayons or colored pencils

pencil

Create a comic strip that tells the story of the rock cycle. Draw pictures and use labels to show each part of the cycle. Be sure you describe each rock stage you show.

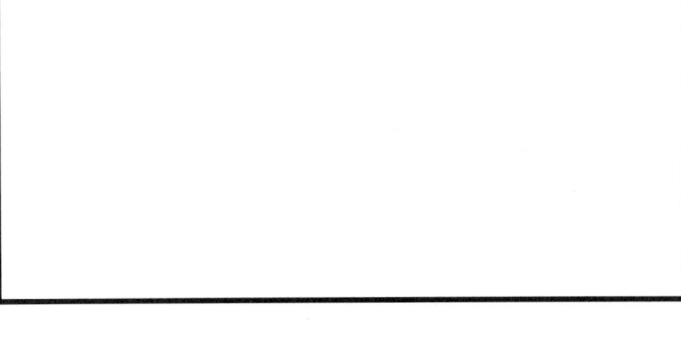

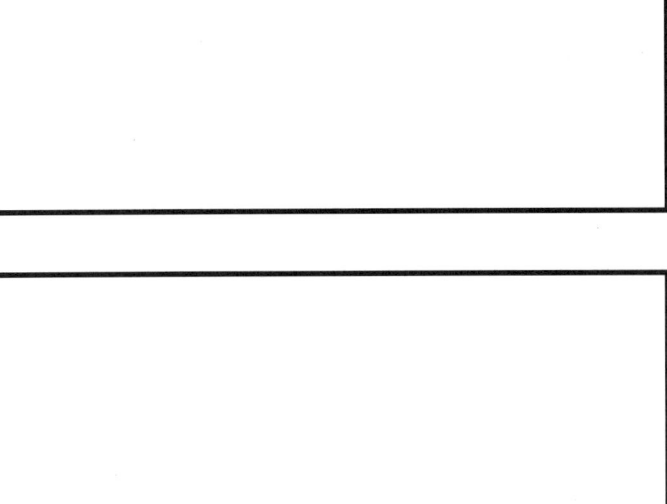

AG 76 **Assessment Guide** Unit C • Chapter 2

Teacher's Directions

The Rock Cycle Story

Materials — Performance Task sheet, crayons or colored pencils, pencils

Time — 20–30 minutes

Suggested Grouping — individuals

Science Processes — make a model, communicate, classify

Preparation Hints — Collect several samples of rocks to share with students. You may wish to provide narrow strips of construction paper folded into sections for the comic strip.

Introduce the Task — Explain to students that a storyboard is a tool that cartoon creators and movie directors use to plan how they will tell a story. Review the rock cycle with students. Discuss how rocks are formed. Give each student a copy of the Performance Task sheet, and read the directions as a class. Remind students to label the various stages so that others can understand what is happening in each panel.

Promote Discussion — Ask students to share their storyboards in small groups. Ask volunteers to present theirs to the class. In a class discussion, have students compare the three parts of the rock cycle. Ask students to summarize what they know about how rocks are formed.

Scoring Rubric

Performance Indicators

_____ Draws example of igneous rock changing to sedimentary rock.

_____ Draws example of sedimentary rock changing to metamorphic rock.

_____ Draws example of metamorphic rock changing to igneous rock.

_____ Writes an accurate description for each picture drawn.

Observations and Rubric Score

| 3 | 2 | 1 | 0 |

Unit C • Chapter 2

Name _____
Date _____

Weather and Climate

Part I Vocabulary

Write the letter of the correct term in each blank below.

A climate	D greenhouse effect	F microclimate
B El Niño	E local winds	G prevailing winds
C global warming		

The **1.** ____ is the average of weather conditions in an area through all seasons over a period of time. It remains fairly stable because of **2.** ____ that blow constantly from the same direction. A short-term climate change is the **3.** ____ effect.

The climate changes all the time. Even a **4.** ____, the climate of a very small area, may change. **5.** ____ can change because a new building or parking lot is built in an area. But a large change in climate usually takes a long time. **6.** ____, an abnormal rise in Earth's average temperature, can happen because too much carbon dioxide absorbs some of the heat given off by the Earth, causing a **7.** ____.

H air pressure	J condensation	L humidity	N air masses
I atmosphere	K evaporation	M precipitation	O fronts

Almost all weather occurs in the lowest layer of air, or the **8.** ____. The sun heats the oceans, causing **9.** ____ of water. The invisible water vapor cools and turns back into liquid water in a process called **10.** ____. When the **11.** ____ is high enough, the droplets fall as **12.** ____. Usually, rain or snow can be predicted if the surrounding **13.** ____ drops. Most weather changes occur at **14.** ____, the boundaries between large bodies of air called **15.** ____.

Name _____

Part II Science Concepts and Understanding

Use the following diagram to answer Questions 16–19.

___ 16. What is happening at Point I?
   A condensation
   B precipitation
   C evaporation
   D humidity

___ 17. What is happening at Point II?
   F humidity
   G evaporation
   H precipitation
   J condensation

___ 18. What is happening at Point III?
   A evaporation
   B humidity
   C condensation
   D precipitation

___ 19. What process is shown in the diagram above?
   F condensation
   G water cycle
   H cloud formation
   J humidity

Write the letter of the best choice.

___ 20. Which is a type of cloud?
   A stratus
   B precipitation
   C novas
   D condensed

___ 21. What is **NOT** observed or measured by weather forecasters?
   F temperature
   G atmosphere height
   H humidity
   J wind speed and direction

Unit C • Chapter 3   (page 2 of 5)   Assessment Guide   AG 79

Name _____

Use the following picture to answer Questions 22–25.

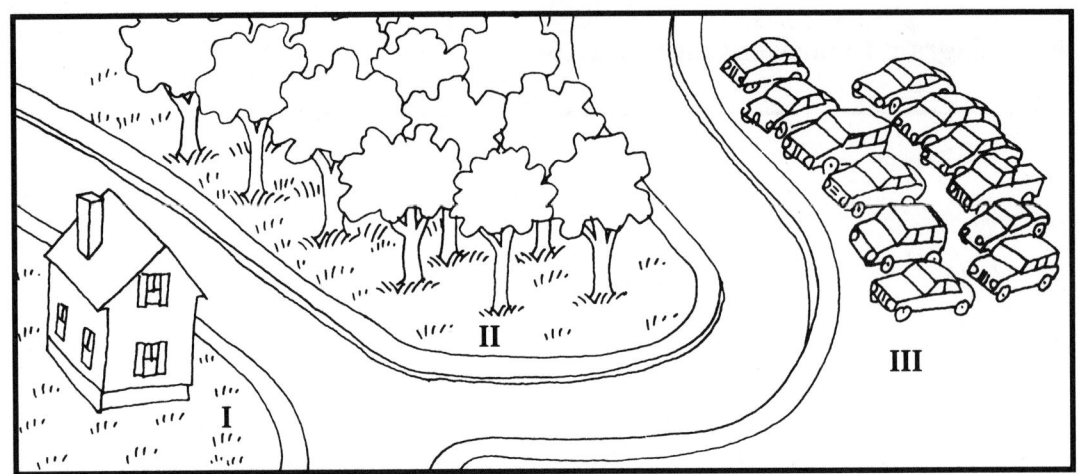

_____ 22. How would the temperature and humidity probably change if you were to walk from Area I to Area II?
  A It would get warmer, with more humidity.
  B It would get cooler, with more humidity.
  C It would get warmer, with less humidity.
  D It would get cooler, with less humidity.

_____ 23. How would the temperature and humidity probably change if you were to walk from Area II to Area III?
  F It would get warmer, with more humidity.
  G It would get cooler, with more humidity.
  H It would get warmer, with less humidity.
  J It would get cooler, with less humidity.

_____ 24. In which area would you expect the humidity to be the highest?
  A Area III
  B Area II
  C Area I
  D They will all have the same level of humidity.

_____ 25. What are Areas I, II, and III called?
  F microclimates
  G temperate zones
  H stratospheres
  J climate zones

Name _____

Look at each picture below. Write *toward the land* or *toward the sea* to describe which way the wind is likely to be blowing.

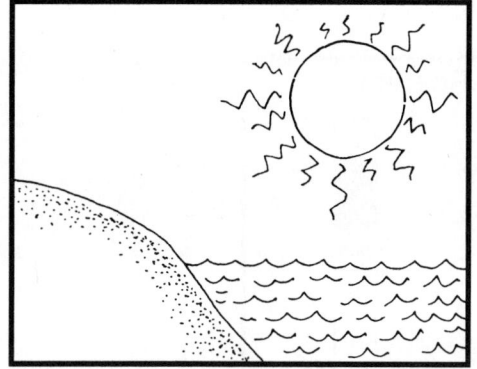 

26. _____   27. _____

Part III   Critical Thinking

28. Most weather forecasts are for large areas. Why is it sometimes more difficult to predict local weather conditions?

_____
_____
_____

29. How do fronts affect weather changes?

_____
_____
_____

30. How can human activities affect local and global climates?

_____
_____
_____

Name _____

Part IV Process Skills Application

Use the following table to answer Questions 31–36.

City's Five-Day Temperature and Rainfall Readings

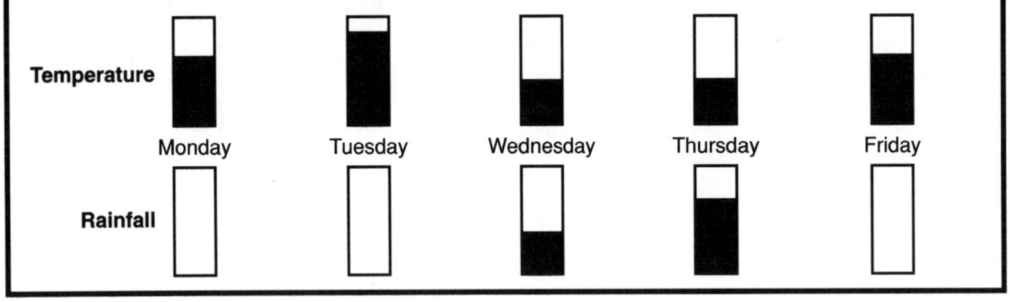

Temperature / Rainfall readings for Monday, Tuesday, Wednesday, Thursday, Friday

Using your *observations*, describe the weather.

31. From Monday to Tuesday:

_____

32. From Tuesday to Wednesday:

_____

33. From Wednesday to Thursday:

_____

34. From Thursday to Friday:

_____

35. Based on the information above, can you **predict** what is going to happen on Saturday? Why or why not?

_____

_____

36. If it is raining in the city on a summer day, what can you **infer** about the temperature?

_____

_____

Name _____ Date _____

Map It!

Materials

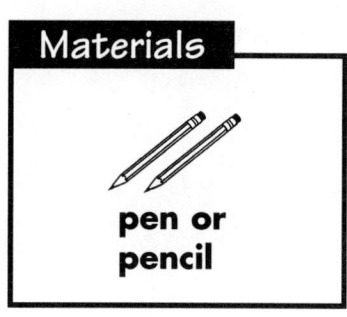

pen or pencil

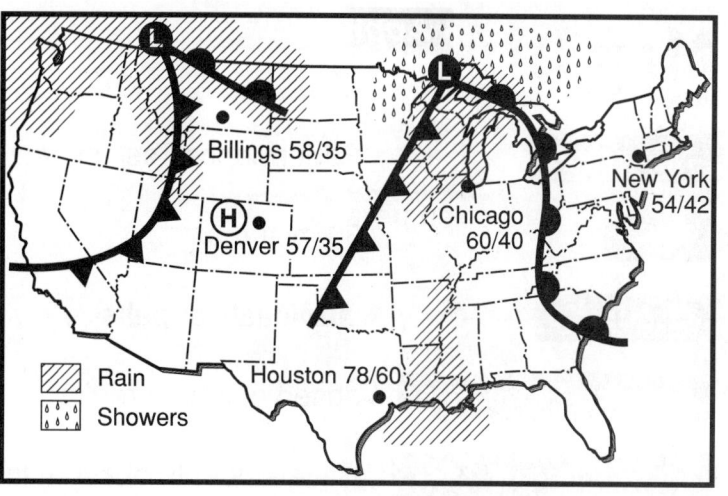

Study the weather map. Fill in the chart and answer the questions.

City	Today's Weather			Prediction for Tomorrow		
	High Temp.	Low Temp.	Precip.	High Temp.	Low Temp.	Predicted Precip.
Billings						
Chicago						
Houston						
New York						

1. In what direction do weather systems in the United States generally move? Why? _____

2. What information other than that on the map would help you make a more accurate weather prediction?
   _____

3. How would knowing whether the barometer is rising or falling help you predict the weather?
   _____
   _____

4. Predict what the weather will be like in Denver in a day or two.
   _____

Unit C • Chapter 3   **Assessment Guide AG 83**

PERFORMANCE TASK

Teacher's Directions

Map It!

Materials — Performance Task sheet, pen or pencil

Time — 30 minutes

Grouping — individuals or pairs

Science Processes — observe, infer, predict

Introduce the Task Have students observe the map. Help them interpret the high and low temperatures and precipitation at each city named. Point out that the curved lines across the map stand for fronts. The lines with the triangles stand for cold fronts; those with half circles stand for warm fronts. A warm front is often followed by precipitation. Accept responses within a reasonable range. Predictions for tomorrow: Billings: 50°–55°; 38°–40°; rain. Chicago: 50°–55°; 35°–40°; none. Houston: 75°–80°; 55°–60°; none. New York: 55°–60°; 45°–50°; none.

Promote Discussion When students have finished, have volunteers share their weather predictions. Have them give justifications for the predictions.

Scoring Rubric

Performance Indicators

_____ Makes logical or justifiable predictions of temperature and precipitation in four cities.

_____ Identifies the movement of weather patterns in the country as moving from west to east.

_____ Identifies cloud cover, types of clouds, and wind speed and direction as observations that assist in weather prediction.

_____ Predicts that within a few days Denver will experience a drop in temperature and there will probably be some type of precipitation.

Observations and Rubric Score

| 3 | 2 | 1 | 0 |

Name _____
Date _____

Exploring the Oceans

Part 1 Vocabulary

Match each term in Column B with its meaning in Column A.

Column A

____ 1. Wall of rocks built out into the ocean

____ 2. Up-and-down movement of surface water

____ 3. Repeated rise and fall in the level of the ocean

____ 4. Stream of water that flows like a river through the ocean

____ 5. Self-contained underwater breathing apparatus

____ 6. Area where ocean and land meet

____ 7. Small underwater vehicle

____ 8. Rocky point along a shore

____ 9. Pool of sea water found along a rocky shoreline

____ 10. Removal of salt from sea water

____ 11. Sound waves that can be used to map the ocean floor

____ 12. Weight of water pressing on an object

____ 13. Percent of salt in ocean water

Column B

A tide

B salinity

C current

D shore

E desalination

F jetty

G wave

H headland

I sonar

J submersible

K tide pool

L scuba

M water pressure

Name _____

Part II Science Concepts and Understanding

Write the letter of the best choice.

___ 14. Waves form because —
   A Earth spins on its axis
   B currents flow through the ocean
   C wind blows over the surface of the water
   D Earth's gravity pulls the water up and down

___ 15. Earth's rotation causes ocean currents —
   F to bend to the right in the Northern Hemisphere
   G to bend to the right in the Southern Hemisphere
   H to form larger tides
   J to spread out over the equator

___ 16. Differences in _____ cause deep-ocean currents.
   A air temperature
   B wind speed
   C current direction
   D water temperature

___ 17. Tides are caused by —
   F Earth's rotation and the gravitational pull of the moon and sun
   G the effect of wind on both hemispheres
   H uneven heating of Earth's surface
   J deep-ocean currents

___ 18. Scientists discovered the presence of vents along the mid-Atlantic ridge by using the submersible —
   A *Scuba*
   B *Titanic*
   C *Trieste*
   D *Alvin*

___ 19. A rip current —
   F moves along the surface of the ocean
   G carries huge amounts of beach materials
   H flows away from the beach
   J varies with high and low tides

Name _____

___ 20. A headland may be all that remains when —
   A soft rock erodes
   B arches erode
   C soft rock and hard rock become layered
   D hard rock is layered

___ 21. Sonar is used to —
   F scrape samples from the ocean floor
   G collect objects at sea level
   H measure the depth of the ocean
   J help people breathe under water

___ 22. When a submarine explores the ocean bottom, what type of currents affect it?
   A surface currents
   B tidal currents
   C ebb currents
   D deep-ocean currents

___ 23. Why does a tsunami pass unnoticed under ships but destroy everything when it reaches the shore?
   F Increased friction with the ocean bottom decreases the speed of the wave, causing it to grow.
   G The tsunami speeds up and gets larger when it reaches the shore.
   H The tsunami splits into many waves that join into one large wave when they reach the shore.
   J Tsunami waves continue to combine and grow until they reach the shore.

___ 24. The salinity of ocean water comes from —
   A the gravitational pull of the moon
   B minerals weathered from Earth's crust
   C seaweed and other ocean plants
   D water pressure on the ocean's floor

___ 25. How does water in a wave move?
   F in a circle
   G back and forth
   H down to the bottom of the sea
   J up from the bottom of the sea

Name _____

___ 26. The deeper you go in an ocean, the ___ the water pressure becomes.
   A less
   B greater
   C deeper
   D shallower

___ 27. The removal of salt from ocean water is called —
   F saline removal
   G estuarial
   H desalination
   J sodium chloride

___ 28. Resources such as ___ can be found in the ocean.
   A petroleum
   B salt
   C coal
   D natural gas

___ 29. Because of erosion, a rocky beach may become —
   F an estuary
   G a mountain
   H a valley
   J a sandy beach

Part III   Critical Thinking

Answer Questions 30–33 on a separate sheet of paper.

30. Even though Cape Hatteras has had three jetties built to protect a lighthouse, the lighthouse is threatened by increased erosion. How might the erosion problem be fixed?

31. Suppose a boater sails a large boat almost onto shore during high tide. Explain what will happen if the boater tries to leave during low tide.

32. Are tides higher when the moon is full? Why or why not?

33. If a bottle is dropped into the ocean near England, where might the bottle wash ashore? Why?

Name _____

Part IV   Process Skills Application

Observe the following pictures to answer Question 34.

A

B
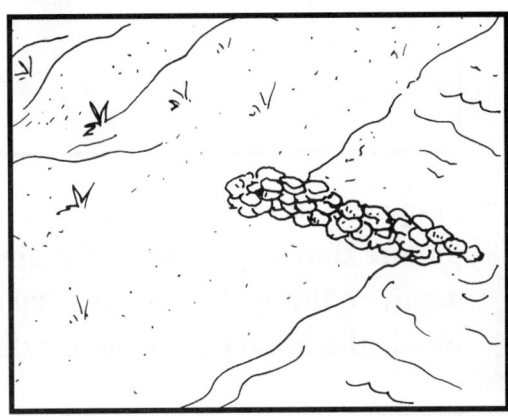

34. **Compare** Picture A with Picture B.

_____

_____

_____

35. Which is a better **model** of sonar—an echo or a reflection in a mirror? Why?

_____

_____

_____

36. Rainwater flows along the sides of the street, carrying leaves and twigs and depositing them where the flow turns a corner. Is this a good **model** for longshore currents that carry beach materials? Why or why not?

_____

_____

_____

Unit C • Chapter 4

Name _____ Date _____

Search!

Materials

pen or pencil

Suppose you are searching for a sunken ship in the area pictured below. The picture shows sonar times for nine different locations. To convert these times to depth, multiply the time by 1500 m/s (the speed of sound in water), and then divide the result by 2 to get the depth. Use a calculator to find your answers.

Time = 5.0 s Depth = 1. ____	Time = 3.1 s Depth = 2. ____	Time = 2.2 s Depth = 3. ____
Time = 1.9 s Depth = 6. ____	Time = 2.4 s Depth = 5. ____	Time = 4.6 s Depth = 4. ____
Time = 3.8 s Depth = 7. ____	Time = 1.9 s Depth = 8. ____	Time = 1.0 s Depth = 9. ____

You don't have time to search all nine locations, and the pressure becomes too great for your submersible to search locations below 1750 meters.

10. Which locations can you search with your submersible?

_____

_____

11. Infer why searching the ocean depths might be expensive.

_____

_____

_____

Teacher's Directions

Search!

Materials Performance Task sheet, pens or pencils

Time 25–30 minutes

Suggested Grouping individuals or pairs

Science Processes observe, compare, use numbers, measure

Preparation Hints Go over the math operations with students. Some may need help reading the answers if they contain decimal points.

Introduce the Task Tell students they will be converting sonar times to depth measurements to determine whether they can use a submersible to explore different locations.

Promote Discussion When students finish, have them compare results. Discuss that searching the ocean depths might be expensive because of the time and difficulty of finding an object under water.

Scoring Rubric

Performance Indicators

____ Calculates depth measurements. (Answers: 1. 3750 m; 2. 2325 m; 3. 1650 m; 4. 3450 m; 5. 1800 m; 6. 1425 m; 7. 2850 m; 8. 1425 m; 9. 750 m)

____ Analyzes calculations to find where a submersible can reach.

____ Demonstrates an understanding that searching the ocean can be expensive.

Observations and Rubric Score

3	2	1	0

Unit C • Chapter 4

Name _____
Date _____

Processes That Change the Earth

Write the letter of the best choice.

___ 1. Breaking rock into silt and other tiny pieces is known as —
  A erosion
  B weathering
  C deposition
  D mass movement

___ 2. Which of the following is **NOT** an example of changing landforms?
  F wind creating sand dunes
  G floodplains at the end of rivers
  H terminal moraines from glaciers
  J the sun warming desert sands

___ 3. Which would most likely cause the highest mountain to form?
  A two continental plates colliding
  B a continental and an oceanic plate colliding
  C magma bubbling up between plates that are pulling apart
  D the sudden release of energy as plates scrape past each other

___ 4. The difference between magma and lava is —
  F lava is always hotter than magma
  G lava is magma that reaches the surface of Earth
  H lava is inside a volcano and magma is outside
  J magma is found only under oceanic plates

___ 5. When the plates in Earth's crust grind past each other, the result is —
  A earthquakes C volcanoes
  B mudslides   D mountains

___ 6. The position of a rock layer in the Grand Canyon, as compared to those above and below it, can tell us —
  F which direction is north
  G whether or not there is coal nearby
  H how the Grand Canyon was formed
  J the age of the layers in relation to the other layers

AG 92 Assessment Guide   (page 1 of 4)   Unit C

Name _____

_____ 7. If similar fossils are found in North America and in Europe, which conclusion could be drawn?
   A The two land masses were once joined together.
   B At one time there were no oceans on Earth.
   C The fossils formed at the same time.
   D Ancient animals could swim long distances.

_____ 8. Which of the following best describes a mineral?
   F a compound made from living matter
   G a solid material arranged in a repeating pattern
   H the remains of organisms found in sedimentary rock
   J hot, soft rock from Earth's mantle

_____ 9. On Mohs' hardness scale, quartz has a hardness of 7 and glass has a hardness of 6. If they are rubbed together —
   A the quartz and glass would scratch each other
   B neither rock would get scratched
   C the quartz would scratch the glass
   D the glass would scratch the quartz

_____ 10. Scientists use a streak plate to —
   F measure the hardness of a mineral
   G observe the true color of a mineral
   H categorize the luster of a mineral
   J measure the clarity of a mineral

_____ 11. Which item includes a use for copper?
   A a stereo   C a pencil
   B a bicycle   D a pair of scissors

_____ 12. Rocks that are formed when magma hardens are known as —
   F frozen rocks   H sedimentary rocks
   G solid rocks   J igneous rocks

_____ 13. Shale is a —
   A fossilized rock
   B igneous rock
   C metamorphic rock
   D sedimentary rock

_____ 14. Marble is often used in —
   F chalkboards   H roofs
   G statues   J paper

_____ 15. What is needed to change a sedimentary rock into a metamorphic rock?
   A erosion
   B heat and pressure
   C compaction and cementing
   D melting

Name _____

_____ 16. Which one does **NOT** help to change rocks in the rock cycle?
F wind
G rivers
H volcanoes
J sunlight

_____ 17. Most of Earth's weather occurs in the —
A substratosphere
B hemisphere
C troposphere
D stratosphere

_____ 18. How does warm air compare to cold air?
F Warm air has low air pressure.
G Warm air has less humidity.
H Warm air weighs more.
J Warm air is drier.

_____ 19. If a meteorologist predicts that the barometric pressure is going to drop, what will most likely happen?
A It will be sunny and clear.
B The weather will be rainy.
C An earthquake will occur.
D There will be a drought.

_____ 20. Clouds form when —
F water evaporates
G air pressure increases
H water vapor condenses
J humidity decreases

_____ 21. Which type of wind will affect South America as well as Africa?
A local wind
B prevailing wind
C stratospheric wind
D breeze wind

_____ 22. Because of the prevailing westerly winds in the United States, most air masses tend to move from —
F west to east
G north to south
H east to west
J south to north

_____ 23. What changes when you walk from a city street to a park with a pond?
A El Niño   C microclimate
B global winds D climate zone

_____ 24. If humans continue to burn fossil fuels at the current rate, how will Earth's temperature be affected?
F no change at all
G a significant decrease
H a slight decrease
J a significant increase

_____ 25. Which of the following is a type of current?
A shore   C hemispheric
B jetty   D longshore

_____ 26. A boat about 15 miles offshore is above the —
F continental shelf
G abyssal plain
H continental slope
J continental plain

_____ 27. Most waves are caused by —
A ocean water moving forward
B wind blowing over the water
C extremely high air pressure
D differences in water temperature

Name _____

_____ 28. What does desalination remove from ocean water?
- F sand
- G salt
- H water
- J oil

Answer in complete sentences.

29. Explain the theory of "continental drift," starting with Pangea.

_____
_____
_____
_____

30. You find a rock in your back yard. Explain how you could determine the hardness of this unknown rock, using rocks that you have already identified.

_____
_____
_____
_____
_____

31. The shoreline of Olympic National Park in Washington has many headlands, sea caves, and sea arches. Explain how these occur and change with time.

_____
_____
_____
_____
_____

Name _____
Date _____

Earth, Moon, and Beyond

Part 1 Vocabulary

Use the letters of the terms in the Word Bank to complete the sentences.

A axis	D revolves	G space probes	J asteroids	M solstice
B eclipse	E rotates	H telescope	K planets	
C orbit	F satellite	I comets	L equinox	

Early robotic **1.** _____ that were sent into deep space could not report how it felt to be in space. They could only provide data and pictures. At first, even a simple **2.** _____ could provide a better view of space objects than they could.

The moon **3.** _____ in a closed path around Earth and is Earth's only natural **4.** _____. Its path around Earth is its **5.** _____. Earth **6.** _____, or turns, on an imaginary line called an **7.** _____. It is daytime for locations that face toward the sun, and it is nighttime for locations that face away from the sun. At times, an **8.** _____ occurs when Earth or the moon passes into the other's shadow.

Earth is one of nine **9.** _____ that orbit the sun. Other objects in the solar system include thousands of rocks called **10.** _____ and balls of ice and rock called **11.** _____. Each point in Earth's orbit at which the daylight hours are at their greatest or fewest is called a **12.** _____. Each point at which they are equal is the **13.** _____.

Name _____

Part II Science Concepts and Understanding

Write the letter of the best choice.

___ 14. Earth and the moon are alike in that both —
   A have liquid water
   B have satellites
   C have an atmosphere
   D are made of rock

___ 15. The three main types of landforms that make up the moon's surface are —
   F craters, equators, and gyrators
   G volcanoes, highlands, and eclipses
   H marias, santas, and domes
   J highlands, craters, and marias

___ 16. The moon landings were part of what program of space exploration?
   A Galileo   C Apollo
   B Mercury   D Newton

___ 17. The first artificial satellite launched into space was —
   F Viking   H Hubble
   G Sputnik   J Apollo

___ 18. Choose the order in which the following things were used to study space.
   A telescope, satellite, space probe, space shuttle
   B space probe, telescope, satellite, space shuttle
   C space probe, satellite, space shuttle, telescope
   D telescope, space probe, satellite, space shuttle

___ 19. The first Americans were sent into space in what program?
   F Apollo   H Voyager
   G Viking   J Mercury

Name _____

_____ 20. The first scientist to use a telescope to observe the sky was —
   A Armstrong
   B Galileo
   C Copernicus
   D Glenn

_____ 21. Timekeeping on Earth is based on Earth's —
   F hemispheres
   G time zones
   H satellites
   J distance from the sun

Use the following picture to answer Questions 22–23.

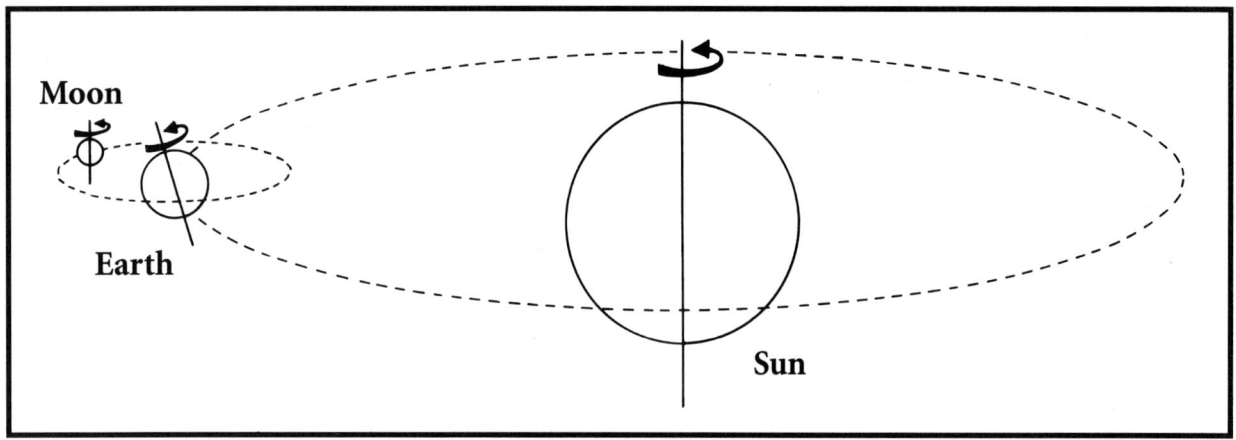

_____ 22. What does the symbol ↻ represent in the diagram above?
   A a revolution
   B an eclipse
   C an orbit
   D a rotation

_____ 23. What paths do the dotted lines represent in the diagram above?
   F revolutions
   G eclipses
   H orbits
   J rotations

Name _____

____ 24. Which of the following shows the correct order for phases of the moon?

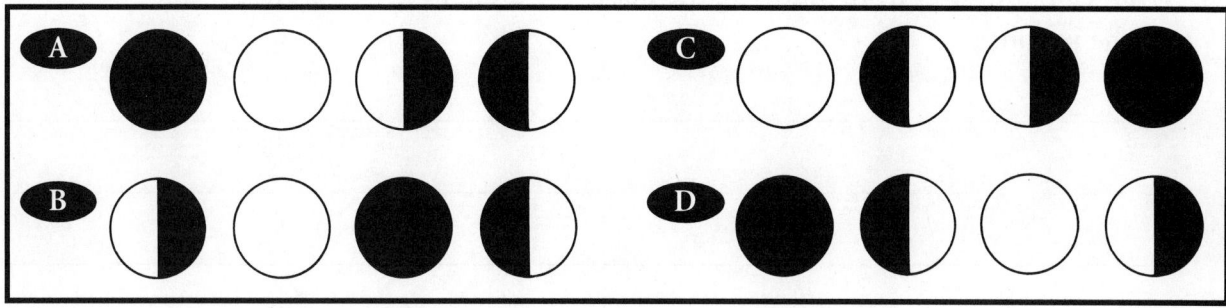

Use the following diagrams to answer Questions 25–26. What is happening in each picture?

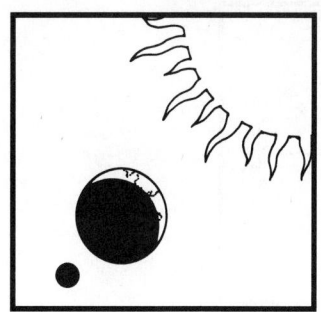   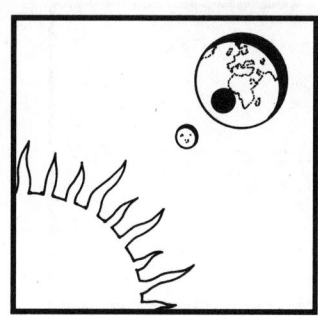

25. _____   26. _____

Part III   Critical Thinking

Answer the following on a separate sheet of paper.

27. Does a total solar eclipse block all of the sun from the Earth? Explain.

28. Compare the advantages and disadvantages of crewed space exploration and space probes.

29. Describe the relationships of the Earth-moon-sun motions.

Unit D • Chapter 1   (page 4 of 5)   Assessment Guide   AG99

Name _____

Part IV Process Skills Application

30. What can you **infer** from studying the depths and diameters of craters on the moon?

_____
_____
_____

Use the following pictures to answer Questions 31–32.

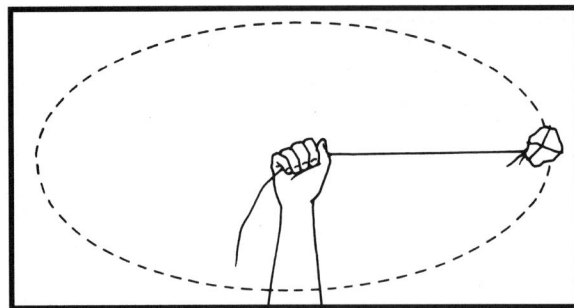 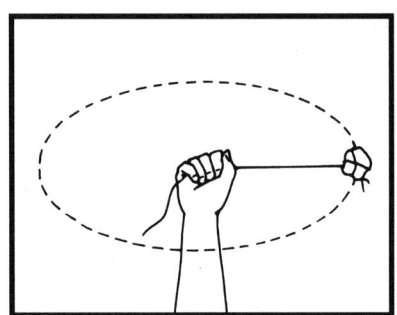

31. If you tie a string to a rock and spin the string and rock in a circle, you are **modeling** the orbit of Earth (the rock) around the sun (your hand). **Infer** what would happen if the string were only half as long and still being turned with the same force. What would the shorter string **model**?

_____
_____
_____

32. Use time and space relationships to **compare** the two pictures with the moon's orbit around Earth and Earth's orbit around the sun.

_____
_____
_____

Name _____ Date _____

It's Just a Phase!

Materials

lamp without a shade

softball or baseball

With your group, you are going to model the phases of the moon, using a lamp without a shade and a small ball.

1. When the teacher darkens the room, turn on the lamp.

2. Stand with your back to the lamp.

3. Hold the ball at arm's length above your head so that it is in the light.

4. Rotate counterclockwise, keeping the ball in the same position. Stop each eighth of the way around, and draw a picture that shows how much of the ball appears lighted.

5. What does the lamp represent? What does the ball represent?

   _____
   _____

6. Describe how much of the lighted half of the ball you could see and your position at each stopping point in your rotation. What is each similar phase of the moon called?

   _____
   _____

7. In a short paragraph, explain what causes the phases of the moon.

   _____
   _____

Unit D • Chapter 1   Assessment Guide AG101

PERFORMANCE TASK

Teacher's Directions

It's Just a Phase!

Materials — Performance Task sheet, lamp without a shade, softball or baseball

Time — 25–30 minutes

Suggested Grouping — groups of three

Science Processes — formulating and using models

Preparation Hints — none

Introduce the Task — Tell students that they will be modeling the phases of the moon. One student in each group will rotate the ball and the other two will draw what is happening. Students will answer questions on the Performance Task sheet individually, after a small-group discussion.

Promote Discussion — When students finish, ask why it was important to hold the ball above the head. (to keep it in the light; to prevent the person's shadow from falling on the ball)

Scoring Rubric

Performance Indicators

_____ Works with group to model the phases of the moon according to directions.

_____ Works with group to create drawings of the moon's cycle.

_____ Can identify and name the phases of the moon.

_____ Writes a clear paragraph explaining the phases of the moon's cycle.

Observations and Rubric Score

3   2   1   0

Name _____
Date _____

The Sun and Other Stars

Part I   Vocabulary

Match each term in Column B with its meaning in Column A.

Column A

____ 1. Dark areas on the surface of the sun

____ 2. Burst of energy from the sun's atmosphere

____ 3. Type of most stars

____ 4. Distance light travels in one year

____ 5. Everything that exists

____ 6. Particles thrown into space by the sun

____ 7. Group of stars, gas, and dust

____ 8. Brightness of a star

____ 9. Surface of the sun

____ 10. Atmosphere of the sun

Column B

A   corona

B   galaxy

C   light-year

D   magnitude

E   main-sequence

F   photosphere

G   solar flare

H   solar wind

I   sunspots

J   universe

Part II   Science Concepts and Understanding

Write the letter of the best choice.

____ 11. Solar energy is produced by —
   A hot gas   B fusion   C electricity   D waves

____ 12. The sun is the original source of energy for fossil fuels because —
   F organisms that died long ago depended on the sun for energy
   G heat from the sun caused dead organisms to turn into fossils
   H the sun dried out fossils and turned them into fuel
   J the sun caused Earth to form, and pressure from Earth turned fossils into fossil fuel

Unit D • Chapter 2

Name _____

____ 13. Energy from the sun travels in —
  A *aurora borealis*   C particles of helium
  B particles of hydrogen D waves

Use the following picture to answer Questions 14–16.

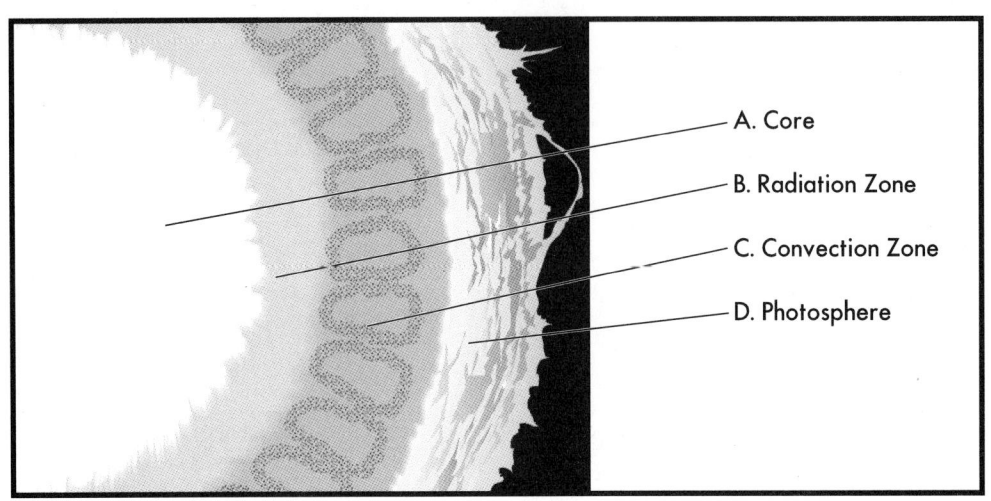

____ 14. In which layer do sunspots occur?

____ 15. Which layer is the hottest part of the sun?

____ 16. In which layer are cooler particles pulled down by gravity?

Write the letter of the best choice.

____ 17. The absolute magnitude of a star depends on —
  F its absolute brightness   H the amount of light it produces
  G its closeness to Earth   J whether you use a telescope

____ 18. What evidence is there that the sun rotates?
  A Solar wind causes magnetic storms.
  B Sunspots move across the sun, disappear, and reappear on the other side.
  C Granules, which are the tops of gas columns, rise through the convection layer.
  D Cycles of sunspots occur every 11 years.

____ 19. If you know the mass of a star, you know —
  F how bright it is   H the surface temperature
  G how much hydrogen it has   J nothing except its mass

Name _____

____ 20. Which of these energy waves are **NOT** released by the sun?
    A microwaves   C X rays
    B infrared waves   D radio waves

Use the diagram below to answer 21–24 in the table.

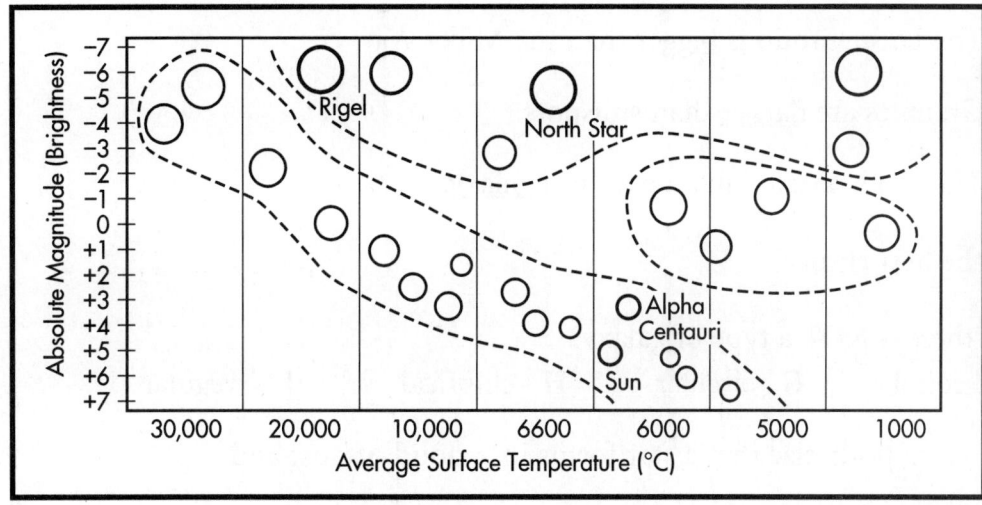

Star	Absolute Magnitude	Temperature (°C)
North Star	–5	23.
Rigel	21.	20,000
Sun	+5	24.
Alpha Centauri	22.	6000

Number the statements below from 1 to 4 to describe the sequence of change for a star like our sun.

____ 25. The star shrinks and becomes a white dwarf.

____ 26. The star uses up most of its fuel and grows to become a red giant.

____ 27. A swirling cloud of dust, a nebula, becomes a small, cool star.

____ 28. A protostar grows in mass and its temperature rises until it begins to glow.

Unit D • Chapter 2   (page 3 of 5)   Assessment Guide AG 105

Name _____

If the statement is true, write *true*. If the statement is false, change the underlined term to make it true.

_____ 29. <u>Absolute</u> magnitude is how bright the star appears from Earth.

_____ 30. <u>A galaxy</u> is bigger than the universe.

_____ 31. The Local Group is <u>bigger</u> than the Milky Way.

_____ 32. Granules are <u>darker</u> than sunspots.

_____ 33. The sun is located in an <u>elliptical galaxy</u>.

Write the letter of the best choice.

____ 34. Which of these is **NOT** a type of galaxy?
      F barred spiral   G circular   H elliptical   J irregular

____ 35. Astronomers hypothesize that a star forms in a cloud of dust and gas called a —
      A Local Group   B universe   C galaxy   D nebula

Part III   Critical Thinking

36. The sun makes one complete revolution around the center of the Milky Way Galaxy about every 250 million years. Telescopes often see objects more than 250 million light-years away. Why, then, can't we see the light from the sun through a telescope?

_____

_____

37. Why is a star said to be "dead" when it becomes a white dwarf?

_____

_____

38. Why are older stars located at the center of a spiral galaxy, while younger stars make up the arms of a spiral galaxy?

_____

_____

Name _____

39. Why do scientists think that studying the sun helps us learn about other stars?

_____
_____

Part IV   Process Skills Application

40. The solar wind disturbs compasses. What materials would you use to **model** this disturbance? Explain what you would do.

_____
_____

41. Suppose a large solar flare has just occurred. **Hypothesize** about the presence of one or more sunspots in the area of the solar flare.

_____
_____

42. Earth's atmosphere deflects many harmful energy waves from the sun. **Draw conclusions** about why astronauts on a mission need protection from this energy.

_____
_____

43. Sunspots appear to move across the sun's surface from west to east. What can you **infer** about the sun from this observation?

_____
_____

44. A massive, hot blue star was formed about the same time as our sun. **Predict** which star will last longer. What information did you use to make your prediction?

_____
_____

Unit D • Chapter 2   (page 5 of 5)   **Assessment Guide AG 107**

Name _____ Date _____

PERFORMANCE TASK

Seeing Stars

Materials

variety of art materials, such as assorted colors of construction paper, paper stars, cotton, sawdust, chenille sticks, scissors, paste, box lids, plastic supermarket trays

Your task is to compare two basic types of galaxies. To do this, you will make a model of each one.

1. Write the names of the two types of galaxies you will compare.

   _____   _____

2. List the materials you will use in your models and what each material will represent.

   _____
   _____

3. Use your materials to make models of the two galaxies. Add a title and labels to each model to tell what each one shows.

4. Compare the galaxies in your models. How are they alike?

   _____
   _____

   How are they different?

   _____
   _____

5. Present your models to the class. Compare and explain them.

AG 108 Assessment Guide Unit D • Chapter 2

Teacher's Directions

Seeing Stars

Materials   Performance Task sheet, variety of art materials, such as assorted colors of construction paper, paper stars, cotton, sawdust, chenille sticks, scissors, paste, box lids, plastic supermarket trays

Time   20–35 minutes

Suggested Grouping   pairs

Science Processes   make a model, compare

Preparation Hints   Set out the materials for constructing models.

Introduce the Task   Tell students they are going to make models to compare two types of galaxies. Discuss the types of galaxies they may choose, and identify the materials they may use. Tell students they will demonstrate their models after they have completed them. Answer students' questions about the task. Divide the class into pairs.

Promote Discussion   When students finish their demonstrations, ask the class to point out any unique ways students demonstrated their models (for example, rotated their model of the spiral galaxy to show how it moves).

Scoring Rubric

Performance Indicators

_____ Uses appropriate materials for the components of the models.

_____ Makes a model that shows the correct shape of each galaxy.

_____ Compares the two galaxies, citing similarities and differences.

_____ Clearly explains the models to the class.

Observations and Rubric Score

| 3 | 2 | 1 | 0 |

Name _____
Date _____

The Solar System and Beyond

Write the letter of the best choice.

_____ 1. How does the moon move in relation to Earth?
   A The moon revolves around Earth in a circle-shaped orbit.
   B Earth revolves around the moon in an ellipse-shaped orbit.
   C The moon revolves around Earth in an ellipse-shaped orbit.
   D The moon revolves around the sun, but not around Earth.

_____ 2. Earth passes into the shadow of the moon during —
   F a solar eclipse
   G a lunar eclipse
   H nighttime only
   J a waxing crescent

_____ 3. What exists on Earth but **NOT** on the moon?
   A aluminum   C craters
   B rocks   D air

_____ 4. The moon appears bright in the night sky because it —
   F gives off its own light
   G reflects light from the sun
   H reflects light from Earth
   J absorbs light from the stars

_____ 5. If it is 11 A.M. in New York, what time is it in California?
   A 5 A.M.   C 11 A.M.
   B 8 A.M.   D 2 P.M.

_____ 6. The date is September 21, and there is an equal time of day and night. Which of the following has occurred?
   F autumn equinox
   G spring equinox
   H autumn solstice
   J spring solstice

_____ 7. Earth has seasons because it —
   A revolves around the moon
   B rotates around the sun
   C is tilted on its axis
   D rotates on its axis

_____ 8. Chunks of rock, perhaps left over from the formation of planets, are —
   F comets   H moons
   G asteroids   J stars

_____ 9. Which was used first by scientists to explore outer space?
   A satellites   C space probes
   B spacesuits   D telescopes

AG 110 Assessment Guide   (page 1 of 4)   Unit D

Name _____

___ 10. The future plans of space exploration start with the completion of a —
   F space station   H Mars base
   G moon base   J warp drive

___ 11. The sun's energy causes which of the following on Earth?
   A thunderstorms
   B the oceans' tides
   C greenhouse gases
   D air pollution

___ 12. (2.1) Sunspots occur on what layer of the sun?
   F radiation zone
   G corona
   H photosphere
   J core

___ 13. The temperature of a star can be detected by its —
   A color   C orbit
   B distance   D rotation

___ 14. Which of the following sequences is the correct order for the first five stages of a star?
   F nebula, red giant, protostar, main sequence, expanding star
   G red giant, nebula, main sequence, expanding star, protostar
   H nebula, protostar, main sequence, expanding star, red giant
   J protostar, nebula, main sequence, expanding star, red giant

___ 15. The largest group of objects in space is —
   A a solar system
   B a galaxy
   C the Milky Way Galaxy
   D the universe

___ 16. Which of the following is NOT a type of galaxy?
   F irregular
   G barred
   H regular
   J spiral

___ 17. The Milky Way Galaxy is —
   A a spiral galaxy
   B a barred galaxy
   C an elliptical galaxy
   D an irregular galaxy

___ 18. If you want to locate a galactic cluster in the night sky, you should look for a —
   F twinkling yellow star
   G red supergiant star
   H faint blur of stars
   J group of bright stars

Name _____

_____ 19. About 95 percent of the stars
scientists have observed are
organized into a band called
the —
A barred galaxy
B main sequence
C solar system
D Milky Way

_____ 20. What is true about the brightness
of stars?
F The closer a star is, the
   brighter it appears.
G Brighter stars have hotter
   surface temperatures.
H Red stars are the hottest and
   brightest stars.
J The sun is the brightest star in
   the universe.

_____ 21. The absolute magnitude of a star
depends on —
A its absolute brightness
B its closeness to Earth
C the amount of light it
   produces
D whether you use a telescope

_____ 22. Which of these energy waves are
NOT released by the sun?
F X rays
G radio waves
H infrared waves
J microwaves

Name _____

Answer in complete sentences.

23. In terms of energy, how are we dependent on the sun?

_____

_____

_____

24. Two stars have the same brightness when viewed from Earth. Is it correct to say the stars are the same distance from Earth and have the same temperature? Explain.

_____

_____

_____

25. What is the difference between a solar eclipse and a lunar eclipse?

_____

_____

Name _____
Date _____

Matter and Its Properties

Part 1   Vocabulary

Use the letters of the terms in the Word Banks to complete the sentences.

A gas	C liquid	E mass	G matter
B solid	D volume	F weight	H solubility

All material that takes up space is called **1.** ____. The amount of material in an object is called the object's **2.** ____. An object's **3.** ____ is the pull of gravity on the object.

All material takes the form of a solid, a liquid, or a gas. A **4.** ____ has a definite volume but no definite shape. A **5.** ____ does not have a definite volume or a definite shape. A **6.** ____ has both definite volume and shape. You can measure the amount of space a solid object takes up, or the **7.** ____ of a solid object, by placing the object in a graduated cylinder with water and measuring how much water is displaced. Sometimes the ability to be dissolved, or **8.** ____, can be used to identify a substance.

I condensation	K density	M evaporation
J physical properties	L reactivity	N combustibility

A liquid can change into a gas. This process is called **9.** ____. A gas can also turn into a liquid. This reverse process is called **10.** ____.

Other **11.** ____ of substances, like color, size, and hardness, can be found without changing the substance into something else. You can divide the mass of an object by its volume to find the object's **12.** ____.

Chemical changes can turn substances into other substances. The ability of a substance to go through a chemical change is called **13.** ____. The ability of a substance to burn is called **14.** ____.

AG 114 Assessment Guide

Name _____

Part II Science Concepts and Understanding

Write the letter of the best choice.

____ 15. Which of the following is **NOT** a physical property?
   A color   B density   C solubility   D reactivity

____ 16. When iron rusts, it no longer conducts electricity. This is because it —
   F changed chemically   H is in water
   G changed physically   J lost its luster

____ 17. The density of an object is a —
   A combustible property   C chemical property
   B reactive property   D physical property

____ 18. Weight is measured on a scale. Mass is measured on a —
   F thermometer   H barometer
   G balance   J scale

____ 19. Changing the shape and amount of a substance does **NOT** change its —
   A volume   B density   C mass   D appearance

____ 20. In which of the pictures below is a substance undergoing a chemical change?
   F I   G II   H III   J IV

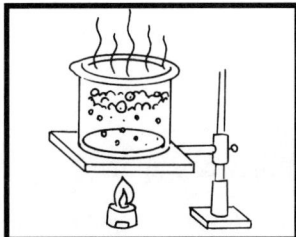
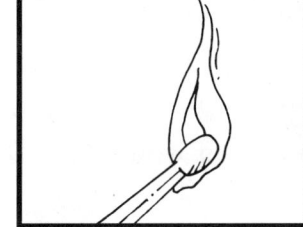

Name _____

___ 21. A person's ___ is different on a high mountain than it is at sea level.
   A mass
   B weight
   C chemical property
   D density

___ 22. A solution is a type of —
   F balance
   G matter
   H mixture
   J combustibility

___ 23. Which of the following does **NOT** signal a chemical change?
   A color change
   B production of light and heat
   C production of a gas
   D change in state

___ 24. Making skim milk is an example of —
   F using physical properties to separate a mixture
   G using chemical properties to separate a mixture
   H solubility
   J combustibility

Use the following pictures to answer Question 25.

___ 25. What do the pictures show about the solubility of these substances?
   A Sugar is soluble in water, but pepper is not.
   B Pepper is soluble in water, but sugar is not.
   C Sugar and pepper have the same solubility.
   D If stirred, the pepper would have the same solubility as sugar.

Name _____

____ 26. Two similar-looking substances are burned. One produces a red flame, and the other produces a yellow flame. This is an example of—
    F a combustibility test   H a flame test
    G an indicator test   J a reactivity test

____ 27. A pure substance always has ____ density when measured under ____ conditions.
    A the same; the same   C the same; different
    B a different; different   D a different; the same

Part III Critical Thinking

28. How does the volume of liquid water change when it turns to water vapor? Explain.

_____

_____

_____

29. Can water be used to separate salt from sugar? Why or why not?

_____

_____

_____

30. Describe what would happen to a cold empty glass if it was suddenly placed in a hot, humid room. Explain your answer.

_____

_____

_____

Name _____

Part IV Process Skills Application

31. Suppose you had 5 g of paper. You burned it and found that its new mass was 3 g. **Infer** where the 2 g of mass went.

_____

_____

_____

32. Suppose two substances are combined. You observe bubbles forming from the mixture. **Draw a conclusion** about what is happening.

_____

_____

_____

33. How do you **measure** density?

_____

_____

_____

Name _____   Date _____

A Disappearing Act!

Materials

4 small glass beakers

4 sugar cubes

4 packages of granulated sugar

stopwatch

spoon

warm water

Do sugar cubes dissolve faster than loose sugar? Does stirring the water have any effect on which form of sugar dissolves faster? Do this activity to find out.

1. Find out whether sugar cubes dissolve faster than loose sugar. You may use the materials in front of you. Each package of sugar contains the same amount of sugar as one cube.

2. Briefly describe what you did to conduct a fair test to compare how fast the two kinds of sugar dissolved.

   _____
   _____
   _____

Fill in the blanks in the sentences below to tell what you found out.

3. When the water was stirred, the _____ dissolved faster.

4. When the water was not stirred, the _____ dissolved faster.

5. Write your explanation of the results.

   _____
   _____
   _____

Unit E • Chapter 1   **Assessment Guide AG 119**

PERFORMANCE TASK

Teacher's Directions

A Disappearing Act!

Materials Performance Task sheet; 4 small glass beakers; 4 sugar cubes; 4 packages of granulated sugar, each containing the same mass as one cube of sugar; stopwatch; warm water; spoon

Time 10–15 minutes

Suggested Grouping individuals or pairs

Science Processes experimenting, measuring, observing, comparing, inferring

Preparation Hints You will need one set of materials for each student or pair. Make sure the water is warm enough for the sugar to dissolve but not too hot to burn the students. If you do not have access to a sink with warm water, store some water in a thermos.

Introduce the Task Tell students that they will conduct an experiment that is explained on their task sheet. Suggest that before they begin the experiment, they think carefully about what they need to do to conduct a fair test.

Promote Discussion Students should realize that variables such as the amount of water, the temperature, and the rate of stirring were controlled. They should be able to explain that loose sugar will dissolve faster because it is in separate grains; the cube has to break up into separate grains before it can dissolve.

Scoring Rubric
Performance Indicators

_____ Describes how the test conducted is fair.

_____ Explains the effect stirring has on how fast the sugar dissolves.

_____ Compares the dissolving rate of a sugar cube to that of loose sugar.

_____ Writes a clear explanation of the results of the sugar test.

Observations and Rubric Score

| 3 | 2 | 1 | 0 |

Name _____
Date _____

Atoms and Elements

Part I Vocabulary

Match each term in Column B with its meaning in Column A.

Column A

____ 1. Center of an atom

____ 2. Substance made up of only one kind of atom

____ 3. Subatomic particle with a positive charge

____ 4. Smallest unit of an element with all the properties of that element

____ 5. Subatomic particle with no charge

____ 6. Arrangement of elements by similar properties

____ 7. Substance made up of the atoms of two or more elements

____ 8. Two or more atoms joined together

____ 9. Subatomic particle with a negative charge

Column B

A atom

B compound

C electron

D element

E molecule

F neutron

G nucleus

H Periodic Table

I proton

Part II Science Concepts and Understanding

Write the letter of the best choice.

____ 10. Atoms are held together by the attraction between —
  A protons and neutrons
  B protons and the nucleus
  C electrons and neutrons
  D electrons and protons

Unit E • Chapter 2   (page 1 of 5)   Assessment Guide AG 121

Name _____

_____ 11. The atomic number of an element is the number of _____ in its nucleus.
   F electrons
   G neutrons
   H protons
   J atoms

_____ 12. In the Periodic Table, elements are arranged by atomic number and —
   A color
   B size
   C similar properties
   D atomic mass

_____ 13. Which is **NOT** true of metals?
   F They conduct electricity.
   G They are good insulators.
   H They are ductile.
   J They conduct heat.

_____ 14. What is the formula for a molecule with 1 carbon atom, 2 hydrogen atoms, and 3 oxygen atoms?
   A H_2CO_3
   B H_3CO_2
   C HC_2O_3
   D H_3C_2O

Use the diagram on the right to answer Questions 15–17.

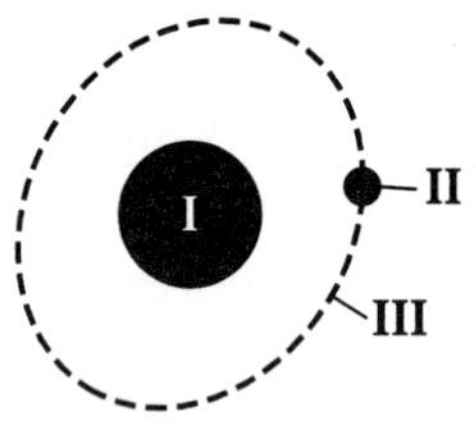

_____ 15. In this model, the I represents —
   F an atom
   G a proton
   H a neutron
   J an electron

_____ 16. The II represents —
   A an atom
   B a proton
   C a neutron
   D an electron

_____ 17. The III represents —
   F a nucleus
   G a subatomic particle
   H a neutron path
   J an energy level

Hydrogen Atom

Use the following formula to answer Questions 18–19.

$MgCO_3$

_____ 18. How many atoms of oxygen are in the chemical formula?

_____ 19. How many total atoms are in the chemical formula?

Name _____

Use the part shown of the Periodic Table to answer Questions 20–22.

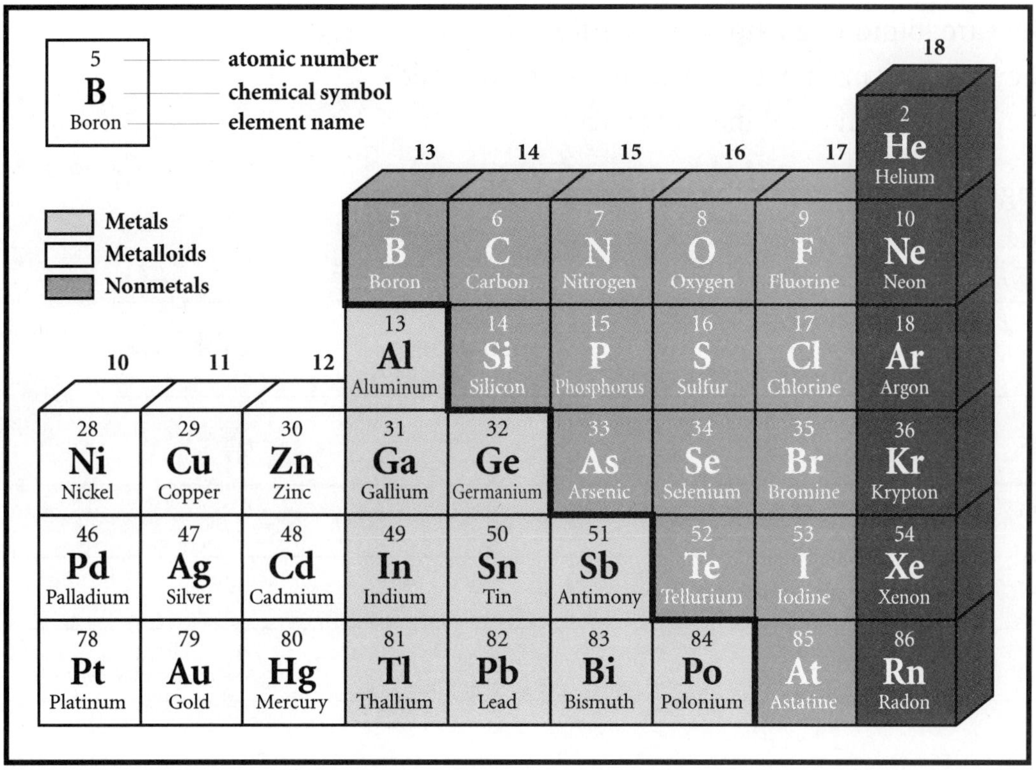

_____ 20. All elements listed in Column 18 of the table have the same physical state, so they are all —
   A liquids   B metals   C gases   D neutrons

_____ 21. All elements listed in Columns 10–12 are —
   F liquids   H nonmetals
   G metalloids   J neutrons

_____ 22. What are the atomic number and the chemical symbol for silver?
   A 14, Si   B 16, S   C 52, Te   D 47, Ag

Write the letter of the best choice.

_____ 23. If an element has electrons bound tightly to their atoms and conducts hardly any electricity, it can be used in —
   F lusters
   G transfers
   H ductiles
   J insulators

Unit E • Chapter 2

Name _____

____ 24. Which of the following is true of all compounds?
    A They are made of atoms of two or more elements.
    B They are found in all atoms in nature.
    C They can be mixed with molecules to form liquids.
    D They react when combined with acids.

25. Write a paragraph using each of the following words in the correct context.

| alloy | conductor | ductile | insulator | malleable |

_____
_____
_____
_____
_____
_____
_____

Part III Critical Thinking

26. Are protons from two different elements alike? Explain why or why not.

_____
_____

27. If you added a proton, a neutron, and an electron to an atom, explain why the atom would not still be the same element.

_____
_____

Name _____

28. Would you want a plastic, a metal, or a metalloid handle for a metal pot? Why?

_____

_____

Part IV   Process Skills Application

Use the following table to answer Questions 29–31.

Element Number	Symbol	Name	Melting Point	Boiling Point
1	H	Hydrogen	−259°C	−253°C
2	He	Helium	−272°C	−269°C
3	Li	Lithium	181°C	1342°C
4	Be	Beryllium	1287°C	2472°C
5	B	Boron	2027°C	4002°C
6	C	Carbon	3827°C	4197°C

29. Normal room temperature is 25°C. If the elements listed in the table are at room temperature, **infer** which elements are solids.

_____

_____

30. Observe the boiling points of elements 1 and 2. **Infer** what state they would be in at room temperature.

_____

_____

31. Predict the state of lithium at 50°C.

_____

_____

Unit E • Chapter 2

Name _____ Date _____

Model an Element

PERFORMANCE TASK

Materials

 beach balls
 ball bearings

If you could magnify a proton one billion times, it would be about 1 m in diameter. Under the same magnification, a neutron also would be about 1 m in diameter, and an electron would be about 0.001 m in diameter.

Work as a group to answer the questions.

1. How could you use the above materials to make a model of a helium atom?

   _____
   _____
   _____

2. What facts about atoms will you model in your helium atom?

   _____
   _____
   _____

3. With your group, use the materials to demonstrate a model of the helium atom to your teacher. Do not let the other groups see your model. Explain what your model shows. Then tell what it does not show.

4. Make a drawing of your model.

Teacher's Directions

Model an Element

Materials Performance Task sheet, four beach balls (approximately 1 meter in diameter), two ball bearings (approximately 1 millimeter in diameter)

Time 10–15 minutes

Suggested Grouping pairs or small groups

Science Processes communicate, use models

Preparation Hints Inflate the beach balls, and display them and the ball bearings. Set up a place where groups can demonstrate their models to you without being seen by the rest of the class. You may want to use smaller materials, such as tennis balls and BBs.

Introduce the Task Tell students they are going to think about the size of subatomic particles and the helium atom. Ask a volunteer to define what subatomic particles are. Then have all students read the Performance Task sheet. Divide the class into pairs or small groups, and tell them where you are going to view their demonstrations.

Promote Discussion Call on volunteers to explain what they did to demonstrate characteristics of the helium atom (vibrating nucleus, electrons traveling in three dimensions).

Scoring Rubric

Performance Indicators

_____ Uses the four beach balls as the protons and neutrons in the nucleus.

_____ Uses the two ball bearings as the electrons that move around the nucleus.

_____ Demonstrates understanding of the movement of atoms and their electrons.

_____ Models several characteristics of the helium atom.

Observations and Rubric Score

| 3 | 2 | 1 | 0 |

Unit E • Chapter 2

Name _____
Date _____

Building Blocks of Matter

Write the letter of the best choice.

_____ 1. What do all of the following have in common? water, wood, cement, animals, plants, glass
  A They are all found in nature.
  B They are all made of matter.
  C They are all made of minerals.
  D They are all living things.

_____ 2. You observe that a ball is red. What type of property is the red color?
  F elemental
  G chemical
  H organizational
  J physical

_____ 3. What do we call the measurement of the gravitational pull on an object?
  A weight   C density
  B mass   D volume

_____ 4. If an object has a mass of 100 kg and a volume of 2 cubic meters, what is its density?
  F 200 kg/m^3 H 100 kg/m^3
  G 50 kg/m^3 J 10 kg/m^3

_____ 5. You have two blocks of aluminum. One has a volume twice that of the other. Which measurement is identical for both blocks?
  A mass   C volume
  B density   D weight

_____ 6. Which is a characteristic of solids?
  F A solid does not have a definite shape.
  G A solid floats on water.
  H A solid takes the shape of its container.
  J A solid has a definite shape.

_____ 7. When water changes from a gas into a liquid, it —
  A condenses   C boils
  B evaporates   D melts

_____ 8. The melting point of table salt is 801°C, so its boiling point is —
  F greater than 801°C
  G less than 801°C
  H also 801°C
  J less than 500°C

AG 128 Assessment Guide   (page 1 of 4)   Unit E

Name _____

_____ 9. Which is an example of a chemical change?
   A water boiling
   B a nail rusting
   C iron melting
   D glass shattering

_____ 10. What occurs when two or more elements come together and make a new substance?
   F a physical change
   G a biological change
   H a chemical change
   J an elemental change

_____ 11. Chlorine's ability to combine with elements chemically is known as its —
   A combustibility
   B reactivity
   C physical activity
   D mechanical ability

_____ 12. Which has the chemical property of combustibility?
   F salt   H aluminum
   G iron   J charcoal

_____ 13. In a chemical reaction, the mass of the products will be ____ the mass of the reactants.
   A equal to
   B less than
   C greater than
   D much greater than

_____ 14. A subatomic particle with a positive charge is —
   F a neutron   H an electron
   G a proton   J an atom

_____ 15. Which item would be considered an element?
   A sugar
   B water
   C table salt
   D aluminum foil

_____ 16. Which of the following is NOT a property of a metal?
   F luster   H malleability
   G size   J ductility

_____ 17. An atom's nucleus is made up of —
   A protons and electrons
   B neutrons and electrons
   C protons and neutrons
   D neutrons only

_____ 18. What determines what kind of element an atom is?
   F the number of protons
   G the number of atoms
   H the number of neutrons
   J the number of molecules

Name _____

_____ 19. What makes a compound different from an element?
  A A compound has only one type of element in it.
  B A compound has more than one type of element in it.
  C A compound always has more atoms.
  D A compound always weighs more than an element.

_____ 20. The modern periodic table has elements arranged —
  F in order of decreasing atomic weight
  G in order of increasing atomic number
  H alphabetically by element name
  J alphabetically by chemical symbol

_____ 21. Which type of grouping is used on the periodic table?
  A nonmetal/metal/metalloid
  B solid/liquid/gas
  C dark/light colors
  D heavy/light weight

_____ 22. Which of the following is a compound?
  F gold
  G helium
  H water
  J carbon

Name _____

Answer in complete sentences.

23. Do all substances have a solid, liquid, and gas phase? Explain.

_____
_____
_____
_____
_____

24. You are given a solid cube of an unknown substance. Describe at least three measurements you would take and which physical properties you could use to help identify the substance.

_____
_____
_____
_____
_____

Name _____
Date _____

Forces

Part 1 Vocabulary

Match each term in Column B with its meaning in Column A.

Column A

____ 1. Push or pull that causes an object to move, stop, or change direction

____ 2. Use of force to move an object through a distance

____ 3. Force that pulls all objects toward each other

____ 4. A thing that makes work seem easier by changing the size or direction of a force

____ 5. Forces equal in size and opposite in direction

____ 6. Force that opposes motion when two surfaces rub against each other

____ 7. Force of pushing or pulling between magnetic poles

____ 8. Opposing forces of which one force is greater than the other

____ 9. Value of combined forces on an object

____ 10. Amount of work done for each unit of time

Column B

A work

B friction

C magnetism

D gravitation

E force

F machine

G balanced forces

H unbalanced forces

I power

J net force

AG 132 Assessment Guide   (page 1 of 5)   Unit F • Chapter 1

Name _____

Part II Science Concepts and Understanding

Write the letter of the best choice.

_____ 11. Which of the following is **NOT** a force?
   A newton   C friction
   B gravity   D magnetism

_____ 12. What force causes a teardrop to roll down someone's cheek?
   F friction   H magnetism
   G gravity   J water

_____ 13. What force slows a skateboard when a skateboarder puts a foot down to brake?
   A motion   C gravity
   B magnetism   D friction

_____ 14. What do magnets have that acts on objects without touching them?
   F a power   H a force
   G a machine   J a current

_____ 15. If two arm wrestlers exert a force on each other's hands and the hands don't move, the forces must be —
   A balanced   C weak
   B unbalanced   D strong

_____ 16. If a refrigerator magnet can't hold a piece of paper against a refrigerator, the forces acting on the magnet must be —
   F balanced   H weak
   G unbalanced   J strong

_____ 17. Two people try to push a 2000-newton crate, but it doesn't move. They have done —
   A 4000 joules of work   C zero joules of work
   B 1000 joules of work   D balanced work

_____ 18. When you lift a 2-newton book 1 meter off of your desk, you do —
   F 1 joule of work   H 3 joules of work
   G 2 joules of work   J 4 joules of work

Name _____

___ 19. Which of the following can change the size or direction of a force?
     A friction   **B** a magnet   **C** a machine   **D** speed

___ 20. A shovel is a compound machine made up of—
     F a lever and a wedge
     G a pulley and a screw
     H a wedge and a pulley
     J a screw and a wedge

Part III Critical Thinking

21. Suppose you are playing a game of catch with a friend. What forces act on the ball when it is in the air?

_____
_____
_____
_____

22. Suppose a shoe on the top shelf of your closet falls to the floor when you open the closet door. How do you know a force has acted on the shoe?

_____
_____
_____
_____

23. Which requires more work—running around the block or walking around the block? Which requires more power? Explain your answers.

_____
_____
_____
_____

Name _____

Part IV Process Skills Application

The following table shows data gathered when a dog chases three cats.

	Force Needed (Weight of Object)	Distance	Work (Force × Distance)	Time	Power (Work ÷ Time)
Cat 1	40 newtons	10 m	400 joules	4 sec	100 watts
Cat 2	55 newtons	10 m	550 joules	5 sec	110 watts
Cat 3	45 newtons	10 m	450 joules	5 sec	90 watts
Dog	100 newtons	10 m	1000 joules	10 sec	100 watts

____ 24. **Interpret the data** to determine which animal does the most work.
   A Cat 1   B Cat 2   C Cat 3   D Dog

____ 25. **Compare** the animals to find which one uses the most power.
   F Cat 1   G Cat 2   H Cat 3   J Dog

Use the following graph to answer Questions 26–27.

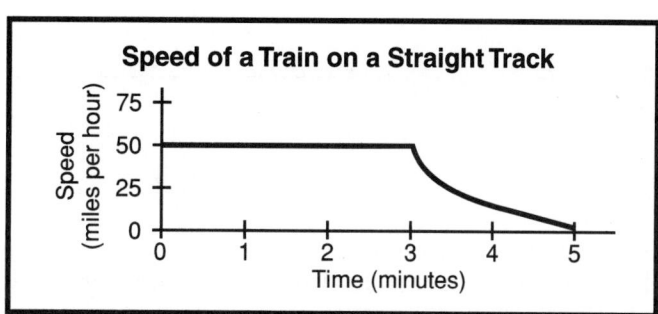

26. **Interpret the data** to determine when the train's brakes started exerting force on the train's wheels. Explain your answer.

   _____

   _____

27. What **conclusion** can you **draw** about the forces on the train during the time its speed stayed the same?

   _____

Name _____

The following picture shows two plans for investigating the force of friction. Study the plans before answering Questions 28–29.

> How many blocks must you stack under the end of the board before the book begins to move?
>
> | | Trial 1 | Trial 2 |
> |---|---|---|
> | Plan A | (book on board, blocks under one end) | (book on board with sandpaper, blocks under one end) |
> | Plan B | (book on board, taller stack of blocks) | (book on board with sandpaper, taller stack of blocks) |

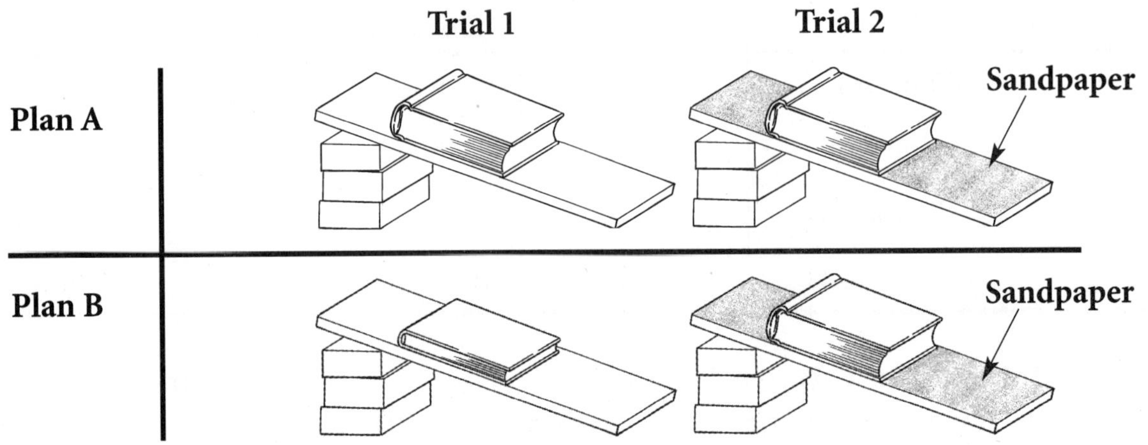

28. Which of the two plans is a better **plan for investigating** the force of friction? Why?

   _____
   _____
   _____
   _____

29. Study the better plan, and **draw a conclusion** about whether Trial 1 or Trial 2 will take more blocks to make the book move. **Hypothesize** why.

   _____
   _____
   _____
   _____

AG 136 Assessment Guide   (page 5 of 5)   Unit F • Chapter 1

Name _____ Date _____

Force Hero

Materials

drawing paper   crayons or colored pencils   pencils

You work for a children's science magazine. The next issue is on forces. Draw a cartoon that shows how a hero uses a force or a simple machine to solve a problem.

1. To plan your cartoon, answer the following questions.

   A. Who will be the hero in your cartoon?

   _____

   B. What problem will your hero need to solve?

   _____

   _____

   C. What force or simple machine will your hero use to solve it?

   _____

   D. How will the force or simple machine help solve the problem? Be sure to show the solution in your cartoon.

   _____

   _____

2. Draw your cartoon on a separate sheet of paper.

3. Label important objects in the cartoon.

4. Be ready to explain how your hero uses a force or machine to solve the problem presented in your cartoon.

Unit F • Chapter 1   Assessment Guide AG 137

PERFORMANCE TASK

Teacher's Directions

Force Hero

Materials — Performance Task sheet, drawing paper, crayons or colored pencils, pencils

Time — 20–30 minutes

Suggested Grouping — individuals or pairs

Science Processes — communicate, hypothesize, draw conclusions

Preparation Hints — Display on the board various scenes that show action, such as people moving heavy objects.

Introduce the Task — Explain to students that they will make a cartoon that shows what they have learned about forces. Explain that students are to include a hero who uses a force or simple machine to solve a problem. Point out that students must label the different elements included in the cartoon and explain how the force or simple machine affects the situation. Tell students that depicting violence (people hurting each other or other living things) is not acceptable. Have volunteers read the Performance Task directions aloud.

Promote Discussion — Display students' cartoons on the board, and have volunteers explain theirs. Discuss how a force or simple machine helped the hero in each cartoon. Extend the discussion to include what students learned about forces throughout the chapter.

Scoring Rubric

Performance Indicators

- _____ Identifies a problem that involves a force or a simple machine.
- _____ Labels important objects in the cartoon.
- _____ Explains how a force or simple machine is used to solve a problem.
- _____ Demonstrates an understanding of concepts such as *force*, *power*, and *machine*.
- _____ Communicates ideas effectively through a cartoon.

Observations and Rubric Score

| 3 | 2 | 1 | 0 |

Name _____
Date _____

Motion

Part 1 Vocabulary

Use the letters of the terms in the Word Banks to complete the sentences.

A velocity	C position	E speed
B momentum	D acceleration	

To measure the movement of an object, one must first locate the **1.** ____ of that object. The **2.** ____ of an object is the distance it travels in a given period of time. The term used to describe the speed of an object in a certain direction is **3.** ____. A change in the direction or speed of an object is called **4.** ____. A truck that is moving at a high rate of speed is difficult to stop because of its **5.** ____, which is a product of its velocity and mass.

F action force	I law of universal gravitation
G orbit	J reaction force
H inertia	

The first law of motion states that an object that is not moving will remain at rest because of **6.** ____. The force that you exert on an object at rest is called an **7.** ____. That object exerts a force on you, called a **8.** ____. An object in motion will travel in a straight line unless another force acts on it. An object in an **9.** ____ travels around another object as a result of inertia and gravity working together. According to the **10.** ____, all objects are attracted to all other objects.

Name _____

Part II Science Concepts and Understanding

Write the letter of the best choice.

____ 11. The first law of motion says that an object at rest will remain at rest unless —
  A it continues in a straight line
  B a nearby star acts on it
  C an outside force acts on it
  D it is placed on a flat surface

____ 12. According to the third law of motion, for every action there is —
  F a force sending it backward
  G an equal and opposite reaction
  H a greater force pushing on it
  J a movement in all directions

____ 13. When you observe an object, how do you know if it is moving?
  A Its mass and velocity change.
  B Its frame of reference changes.
  C Its position changes.
  D Its momentum changes.

____ 14. Suzette keeps her schoolbooks in a basket on the handlebars of her bicycle. When she rides, why do the books seem not to be moving?
  F Her eyes must be playing tricks on her.
  G Books cannot move by themselves.
  H From her frame of reference, the books are stationary.
  J From her frame of reference, the books are accelerating.

____ 15. If one car moves ahead of another car that is traveling in the same direction, do the cars have the same velocity?
  A No, they are traveling in different directions.
  B Yes, they are traveling in the same direction.
  C Yes, the direction and speed of the cars are the same.
  D No, the cars are traveling at different speeds.

Name _____

___ 16. Do two skaters traveling in different directions at the same speed have the same velocity?
   F no, because the direction is different
   G no, because the skaters are different
   H yes, because the speed is the same
   J yes, because the acceleration is the same

___ 17. A train traveling on a curved track at a constant speed is accelerating because —
   A the train travels faster around a curved track
   B the direction of the train is constantly changing
   C the train's size will eventually slow it down
   D the clockwise direction of the train is constant

___ 18. The brakes on an adult bicycle must be stronger than the brakes on a children's bicycle because —
   F a child's mass causes more momentum
   G an adult's mass causes less momentum
   H an adult rider is farther from the ground
   J an adult rider will have more momentum

___ 19. What do the laws of motion explain?
   A how *frame of reference* influences movement
   B the relationship between the four basic elements
   C the movement of objects on Earth and in space
   D why all moving objects eventually stop moving

___ 20. Inertia explains why —
   F friction can be overcome for all objects
   G people in a car move forward in their seats when the car stops quickly
   H gravitational forces are stronger on Earth than on the moon or other satellites
   J the ground pushes against your feet when you run

___ 21. If an equal force acts on each of the following objects, which will have the greatest acceleration?
   A a golf ball   C a football
   B a soccer ball   D a baseball

Name _____

_____ 22. When a baseball player strikes a ball with a bat, the ball exerts a force on the bat. What is this an example of?
    F universal law of gravitation
    G frame of reference
    H the second law of motion
    J the third law of motion

_____ 23. *Conservation of momentum* explains how —
    A a spacecraft can travel in space for thousands of years
    B a ball thrown into the air always falls back toward Earth
    C trucks slow down when they are traveling uphill
    D a pole can be knocked down when a moving car hits it

Use the following drawing to answer Questions 24–25.

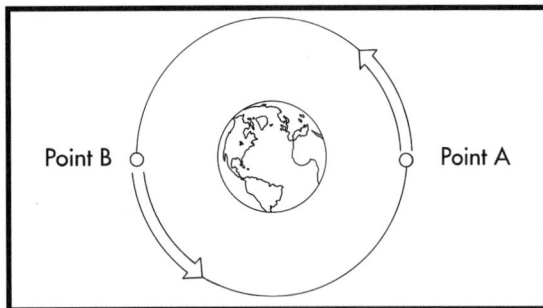

24. Draw an arrow to show what would happen to the path of the moon if it and Earth suddenly lost their gravitational attraction at Point A.

25. Draw an arrow to show what would happen to the path of the moon if its inertia suddenly decreased at Point B.

Part III Critical Thinking

26. At the airport, Sam and Jose are trying to get to their gate on time. They are walking at the same speed. Sam takes the moving sidewalk, but Jose chooses to walk alongside. How can you tell that Sam is in motion even though he is standing still on the sidewalk?

_____

_____

_____

Name _____

27. A clown is performing in front of a crowd. He is pretending to walk, but he is not actually changing his position in front of the crowd. Why can't we measure his speed?

_____

_____

28. If Earth pulls on a puppy with a force of 2 newtons, what amount of force does the puppy exert on Earth? Explain why.

_____

_____

Part IV   Process Skills Application

29. The following observations were made of two cars traveling at various speeds and directions.

   | Car A: 30 mph, 45 mph, 20 mph, north, south, east |
   | Car B: 50 mph, 30 mph, 15 mph, west, south, northeast |

From the information above, **record** in the following table the **data** that will show both cars having the same velocity.

	Speed	Direction
Car A		
Car B		

30. What do you **hypothesize** would happen if you tried to make a shopping cart go around a corner by itself? Explain your answer.

_____

31. Suppose that you are a toymaker who **experiments** to find ways to limit the speed of battery-powered toy cars. **Identify** the **variables** that must be **controlled** in the experiments.

_____

Unit F • Chapter 2   (page 5 of 5)   **Assessment Guide AG 143**

Name _____ Date _____

Mass in Motion

Materials

- tape
- three large marbles
- three small marbles
- piece of poster board
- three or four books
- meterstick

You have already seen firsthand how mass and velocity affect momentum. Now you are going to investigate the relationship between mass and momentum. You and your small group will do this by comparing how far different-sized marbles roll after rolling down an inclined plane.

1. First, create a track for the marbles by folding the poster board in half lengthwise, so a V-shaped channel is formed. On a carpeted area, stack books to raise the height of one end of the channel to about 15–20 millimeters. Use tape to hold the channel in place. Arrange the books and channel so the marbles will run onto the carpet.

2. Carefully hold each marble in the track and release it without pushing. Start with the three large marbles. Measure the distance that each marble travels. Calculate the average distance traveled for the large marbles. Do the same for the small marbles. Record your results as a table on a separate sheet of paper.

3. Compare the average distance traveled by the large marbles with the average distance traveled by the small marbles. What is the relationship of mass to momentum? Write your conclusion in the space below.

_____
_____
_____
_____

Teacher's Directions

Mass in Motion

Materials   Performance Task sheet, three large marbles, three small marbles, piece of poster board, three or four books, tape, meterstick

Time   30 minutes

Suggested Grouping   groups of three or four

Science Processes   observe, compare, identify and control variables, gather data, record data, infer, communicate

Preparation Hints   Place a set of marbles for each group in a plastic bag or envelope. Make sure sufficient space is available for the marbles to roll freely on the carpet or floor.

Introduce the Task   Explain to students that they will collect data to determine the relationship between mass and momentum. They will compare how far two different-sized marbles travel on a flat surface after traveling down a channel. Make sure students hold the marbles very still before releasing them and that the marbles are all released from the same point.

Promote Discussion   When students finish, have each group present its findings. Ask students to explain their conclusions. If any data seems incorrect, ask the students to determine what might have interfered with their data collection or recording.

Scoring Rubric

Performance Indicators

____ Completes all steps in the experiment.
____ Records in a table the distance each marble traveled.
____ Calculates the average distance each size of marble traveled.
____ Concludes that the larger marbles have greater mass, which increases momentum and causes the marbles to travel farther.

Observations and Rubric Score

     3   2   1   0

Name _____
Date _____

Forms of Energy

Part I Vocabulary

Match each term in Column B with its meaning in Column A.

Column A

_____ 1. Iron bar with a coil wrapped around it that becomes a magnet when electric current flows through it

_____ 2. The result of a gain or loss of electrons

_____ 3. Loudness of a sound

_____ 4. Attraction or repulsion of electric charges

_____ 5. Piece of clear material that bends, or refracts, light rays

_____ 6. Energy of motion

_____ 7. Energy an object has because of its location or its condition

_____ 8. Flow of electrons

_____ 9. Bending of light rays

_____ 10. Material that allows electrons to travel easily

_____ 11. Path along which electrons flow

_____ 12. Material that doesn't carry electrons

_____ 13. Light bouncing off an object

_____ 14. Speed with which sound waves move

_____ 15. Material that slows the flow of electrons

_____ 16. Ability to cause change in matter

Column B

A energy

B volume

C electromagnet

D kinetic energy

E lens

F electric charge

G potential energy

H electric circuit

I electric force

J pitch

K reflection

L electric current

M insulator

N refraction

O conductor

P resistor

AG 146 Assessment Guide   (page 1 of 5)   Unit F • Chapter 3

Name _____

Use the letters of the terms in the Word Bank to complete the sentences.

A conduction	C convection	E radiation
B heat	D temperature	

The direct transfer of thermal energy between objects that touch is called
17. ____. The mixing of a gas or liquid causes the transfer of thermal
energy by **18.** ____. **19.** ____ occurs when electromagnetic waves transfer
thermal energy. **20.** ____ is the transfer of thermal energy. The average
kinetic energy of the molecules in an object is called **21.** ____.

Part II   Science Concepts and Understanding

Write the letter of the best choice.

____ 22. What happens when you unscrew a light bulb in a series circuit?
    A All the lights go out.   C You get a shock.
    B All the lights stay on.   D The lights on each side go out.

____ 23. Which of the following is an advantage that an electromagnet
has over a regular magnet?
    F It attracts more types of materials.   H Opposites are attracted to each other.
    G It can be turned on and off.   J It requires an electrician.

____ 24. If you grab the hot handle of a pot on a stove, you
will experience —
    A radiation   C conduction
    B convection   D insulation

____ 25. Which of the following is true of people who are farsighted?
    F They do not need glasses to read fine print.
    G They use concave lenses to correct their vision.
    H They use convex lenses to correct their vision.
    J They use conduction to correct their vision.

____ 26. Which of the following is **NOT** an example of a release of
chemical energy?
    A bouncing a ball   C burning wood
    B using batteries   D digesting food

Name _____

_____ 27. Which of the following describes how sound travels in space?
  F Sound is more intense.   H Sound cannot travel.
  G Sound travels farther.   J Sound bounces off of Earth.

_____ 28. Radiators in homes transfer heat by —
  A conduction   C radiation
  B convection   D insulation

_____ 29. Electric force is like gravitational force because —
  F both forces depend on distance
  G electric force increases when objects are far apart
  H electrons move in the same direction
  J electrons don't move in any direction

_____ 30. How do our bodies maintain a constant body temperature?
  A They convert thermal energy into mechanical energy.
  B They convert mechanical energy into potential energy.
  C They convert chemical energy into thermal energy.
  D They convert kinetic energy into potential energy.

_____ 31. Most of Earth's energy comes from —
  F Earth's center   H plants
  G the sun   J the oceans

_____ 32. Elastic potential energy can be found in —
  A stretched rubber bands   C concrete floors
  B bowling balls   D rocks

_____ 33. What happens when you twirl a jump rope?
  F You give it thermal energy.   H You give it potential energy.
  G You give it kinetic energy.   J You give it chemical energy.

_____ 34. Which of the following does NOT possess kinetic energy?
  A a pitcher winding up for a pitch   C a baseball moving toward center field
  B a swinging baseball bat   D a ball caught in a catcher's mitt

_____ 35. Which of the following is NOT an example of energy changing matter?
  F a baseball player that is about to hit a ball
  G a wooden baseball bat striking a baseball
  H heat from striking a ball warming the air
  J a batter running from home plate to first base

Name _____

_____ 36. The law of conservation of energy states —
    A that energy cannot be transformed from one form to another
    B that transformation of energy happens only at low temperatures
    C that energy can be changed, but it cannot be created or destroyed
    D that energy can be changed only one time during one activity

_____ 37. Which of the following best describes potential energy?
    F It cannot change form more than once.
    G It can be found in many forms.
    H It can be transformed by gravity only.
    J It includes electric energy.

_____ 38. Electrons flowing through a light-bulb filament produce —
    A heat and sound   C light and heat
    B light and movement   D movement and heat

Part III   Critical Thinking

39. Compare the way a blue whale's song can travel hundreds of kilometers underwater to the way a human voice travels through air.

    _____
    _____
    _____

40. Explain how a yo-yo transfers potential energy to kinetic energy and back again as it moves up and down its string.

    _____
    _____
    _____
    _____

41. When a cup of hot chocolate cools, is energy lost? Why or why not?

    _____
    _____

Name _____

Part IV Process Skills Application

42. Study the following diagram. **Predict** what would happen to the angle of reflection if you increased the angle of incidence, and explain why. **Design an experiment** to test your prediction. Be sure to **identify and control variables.**

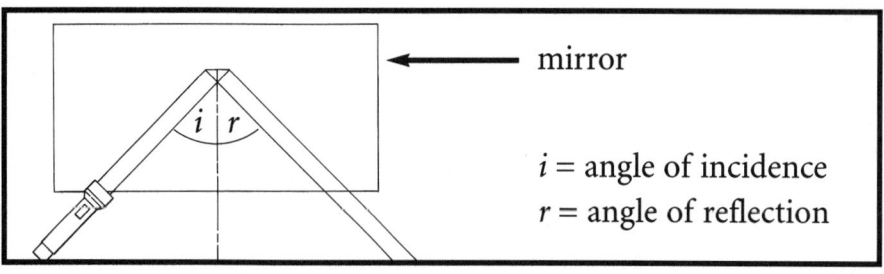

i = angle of incidence
r = angle of reflection

_____
_____

43. Kim used a spring scale and a variety of rubber bands (same length, different widths) to measure the amount of force it took to stretch each band 30 centimeters. Use the following table to **compare the data** and **draw a conclusion** about the relationship between band width and the amount of force used. **Predict** how much force it would take to stretch a 3-centimeter-wide band 30 centimeters. When the bands are stretched, do they have potential or kinetic energy?

Rubber Band Width	Force Required
0.5 cm	0.25 newton
2 cm	1 newton
1 cm	0.5 newton
1.5 cm	0.75 newton
2.5 cm	1.25 newton
3 cm	

_____
_____

Name _____ Date _____

Body Works

Materials: calculator

The amount of energy your body needs each day depends on many things, such as your age and activity level. Study the following tables and answer the questions.

Activity Chart (estimated values)

Activity	Energy Used
Lying Down	540 C in 8 Hours
Walking	360 C in 2 Hours
Running	540 C in 2 Hours
Standing	900 C in 6 Hours
Sitting	540 C in 6 Hours

Potential Energy in Food (in Calories)

Food	Energy
Orange	80 C
Pork Chop	275 C
Oatmeal	105 C
White Bread	65 C
Egg	110 C

1. Calculate the number of calories used during a three-minute run.

   _____

2. Calculate the amount of energy a breakfast of toast, oatmeal, and an egg will give you.

   _____

3. How long would you have to run to use up all of the energy from this breakfast?

   _____

4. What different forms of energy are used during running? Explain the evidence that supports your answer.

   _____

   _____

Unit F • Chapter 3   Assessment Guide AG 151

PERFORMANCE TASK

Teacher's Directions

Body Works

Materials   Performance Task sheet, calculator

Time   30–40 minutes

Suggested Grouping   individuals or pairs

Science Processes   analyze and interpret data, classify, compare

Preparation Hints   none

Introduce the Task   Review with students the different types of energy. Explain that they will interpret data to determine which types of energy might be used when exercising. Remind them that energy cannot be created or destroyed. Using cellular respiration as an example, discuss how energy can be converted from one type to another.

Promote Discussion   When students finish, encourage them to compare their findings. Discuss the energy transformations they identified. Encourage them to consider what further tests could be done.

Scoring Rubric

Performance Indicators

_____ Calculates number of calories used.

_____ Calculates number of calories in food.

_____ Calculates amount of time required to use up calories.

_____ Identifies types of energy used during running.

Observations and Rubric Score

| 3 | 2 | 1 | 0 |

Name _____

Date _____

How People Use Energy

Part I Vocabulary

Use the letters of the terms in the Word Bank to complete the sentences.

A tidal energy	D chemical bonds	G solar energy
B fusion energy	E nuclear energy	H biomass
C hydroelectric energy	F geothermal energy	

The energy of sunlight is **1.** ____, which can be changed into electricity and other forms of energy. In living things, this energy from sunlight is stored in **2.** ____ that join atoms of carbon to each other and to atoms of other elements in living things. Electricity generated from the force of falling water is **3.** ____. One form of this kind of energy, **4.** ____, depends on the difference in water height between high tide and low tide. **5.** ____, or organic matter such as garbage, can be burned for energy. Another source of energy, **6.** ____, comes from heat inside Earth. Yet another source, **7.** ____, comes from splitting nuclei of atoms. One source of energy that may be available in the future is **8.** ____.

Part II Science Concepts and Understanding

Write the letter of the best choice.

____ 9. Which of the following happens when we burn fossil fuels?
  A Turbines turn to generate electricity.
  B Atoms break down to create hydrogen.
  C Molecules break apart and release heat.
  D We produce hydroelectric energy.

____ 10. Gasoline and diesel fuels are —
  F a primary source of electricity in the United States
  G energy sources found only outside the United States
  H renewable energy sources
  J energy sources for transportation

Unit F • Chapter 4   (page 1 of 5)   Assessment Guide AG 153

Name _____

_____ 11. Fossil fuels can easily be —
    A renewed within a few years
    B burned for a variety of uses
    C used to reduce pollution
    D removed from the ground

_____ 12. How do dams help produce hydroelectric energy?
    F They increase the water pressure.
    G They attract fish and other wildlife.
    H They decrease the depth of trapped water.
    J They help to control flooding.

_____ 13. Which of the following is a disadvantage of wind turbines?
    A They don't generate electricity.
    B They create too much wind in the area.
    C They are unpopular with farmers.
    D They don't produce a constant flow of energy.

_____ 14. The energy in fossil fuels that is turned into thermal energy when it burns is —
    F chemical energy
    G light
    H electric energy
    J heat

_____ 15. The main source of energy for transportation is —
    A propane
    B petroleum
    C electricity
    D natural gas

_____ 16. How do fossil fuels add to global warming?
    F They release carbon dioxide.
    G They release oxygen.
    H They make crude oil.
    J They cause nuclear fusion.

Name _____

___ 17. The blades of a generator's turbine would **NOT** be spun by —
    A water
    B steam
    C wind
    D electricity

___ 18. Which of the following releases the least amount of heat per kilogram when burned?
    F hard coal
    G gasoline
    H hardwood
    J propane gas

___ 19. Burning garbage to make steam and then electricity is an inexpensive use of —
    A oil products
    B biomass
    C farm products
    D natural resources

___ 20. Which of the following is a disadvantage of nuclear energy?
    F It requires too many engineers.
    G It uses too many nonrenewable resources.
    H It produces dangerous waste products.
    J It requires large amounts of fuel.

___ 21. What do solar cells use to generate electricity?
    A steam, turbines, and electric generators
    B moving water, dams, and power lines
    C the movement of Earth around the sun
    D the freeing of electrons by sunlight

___ 22. Geothermal energy occurs when underground water is near —
    F burning natural gas
    G magma
    H volcanoes
    J nuclear plants

Name _____

_____ 23. In what form do living organisms and fossil fuels store solar energy?
　　　　A chemical energy　　　C kinetic energy
　　　　B potential energy　　　D wasted energy

Use the letters of the terms in the Word Bank below to label the following diagram.

| A electric generator　　B dam　　C turbine　　D falling water　　E power lines |

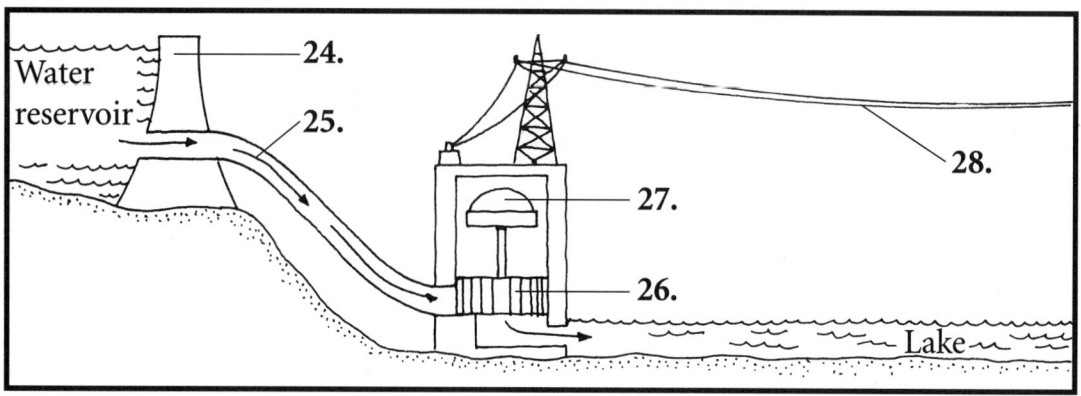

24. _____　　25. _____　　26. _____　　27. _____　　28. _____

Part III　Critical Thinking

29. How could attaching a greenhouse to a building help heat the building?

_____

_____

_____

30. How could computer control of a wind turbine make the turbine more efficient?

_____

_____

31. Why do you think there are fewer nuclear power plants being built today?

_____

_____

Name _____

Part IV   Process Skills Application

32. Compare the data in the graphs below. What do you **observe** about the data?

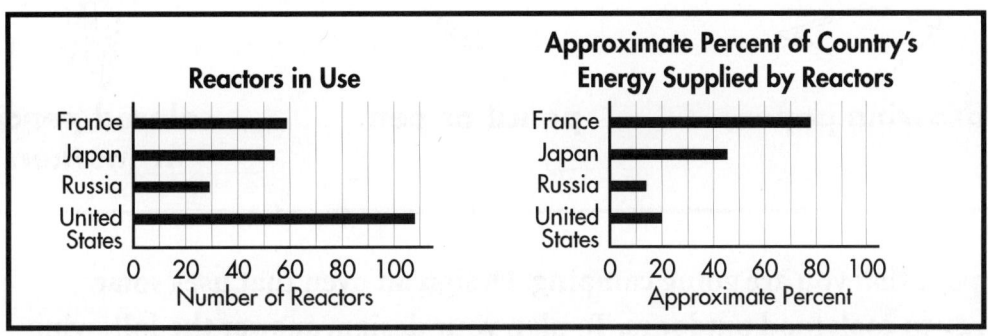

_____
_____

33. Complete the table below to **communicate** the data shown in the two graphs above.

WORLD'S NUCLEAR POWER

Country	Reactors in Use	Approximate Percent of Country's Energy Supplied by Reactors

34. Plan a simple investigation to determine the best spot in your yard or neighborhood to build a small windmill. Describe factors you would consider in picking the best spot. Then **devise an experiment** to determine the size of blades you should use. What **variables** should you **identify and control** as you conduct your experiment?

_____
_____
_____

Name _____ Date _____

PERFORMANCE TASK

Design a Solar Oven

Materials

drawing paper

pencil or pen

colored pencils or markers

Suppose that you are going camping. Design an oven that uses solar energy to cook food outdoors. To plan your design, answer the following questions. Then draw and label a diagram of your solar oven. Explain how the sun's energy generates the thermal energy needed to cook food. Ask your teacher's permission to make and test your design.

1. What is the objective of the project?

2. What is your energy source?

3. How must the energy from the source be changed to provide the energy needed to cook food?

4. What materials are best suited to your project?

5. How can the materials be combined to meet the objective?

Teacher's Directions

Design a Solar Oven

Materials Performance Task sheet, drawing paper, pencil or pen, colored pencils or markers

Time 15–20 minutes

Suggested Grouping individuals

Science Processes communicate, design a model

Preparation Hints You may wish to have students build and test their designs.

Introduce the Task Encourage students to propose simple, inexpensive materials for their designs to collect and concentrate the sun's energy. As an example, point out that lenses or mirrors can be used to start a campfire. Challenge students to explain what makes this possible. Then encourage them to think of how they might apply the same principles to make a solar oven. Direct them to provide a materials list and to label their diagrams clearly.

Promote Discussion Encourage students to present their designs to the class. Have them explain their choice of materials, and have them describe how the materials work together to gather and concentrate solar energy.

Scoring Rubric

Performance Indicators

_____ Labels each important element of the diagram clearly.

_____ Explains how solar energy can be used to cook food.

_____ Demonstrates understanding of unit concepts such as *solar energy* and *thermal energy*.

_____ Communicates ideas effectively through a diagram and explanation.

Observations and Rubric Score

3   2   1   0

Unit F • Chapter 4

Name _____
Date _____

Motion and Energy

Write the letter of the best choice.

___ 1. If the north-seeking pole of one magnet is held close to the north-seeking pole of another magnet, the magnets will —
   A attract each other
   B repel each other
   C attract and then repel each other
   D neither attract nor repel each other

___ 2. The force of gravitation is the strongest between —
   F a small and large object far apart
   G a small and large object close together
   H two large objects close together
   J two small objects close together

___ 3. If you push on a box and it does not move, the forces between you and the box are —
   A unequal forces
   B magnetic forces
   C balanced forces
   D unbalanced forces

___ 4. If you push a cart with 50 lb of force to the left, and someone else pushes with 100 lb of force to the right, the net force is —
   F zero
   G 150 lb to the right
   H 50 lb to the left
   J 50 lb to the right

___ 5. Which two simple machines make up a pair of scissors?
   A a wedge and an inclined plane
   B a lever and a pulley
   C a wedge and a lever
   D a lever and an inclined plane

___ 6. If you lift a box weighing 50 newtons to a height of 2 meters, how much work have you done?
   F 25 joules   H 52 joules
   G 50 joules   J 100 joules

___ 7. If it took you 2 seconds to lift a box weighing 100 newtons to a height of 3 meters, how much power did you use?
   A 50 watts   C 200 watts
   B 150 watts   D 300 watts

AG 160 **Assessment Guide**   (page 1 of 4)   Unit F

Name _____

_____ 8. Which has more momentum, a 300-kilogram motorbike or a 100-kilogram bicycle traveling at the same velocity?
F both
G the bicycle
H the motorbike
J neither one

_____ 9. If an object's velocity is increasing, then —
A its momentum is not changing
B it is experiencing acceleration
C its speed is decreasing
D it is not moving

_____ 10. Which of the following is an example of the conservation of momentum?
F lightning striking a tree
G throwing a dart at a dartboard
H a surfer picking up speed while riding a wave
J a complete transfer of speed between two balls

_____ 11. If you push a chair with your hand, the force from your hand is called —
A inertia   C action force
B manual labor   D reaction force

_____ 12. If an object is moving in an orbit —
F a force is acting on it
G no forces are acting on it
H it is moving in a straight line
J it is rotating on an axis

_____ 13. A car resting at the top of a hill has —
A kinetic energy
B potential energy
C magnetic energy
D thermal energy

_____ 14. The stretched rubber of a blown-up balloon is an example of —
F mechanical energy
G thermal potential energy
H gravitational energy
J elastic potential energy

_____ 15. Electric energy is created by the transfer of —
A protons   C neutrons
B electrons   D atoms

_____ 16. In order for current to flow around a circuit, the circuit must be —
F coiled   H open
G insulated   J closed

_____ 17. When a ray of light passes from one material to another and bends, it is being —
A absorbed   C reflected
B destroyed   D refracted

_____ 18. What can light waves travel through that sound waves cannot?
F air   H water
G space   J soil

Unit F   (page 2 of 4)   **Assessment Guide AG 161**

Name _____

_____ 19. Which word means the transfer of thermal energy from one substance to another?
   A heat   C potential
   B temperature   D kinetic

_____ 20. The transfer of thermal energy by electromagnetic radiation is —
   F conduction   H radiation
   G convection   J absorption

_____ 21. Chemical energy is stored in fuels in the form of —
   A radiation   C electrons
   B thermal energy   D chemical bonds

_____ 22. Which of the following is an example of using fossil fuels?
   F drinking spring water
   G cooking on a gas stove
   H digging fossils with a shovel
   J eating olive oil on a salad

_____ 23. A hydroelectric power plant converts the _____ into electricity.
   A kinetic energy of water
   B thermal energy of water
   C ionic energy of water
   D electromagnetic energy

_____ 24. Which of the following is a disadvantage to using solar power?
   F The energy is directly converted into electricity.
   G Not much energy is produced by the sun.
   H There are many pollutants and byproducts.
   J Large solar collectors and cells are expensive.

Name _____

Answer in complete sentences.

25. Can a car be driven at a constant speed and have a changing velocity? Explain.

_____
_____
_____
_____

26. You are riding a roller coaster. Explain the forms of energy you have at the top of the first hill, at the bottom of the first hill, and somewhere in the middle of the hill.

_____
_____
_____
_____

27. Explain one disadvantage of using fossil fuels as a primary source of energy.

_____
_____
_____
_____

Unit A • Chapter 1

Name _____
Date _____

From Single Cells to Body Systems

Part I Vocabulary   1 point each

Match each term in Column B with its meaning in Column A.

Column A

B 1. Thin cell covering that holds the parts of the cell together

F 2. Movement of water and dissolved materials through the cell membrane

H 3. Tissues that work together

C 4. Organelle that controls a cell's activities

D 5. Jellylike substance that contains many chemicals to keep a cell functioning

I 6. Organs that work together to perform a function

G 7. Cells that work together to perform a specific function

E 8. Process by which particles of a substance move from an area where there are many particles of the substance to an area where there are fewer particles of the substance

A 9. Basic unit of structure and function of all living things

Column B

A cell
B cell membrane
C nucleus
D cytoplasm
E diffusion
F osmosis
G tissue
H organ
I system

Unit A • Chapter 1   (page 1 of 5)   Assessment Guide   AG 1

Name _____

Use the letters of the terms in the Word Bank to complete the sentences.

| A alveoli | C receptors | E bone marrow | G neurons | I capillaries |
| B ligaments | D tendons | F nephrons | H joints | J villi |

The circulatory system transports blood through various-sized tubes called arteries, veins, and 10. __I__. The smallest of these tubes are blood vessels so tiny that blood cells have to move through them in single file. In the respiratory system, air travels into and out of the lungs through tubes. The smallest tubes end in tiny sacs called 11. __A__, which are surrounded by capillaries. Nutrients move from the digestive system into the blood by traveling through 12. __J__, tiny tubes sticking out of the wall of the small intestine. In the body's excretory system, urea and water travel from the blood into the kidneys and diffuse into 13. __F__. Bones have a hard outer membrane and a soft center that contains 14. __E__. This soft material is connective tissue that produces red and white blood cells. Bones are attached to each other in places called 15. __H__. Tough bands of tissue called 16. __D__ attach bones to muscles. Other bands of tissue called 17. __B__ attach bones to each other. To move, a muscle must receive a signal from the nervous system. Specialized cells called 18. __G__ transmit and receive nervous-system signals. Some kinds of nerve cells, called 19. __C__, detect conditions in the body's environment.

Part II Science Concepts and Understanding   2 points each

Write the letter of the best choice.

C 20. Which of the following allows water to flow into the roots of plants?
   A cytoplasm
   B mitochondria
   C osmosis
   D vacuoles

AG 2   Assessment Guide   (page 2 of 5)   Unit A • Chapter 1

Name _____

J 21. Osmosis is one kind of—
   F active transport   H carrier
   G organelle   J diffusion

A 22. Plants and animals grow when cells—
   A reproduce   C get rid of wastes
   B release energy   D repair themselves

H 23. An animal's skin is an example of—
   F connective tissue
   G muscle tissue
   H epithelial tissue
   J nervous tissue

B 24. Oxygen enters the body through the—
   A digestive system
   B respiratory system
   C circulatory system
   D excretory system

G 25. Oxygen travels to every cell in the body through the—
   F respiratory system
   G circulatory system
   H digestive system
   J excretory system

B 26. Which system breaks down food into nutrients?
   A respiratory   C circulatory
   B digestive   D excretory

F 27. The heart is a—
   F muscle   H cartilage
   G nerve   J synapse

C 28. Which of the following is a ball-and-socket joint?
   A knee   C hip
   B elbow   D toe

H 29. The nervous system carries ____ to and from the brain.
   F nutrients   H signals
   G blood   J oxygen

Unit A • Chapter 1   (page 3 of 5)   Assessment Guide   AG 3

Name _____

Use the terms in the Word Bank to label the following diagram.

| nucleus | chromosomes | cell membrane | cell wall |
| chloroplast | vacuole | mitochondria | cytoplasm |

30. chromosomes
31. nucleus
32. chloroplast
33. vacuole
34. cell wall
35. cell membrane
36. mitochondria
37. cytoplasm

Use the terms in the Word Bank to label the following diagram.

| esophagus | stomach | small intestine | liver | large intestine | pancreas |

38. liver
39. pancreas
40. small intestine
41. esophagus
42. stomach
43. large intestine

AG 4   Assessment Guide   (page 4 of 5)   Unit A • Chapter 1

Answer Key

Unit A • Chapter 2

Name _____

Part III Critical Thinking 6 points each

44. Would you expect to find muscle tissue in a plant? Why or why not?
    Possible answer: No, muscles enable an organism to move. Since plants cannot move from place to place, they do not have muscles that contract voluntarily or involuntarily.

45. What kinds of things does the blood transport? Why are these things important to cells in the body?
    Possible answer: The blood transports oxygen, nutrients, and wastes. Each cell needs oxygen and nutrients in order to live and reproduce. Each cell also needs to have its wastes removed.

46. You can contract your voluntary muscles on purpose. Can you contract your smooth muscles and cardiac muscles on purpose? Why or why not?
    Possible answer: No; smooth muscles and cardiac muscles contract involuntarily. They do things that you don't have to think about.

Part IV Process Skills Application 5 points each

47. **Compare** the organelles in a cell to organs in a human body. How are organelles similar to organs?
    Possible answer: Both organelles and organs have specific functions to perform. Organelles do their jobs in cells, while organs carry out their functions in the body.

48. **Hypothesize** how your body's receptors keep you safe.
    Possible answer: Feelings of heat, cold, pressure, touch, and pain, warn you of possible dangers. For example, if you touch a hot stove, the feeling of heat warns you to move your hand.

49. If you are observing cells under a microscope, what would lead you to **infer** that the cells are NOT animal cells?
    Possible answer: the presence of cell walls and chloroplasts, large central vacuoles with a rigid shape, may be green from the presence of chloroplasts

Unit A • Chapter 1   (page 5 of 5)   Assessment Guide AG 5

Name _____

Part II Science Concepts and Understanding 2 points each

Use the pictures to answer Questions 17–19. Write *reptile* if the picture shows an example of a reptile and *amphibian* if it shows an example of an amphibian.

17. reptile   18. amphibian   19. reptile

Use the pictures to answer Questions 20–22. Write *vascular* if the picture shows an example of a vascular plant and *nonvascular* if it shows an example of a nonvascular plant.

20. vascular   21. vascular   22. nonvascular

Write the letter of the best choice.

C 23. Which is an example of a mollusk?
    A spider   C snail
    B bear   D lizard

G 24. All of the following are fungi EXCEPT —
    F mushrooms   H yeasts
    G algae   J molds

Unit A • Chapter 2   (page 2 of 5)   Assessment Guide AG 9

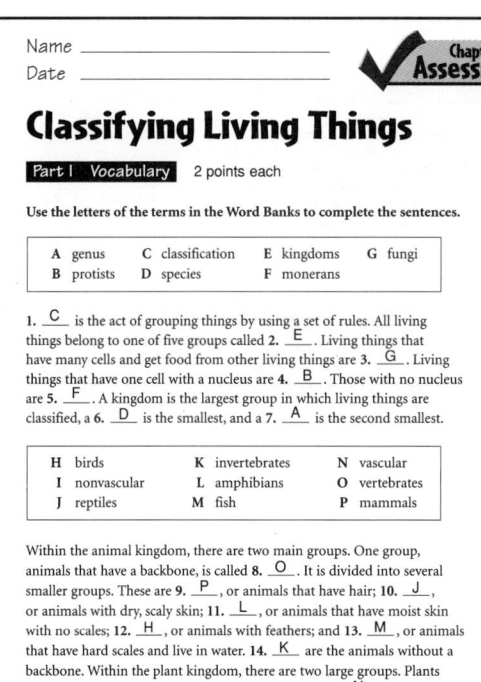

Name _____
Date _____

Chapter Assessment

Classifying Living Things

Part I Vocabulary 2 points each

Use the letters of the terms in the Word Banks to complete the sentences.

| A genus | C classification | E kingdoms | G fungi |
| B protists | D species | F monerans | |

1. __C__ is the act of grouping things by using a set of rules. All living things belong to one of five groups called 2. __E__. Living things that have many cells and get food from other living things are 3. __G__. Living things that have one cell with a nucleus are 4. __B__. Those with no nucleus are 5. __F__. A kingdom is the largest group in which living things are classified, a 6. __D__ is the smallest, and a 7. __A__ is the second smallest.

H birds	K invertebrates	N vascular
I nonvascular	L amphibians	O vertebrates
J reptiles	M fish	P mammals

Within the animal kingdom, there are two main groups. One group, animals that have a backbone, is called 8. __O__. It is divided into several smaller groups. These are 9. __P__, or animals that have hair; 10. __J__, or animals with dry, scaly skin; 11. __L__, or animals that have moist skin with no scales; 12. __H__, or animals with feathers; and 13. __M__, or animals that have hard scales and live in water. 14. __K__ are the animals without a backbone. Within the plant kingdom, there are two large groups. Plants that have tubes in their roots, stems, and leaves are 15. __N__.
16. __I__ plants do not have tubes and pass water and nutrients directly from cell to cell.

AG 8 Assessment Guide   (page 1 of 5)   Unit A • Chapter 2

Name _____

B 25. Where would nonvascular plants most likely be found?
    A under a cactus
    B along a riverbed
    C on the sea floor
    D on a sunny prairie

F 26. Which of the following are one-celled organisms with no nucleus?
    F monerans
    G fungi
    H protists
    J mollusks

D 27. In what living things are sharp senses and large brains usually found?
    A invertebrates
    B vascular plants
    C nonvascular plants
    D vertebrates

J 28. Which are examples of monerans?
    F mushrooms
    G algae
    H ferns
    J bacteria

C 29. Which of these are nonvascular plants?
    A flowers   C mosses
    B grasses   D trees

F 30. Which animal species are NOT vertebrates?
    F spiders   H whales
    G zebras   J lizards

D 31. Which is an invertebrate?
    A shark   C monkey
    B turtle   D clam

AG 10 Assessment Guide   (page 3 of 5)   Unit A • Chapter 2

Answer Key   AG 165 Assessment Guide

Unit A • Chapter 3

Page 1 (AG 11) — Unit A • Chapter 2

H 32. Any plant that has flowers or cones is a —
F hardwood   H vascular plant
G protist   J nonvascular plant

A 33. Which animal is an amphibian?
A frog   C fish
B sea gull   D whale

Part III Critical Thinking 5 points each

34. How would understanding the science of living things be more difficult if they weren't classified?
Possible answer: It would be more difficult to find and share information about living things and how they relate to one another.

35. Why are vascular plants generally taller than nonvascular plants?
Possible answers: Water must soak into nonvascular plants, and it passes slowly from cell to cell, so they must be near the ground. Vascular plants can draw up water, so they can grow tall.

36. What would scientists do if they found an animal that didn't fit into any kingdom?
Possible answer: Talk to other scientists about adding a new kingdom.

37. Why might a break in the main stem of a plant cause it to die?
Possible answers: It would break the tubes that carry water and nutrients from the roots to the leaves; then the leaves could not make food. With a break in the tubes, water and food could not move from the leaves back to other parts of the plant.

Page 2 (AG 15) — Unit A • Chapter 3

Animal Growth and Heredity

Part I Vocabulary 1 point each

Use the letters of the terms in the Word Banks to complete the sentences.

| A mitosis | C asexual reproduction | E life cycle | G sexual reproduction |
| B chromosomes | D direct development | F meiosis | H metamorphosis |

Many primitive organisms require only one parent to produce offspring. This is known as 1. **C**. Yeast is an example. It produces offspring by budding. More complex organisms produce offspring through 2. **G**. In this process, two parents are required. A zygote is formed from the joining of the parents' reproductive cells. The reproductive cells form through 3. **F**. In this process, the cell divides twice. After the first division, the nucleus of each new cell has the same number of 4. **B** as the nucleus of the parent cell. After the second division, the nucleus of each new cell has only half as many as the nucleus of the parent cell.

As organisms grow and mature, some go through distinct stages. A caterpillar, for example, goes through four stages to become a butterfly. This process of development is called 5. **H**. Other animals go through a different kind of development. Young animals that have the same shape as their parents go through 6. **D** to become adults. Each species has its own 7. **E**, a process in which an animal is born unable to reproduce and grows to become a reproducing adult. All animals grow through 8. **A**, a process in which cells make exact copies of themselves.

| I inherited trait | J genes | K dominant trait | L recessive trait |

Eye color is an 9. **I** that parents pass on to their offspring. If one parent has a 10. **L**, such as blue eyes, it may be masked by the stronger 11. **K** of brown eyes. All these characteristics are located on the DNA, which is contained in the 12. **J**. When the offspring become adults, they will pass their characteristics on to their young, continuing the family's unique attributes.

Page 3 (AG 12) — Unit A • Chapter 2

Part IV Process Skills Application

Use the pictures to answer Question 38. Then give the reason for your choice.

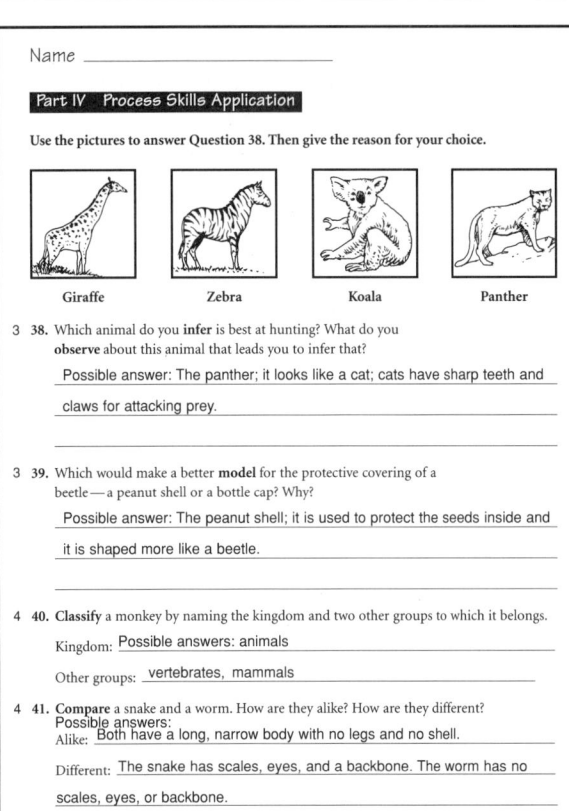

Giraffe   Zebra   Koala   Panther

3 38. Which animal do you **infer** is best at hunting? What do you **observe** about this animal that leads you to infer that?
Possible answer: The panther; it looks like a cat; cats have sharp teeth and claws for attacking prey.

3 39. Which would make a better **model** for the protective covering of a beetle—a peanut shell or a bottle cap? Why?
Possible answer: The peanut shell; it is used to protect the seeds inside and it is shaped more like a beetle.

4 40. **Classify** a monkey by naming the kingdom and two other groups to which it belongs.
Kingdom: Possible answers: animals
Other groups: vertebrates, mammals

4 41. **Compare** a snake and a worm. How are they alike? How are they different?
Possible answers:
Alike: Both have a long, narrow body with no legs and no shell.
Different: The snake has scales, eyes, and a backbone. The worm has no scales, eyes, or backbone.

Page 4 (AG 16) — Unit A • Chapter 3

Part II Science Concepts and Understanding 2 points each

Write the letter of the best choice.

C 13. Cells going through mitosis produce —
A half as many chromosomes
B six new male and female cells
C identical copies of the original cell
D offspring by budding

J 14. What does rapid mitosis allow a lizard to do if its tail is cut off?
F divide a new tail   H fuse a new tail
G spindle a new tail   J regenerate a new tail

A 15. Through the process of metamorphosis, an insect —
A changes the form of its body as it grows
B molts the outer covering of its skeleton
C becomes a hopping, wingless insect
D hatches from an egg in late summer

H 16. What are the three stages of incomplete metamorphosis?
F egg, pupa, chrysalis
G larva, pupa, cocoon
H egg, nymph, adult
J nymph, larva, adult

C 17. Which of the following is required in sexual reproduction?
A siblings   C two parents
B budding   D one parent

G 18. How does the nucleus of a cell prepare for mitosis?
F It divides cells into exact copies.
G It makes exact copies of chromosomes.
H It pinches the cell membrane at the middle.
J Its chromosomes pull apart the DNA coding.

D 19. In sexual reproduction, two cells combine to form a one-cell —
A gamete   C egg
B pupa   D zygote

Answer Key

Unit A • Chapter 4

Name _____

__J__ 20. Genes found on chromosomes contain the DNA codes for —
  F hypothesized factors
  G second-generation offspring
  H Mendel's factors
  J inherited traits

__B__ 21. In direct development, offspring —
  A go through incomplete metamorphosis
  B have the same shape as adults
  C go through complete metamorphosis
  D become nymphs

__H__ 22. One human trait that is **NOT** inherited is —
  F tongue curling   H balance
  G attached earlobes J hair color

__C__ 23. An example of incomplete metamorphosis is the life cycle of the —
  A butterfly   C grasshopper
  B rabbit   D frog

Use the following pictures to answer Question 24.

24. Write *1, 2, 3,* or *4* to indicate the correct order of development.

  2   1   4   3

Use the following pictures to answer Question 25.

25. Write *1, 2, 3,* or *4* to indicate the correct order of mitosis.

  1   3   2   4

Unit A • Chapter 3   (page 3 of 5)   Assessment Guide AG 17

Name _____

Observe the following diagram to answer Questions 31–32.

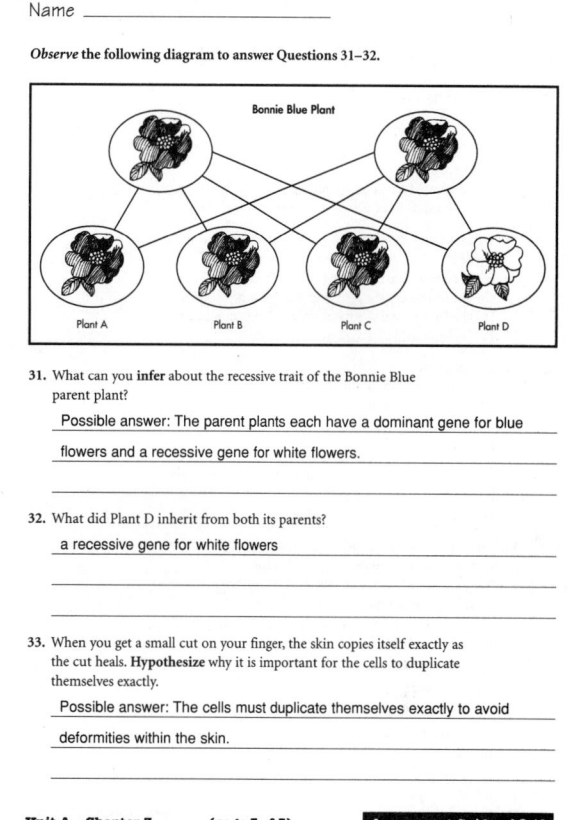

31. What can you **infer** about the recessive trait of the Bonnie Blue parent plant?
    Possible answer: The parent plants each have a dominant gene for blue flowers and a recessive gene for white flowers.

32. What did Plant D inherit from both its parents?
    a recessive gene for white flowers

33. When you get a small cut on your finger, the skin copies itself exactly as the cut heals. **Hypothesize** why it is important for the cells to duplicate themselves exactly.
    Possible answer: The cells must duplicate themselves exactly to avoid deformities within the skin.

Unit A • Chapter 3   (page 5 of 5)   Assessment Guide AG 19

Name _____

Part III Critical Thinking   7 points each

26. Why is it **NOT** a good idea to try to get rid of ocean sponges by chopping them up?
    Possible answer: Each piece can regenerate into a new animal.

27. Why do the cells of an adult continue to divide after the adult has stopped growing?
    Possible answer: to replace dead cells and repair body systems

Part IV Process Skills Application   8 points each

28. **Compare** mitosis with meiosis.
    Both are types of cell division. Both go through similar stages. Mitosis produces body cells; meiosis produces reproductive cells. After mitosis, cells have a complete set of chromosomes; after meiosis, cells have half the number of chromosomes.

29. **Hypothesize** what might happen to an insect larva placed in a glass jar with only grass to eat. What would happen if the insect was in the pupa stage?
    Possible answer: If the grass was not the larva's food, it would starve and die. The pupa does not feed and it probably would survive and emerge as an adult.

30. If a body cell has 22 chromosomes, what would be the chromosome count for the reproductive cells? **Use numbers** to explain your answer.
    Possible answer: It would be 11 because the parent cell contributes half of its chromosomes.

AG 18 Assessment Guide   (page 4 of 5)   Unit A • Chapter 3

Name _____
Date _____

Chapter Assessment

Plants and Their Adaptations

Part I Vocabulary   2 points each

Match each term in Column B with its meaning in Column A.

Column A		Column B
__D__ 1. Process by which plants use light energy to produce sugar		A angiosperm
__J__ 2. Plant material that can be separated into thread		B chlorophyll
__K__ 3. Flower structures that contain the male reproductive cells		C gymnosperm
		D photosynthesis
__B__ 4. Helps plants use light energy to make food		E phloem
__G__ 5. Single reproductive cell that grows into a new plant		F grain
__I__ 6. Tubes in plants that carry water and nutrients		G spore
__A__ 7. Flowering, fruit-producing plant		H germinates
__E__ 8. Tubes in plants that carry food		I xylem
__C__ 9. Plant with unprotected seeds		J fiber
__H__ 10. What a seed does when conditions are right for growth		K pollen
__F__ 11. The seeds of certain grasses from which cereals are made		

AG 22 Assessment Guide   (page 1 of 5)   Unit A • Chapter 4

Answer Key   AG 167 Assessment Guide

Name _____

Part II Science Concepts and Understanding 3 points each

Write the letter of the best choice.

__A__ 12. Quinine and digitalis are examples of —
  A medicines made from plants
  B xylem and phloem
  C plants used for making clothing
  D foods made from the leaves of plants

__J__ 13. Which of the following is NOT a way that a fruit helps the seed inside it?
  F The fruit protects the seed from cold weather.
  G The fruit keeps the seed from being eaten.
  H The fruit provides extra nutrition for the new plant.
  J The fruit helps the seed transfer pollen.

__B__ 14. Root hairs —
  A anchor the plant to the ground
  B take in nutrients and water
  C store food
  D take water directly from the air

__J__ 15. All organisms release _____ as they turn food into energy.
  F oxygen   H nitrogen
  G helium   J carbon dioxide

__A__ 16. More spores are produced from a spore-producing plant than seeds from a seed-producing plant because —
  A spores have less of a chance of growing than seeds
  B there are more spore-producing plants
  C spores don't fall far from the plant that produced them
  D spores are larger than most seeds

__G__ 17. Prop roots —
  F anchor the plant to the soil
  G keep plants from blowing over
  H reach water deep in the ground
  J help make food

Unit A • Chapter 4   (page 2 of 5)   Assessment Guide AG 23

Name _____

__J__ 23. Which of the following is NOT a reason why plants store food?
  F Plants may not get enough water to make food during dry periods.
  G Most plants cannot make food during the winter.
  H Some plants store food to survive brief temperature changes.
  J Plants must store some food to survive in a flood.

__C__ 24. Carrots, sweet potatoes, turnips, and beets are all —
  A storage leaves   C storage roots
  B root hairs   D storage stems

__G__ 25. The leaves of plants take in _____ to use in photosynthesis.
  F oxygen   H chlorophyll
  G carbon dioxide   J bacteria

__D__ 26. The material in old _____ hardens to become the "wood" of a tree.
  A phloem   B branches   C bark   D xylem

__G__ 27. Fibers are —
  F like root hairs in taproots
  G materials that can be separated into thread
  H the xylem "strings" of celery
  J phloem in leaves

Part III Critical Thinking 5 points each

28. Would you expect a plant with large, flat leaves to live in a desert? Why or why not?
   Possible answer: No, because the leaves would cause the plant to lose too much water. Students may also answer that animals would be more likely to eat the leaves to get water.

29. Could a vascular plant live without its roots? Explain.
   Possible answer: No; not unless there was another way for it to take in water and nutrients, store food, and keep from falling over.

Unit A • Chapter 4   (page 4 of 5)   Assessment Guide AG 25

Name _____

Use the diagrams below to answer Questions 18–21.

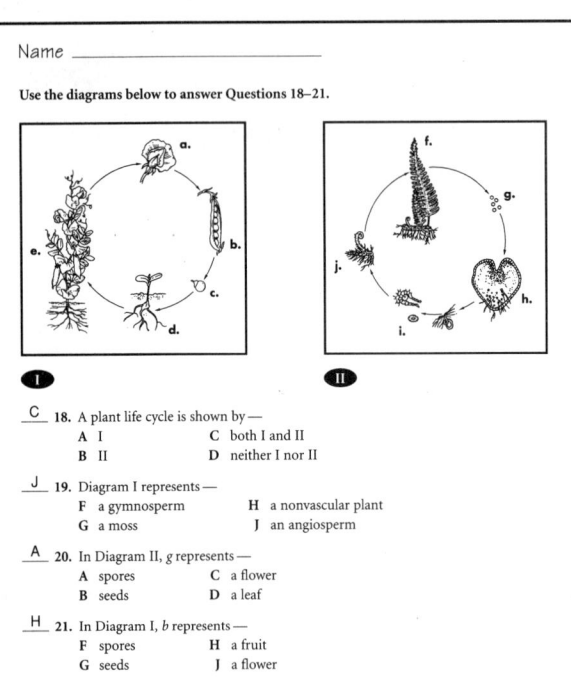

__C__ 18. A plant life cycle is shown by —
  A I   C both I and II
  B II   D neither I nor II

__J__ 19. Diagram I represents —
  F a gymnosperm   H a nonvascular plant
  G a moss   J an angiosperm

__A__ 20. In Diagram II, g represents —
  A spores   C a flower
  B seeds   D a leaf

__H__ 21. In Diagram I, b represents —
  F spores   H a fruit
  G seeds   J a flower

Write the letter of the best choice.

__A__ 22. Xylem and phloem are found only in —
  A vascular plants   C woody plants
  B nonvascular plants   D leaves of large trees

AG 24 Assessment Guide   (page 3 of 5)   Unit A • Chapter 4

Name _____

30. Think of all the things you use in a day that are plant parts or plant products. How would your life be different if there were no plants?
   Possible answer: Without plants there would be no animal life because plants supply oxygen through photosynthesis. Students may also include foods, wood products, medicines, grains, and fibers as being important in their everyday lives.

Part IV Process Skills Application 5 points each

31. **Infer** why a plant from one island begins to grow on a distant island where that kind of plant had never grown before.
   Possible answer: The seed or seeds of the plant may have been carried by wind, water, a bird, a ship, or a person. Also, conditions on both islands would have to be similar for it to grow on the second island.

Interpret the circle graph to answer 32–33.

32. **Observe** the circle graph. What is the total percentage of foods from plants that should be part of a healthful diet?
   82.5%

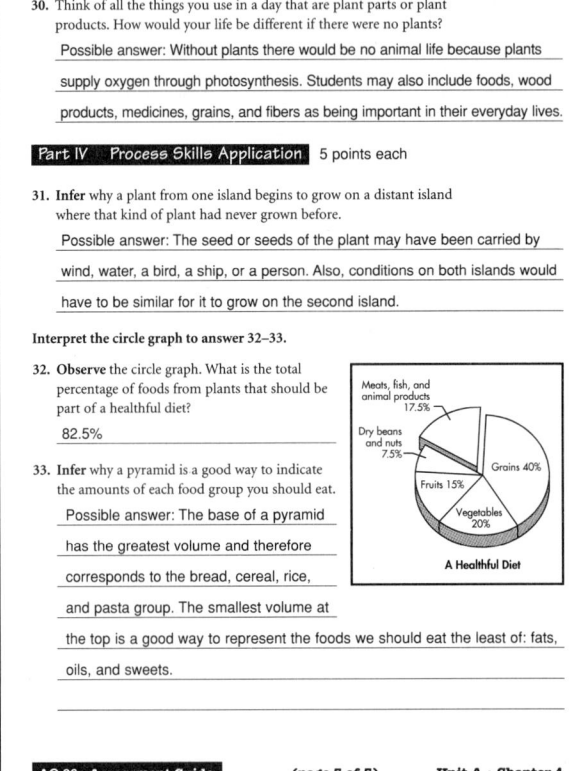

33. **Infer** why a pyramid is a good way to indicate the amounts of each food group you should eat.
   Possible answer: The base of a pyramid has the greatest volume and therefore corresponds to the bread, cereal, rice, and pasta group. The smallest volume at the top is a good way to represent the foods we should eat the least of: fats, oils, and sweets.

AG 26 Assessment Guide   (page 5 of 5)   Unit A • Chapter 4

Unit A

Living Systems

Write the letter of the best choice. 3 points each

__C__ 1. Which organelles are found only in a plant cell?
 A cytoplasm and cell wall
 B chromosomes and chloroplasts
 C chloroplasts and cell wall
 D cell wall and cell membrane

__G__ 2. The passage of water and dissolved materials through a cell membrane is known as —
 F digestion H hydration
 G osmosis J diffusion

__C__ 3. Which organelle is correctly matched with its function?
 A mitochondria – controls all cell activities
 B cytoplasm – separates the cell from its surroundings
 C vacuoles – store food, wastes, or water
 D chloroplasts – release energy from food

__J__ 4. The smallest blood vessels are called —
 F arteries H alveoli
 G veins J capillaries

__B__ 5. What takes place in the alveoli?
 A transportation of blood to cells
 B exchange of oxygen and carbon dioxide
 C excretion of bodily fluids
 D digestion of your food

__G__ 6. How does the body obtain nutrients from food?
 F The stomach absorbs food particles.
 G Nutrients diffuse through the villi in the small intestine.
 H Nutrients are absorbed as they pass through the pancreas.
 J Digested food diffuses through the large intestines.

__B__ 7. The kidney is an organ of which system?
 A digestive C circulatory
 B excretory D respiratory

__H__ 8. Ligaments —
 F produce red blood cells
 G detect conditions in the body
 H hold the skeleton together
 J connect muscle to bone

__C__ 9. Your body uses receptors and produces a reflex when you —
 A listen to soft music
 B lie down and go to sleep
 C touch a hot plate of food
 D jump rope

__G__ 10. Which of the following is NOT one of the five kingdoms?
 F protist H fungi
 G genus J moneran

__B__ 11. Scientists use classification to —
 A make animals easier to find
 B make it easier to categorize living things and to talk about them
 C help protect the environment
 D create an organized environment for plants and animals

__J__ 12. Which group contains only invertebrates?
 F birds H amphibians
 G mammals J arthropods

__A__ 13. Frogs are —
 A amphibians C monerans
 B invertebrates D reptiles

__F__ 14. What is the difference between a vascular plant and a nonvascular plant?
 F A vascular plant has transport tubes.
 G A vascular plant loses its leaves in the winter.
 H A vascular plant needs water.
 J A vascular plant needs light.

__C__ 15. Moss is an example of —
 A a vascular plant
 B a protist
 C a nonvascular plant
 D an invertebrate

__G__ 16. Mitosis —
 F occurs only in sexual reproduction
 G occurs during regeneration
 H reduces the number of chromosomes
 J divides one cell into four cells

__B__ 17. Asexual reproduction requires how many parents?
 A none C two
 B one D three

__G__ 18. What process forms reproductive cells for sexual reproduction?
 F mitosis H regeneration
 G meiosis J photosynthesis

__D__ 19. Which of the following grow through complete metamorphosis?
 A scorpions C grasshoppers
 B spiders D frogs

__H__ 20. If both parent flowers are red but their offspring is white, what does this tell you about flower color?
 F Flower color is not an inherited trait.
 G Red color is a weak trait.
 H White color is a recessive trait.
 J There is no gene for flower color.

__B__ 21. If a cat has white hair when both of its parents have brown hair, how many white-haired genes must it have inherited?
 A one C twenty-three
 B two D forty-six

__F__ 22. Which tubes in a vascular plant transport food?
 F phloem H taproots
 G xylem J prop roots

__A__ 23. Male reproductive cells in gymnosperms are in —
 A pollen C apples
 B spores D flowers

__H__ 24. What gives plants and leaves their green color?
 F stomata H chlorophyll
 G pollen J photosynthesis

__B__ 25. Reproductive cells in nonvascular plants are —
 A seeds C pollen
 B spores D flowers

__J__ 26. What makes angiosperms different from other vascular plants?
 F roots H leaves
 G bark J flowers

__B__ 27. Which of the following is made from the fibers of cotton?
 A perfumes C paper
 B blue jeans D shampoo

__F__ 28. Most breakfast cereals are made of —
 F grains H stems
 G leaves J flowers

Answer in complete sentences.

5 29. A loud noise startles you from behind. Explain how the nervous system, the muscular system, and the skeletal system work together to make you jump.
Possible answer: The receptors in your ears respond to the noise behind you by sending a signal to your central nervous system. Then the nervous system sends a signal through your spinal cord to the muscles in your legs. This signal tells your muscles to contract. When the muscles contract, the bones move, and your body moves away from the noise.

5 30. A new organism is found that is multicellular, does not have a backbone, and has six legs. While studying the organism, you notice that it develops somewhat like a grasshopper. Explain how you would classify this organism, and discuss the stages of its development.
Possible answer: I would classify it as an invertebrate in the animal kingdom. Because it has six legs, it would belong to the arthropod class. The type of development would be incomplete metamorphosis in which there are three stages: egg, nymph, and adult.

6 31. (3.3) Explain how a child can have blue eyes when both parents have brown eyes.
Possible answer: Blue eyes are a recessive trait, while brown eyes are a dominant trait. A child can have blue eyes if each parent has one recessive gene and passes that gene to the child.

Answer Key

Unit B • Chapter 1

Cycles in Nature

Part I Vocabulary — 1 point each

Match each term in Column B with its meaning in Column A.

Column A

- **E** 1. Cycle in which plants turn gas in air into oxygen
- **H** 2. Water falling from clouds
- **B** 3. Water turning into water vapor
- **A** 4. Cycle in which a gas in the air is fixed into a form that plants can use
- **D** 5. Water vapor turning into water
- **G** 6. Plants losing water through their stomata
- **C** 7. Cycle in which water moves through the environment
- **F** 8. Process of releasing energy from food

Column B

A nitrogen cycle
B evaporation
C water cycle
D condensation
E carbon-oxygen cycle
F respiration
G transpiration
H precipitation

Part II Science Concepts and Understanding — 2 points each

Write the letter of the best choice.

- **C** 9. ___ provides energy for plants to grow.
  - A natural gas
  - B sunlight
  - C respiration
  - D carbon dioxide
- **G** 10. Plants release ___ into the atmosphere as a byproduct of photosynthesis.
  - F carbon dioxide
  - G oxygen
  - H nitrogen
  - J helium

Unit B • Chapter 1   (page 1 of 5)   Assessment Guide AG 33

- **D** 11. Plants and animals release ___ as a product of respiration.
  - A oxygen
  - B helium
  - C nitrogen
  - D carbon dioxide
- **F** 12. During ___, plants use sunlight, water, and carbon dioxide to make their own food.
  - F photosynthesis
  - G respiration
  - H decay
  - J transformation
- **C** 13. Which of the following does NOT produce carbon dioxide?
  - A people burning fuels
  - B people breathing
  - C plants using sunlight
  - D animals breathing
- **G** 14. Which of the following return to the soil in animal waste?
  - F nitrates and oxygen
  - G ammonia and nitrates
  - H ammonia and oxygen
  - J oxygen and bacteria
- **B** 15. Plants make proteins from —
  - A water in the soil
  - B nitrates in the soil
  - C nitrogen in the air
  - D oxygen
- **F** 16. In what process do bacteria and fungi break down a dead organism's tissues and use some of the carbon as food?
  - F decay
  - G photosynthesis
  - H water cycle
  - J carbon dioxide–water cycle
- **D** 17. Petroleum is made from —
  - A coal and oil
  - B bacteria and fungi
  - C plants releasing oxygen
  - D decayed organisms
- **J** 18. Burning fuels in cars and factories —
  - F puts oxygen into the air
  - G puts nitrogen into the air
  - H upsets the balance of the nitrogen cycle
  - J upsets the balance of the carbon-oxygen cycle

AG 34 Assessment Guide   (page 2 of 5)   Unit B • Chapter 1

Use the following pictures to answer Questions 19–21.

A   B

C   D

- **B** 19. Which picture represents condensation?
- **A** 20. Which picture represents evaporation?
- **C** 21. Which picture represents precipitation?

Write the letter of the best choice.

- **D** 22. Water falls to Earth as rain after water vapor ___ into clouds.
  - A evaporates
  - B warms
  - C becomes heavy
  - D condenses
- **F** 23. Chemicals and pesticides get into groundwater supplies through —
  - F rain
  - G evaporation
  - H transpiration
  - J water vapor
- **C** 24. Plants return water to the environment through —
  - A photosynthesis
  - B respiration
  - C transpiration
  - D evaporation

Unit B • Chapter 1   (page 3 of 5)   Assessment Guide AG 35

- **H** 25. Which of the following describes a part of the nitrogen cycle?
  - F Plants use nitrogen gas and return it to soil.
  - G Lightning turns fixed nitrogen into nitrogen gas.
  - H Bacteria in the soil fix nitrogen for plants.
  - J Animals turn fixed nitrogen into nitrogen gas.
- **B** 26. Which of the following is **NOT** a part of a natural cycle?
  - A Water evaporates into water vapor and condenses as clouds.
  - B Natural gas burns to produce energy, carbon dioxide, and water.
  - C Carbon dioxide is used in photosynthesis.
  - D Animals eat fixed nitrogen when they eat plants.
- **J** 27. Cold air causes water vapor to ___ and form ___.
  - F precipitate; puddles
  - G evaporate; water vapor
  - H be fixed; lightning
  - J condense; clouds
- **B** 28. Ammonia is a usable form of ___ that bacteria use in the ___.
  - A carbon dioxide; carbon-oxygen cycle
  - B nitrogen; nitrogen cycle
  - C water vapor; water cycle
  - D protein; nitrogen cycle

Part III Critical Thinking — 7 points each

Answer the following on a separate sheet of paper.

29. If plants and animals lived forever, what would happen to the nitrates in Earth's soil? Possible answer: Nothing would die; therefore, nothing would decay, so less nitrate would be returned to the soil. The nitrates in the soil would be used up.
30. What are three ways to help keep the carbon-oxygen cycle in balance? Possible answers: Plant a tree or garden; walk or ride a bicycle instead of driving; carpool; don't burn leaves; use a manual lawn mower; wear a sweater in the house when it's cool, rather than turning up the thermostat.
31. Do rain puddles disappear more quickly on a cloudy day or on a clear day? Why? Possible answer: Puddles disappear more quickly on a clear day because the direct heat from the sun helps the water evaporate.
32. What would happen if the air in the upper atmosphere were warmer than water vapor in the air? Possible answer: If the air were warm, condensation couldn't occur and there would be no precipitation.

AG 36 Assessment Guide   (page 4 of 5)   Unit B • Chapter 1

Answer Key

Unit B • Chapter 2

Name _____

Part IV Process Skills Application   4 points each

33. Rabbits eat lots of green, leafy plants and rarely drink any water. What could you **infer** from this behavior?
    Possible answer: You could infer that green, leafy plants contain most of the water that rabbits need.

34. What did scientists **observe** that made them infer that burning fuels is bad for the air?
    Possible answer: Scientists observed that the additional carbon dioxide in the air wasn't being converted to oxygen.

Observe and *interpret* the following circle graphs to answer Questions 35–38.

[Carbon Dioxide in the Atmosphere: 15% from Natural Processes, 85% from Burning Fuels]
[Gases in Earth's Atmosphere: 21% Oxygen, 0.03% Carbon Dioxide, 0.97% Other, 78% Nitrogen]

35. Which gas makes up most of Earth's atmosphere? __nitrogen__
36. What percentage of Earth's atmosphere is oxygen? __21%__
37. What percentage of Earth's carbon dioxide is produced by natural processes? __15%__
38. What gas do you **infer** would be most affected if human activity increased the burning of fuels?
    carbon dioxide

Unit B • Chapter 1   (page 5 of 5)   Assessment Guide AG 37

Name _____

| M symbiosis | O competition | Q extinct | S instinct |
| N threatened | P endangered | R learned behavior | T exotic |

Because most ecosystems don't have unlimited resources, there may be 13. __O__ for these resources among organisms. Organisms also share resources, however. In some cases, different organisms live together for most or all of their lives. A long relationship between different kinds of organisms is called 14. __M__. Animals behave in certain ways to survive in their communities. An inherited behavior is called an 15. __S__. A behavior that is developed over time is called a 16. __R__. A population of organisms can survive only if enough individuals produce healthy offspring. A population that begins to decline is listed as 17. __N__. A population that is likely to die out unless steps are taken to save it is listed as 18. __P__. A decline in population may result from the importing of 19. __T__, or nonnative, plants, or animals into the community. When the last individual of a population dies, that kind of organism becomes. 20. __Q__.

Part II Science Concepts and Understanding   2 points each

Write the letter of the best choice.

__H__ 21. In a healthy ecosystem, populations of living things are—
   F independent   H interdependent
   G enemies   J large

__A__ 22. The types and number of animals in an ecosystem are determined by the—
   A types and number of plants   C types and number of individuals
   B types and number of communities   D population density

__J__ 23. What do the producers in a community do?
   F hunt prey   H eat other organisms
   G decompose organisms J make food

Unit B • Chapter 2   (page 2 of 5)   Assessment Guide AG 41

Name _____
Date _____

Chapter Assessment

Living Things Interact

Part I Vocabulary   1 point each

Use the letters of the terms in the Word Banks to complete the sentences.

| A individual | C niche | E habitat |
| B ecosystem | D population | F community |

An environment includes all living and nonliving things in an area. A single organism in an environment is called an 1. __A__. Organisms of the same kind living in the same environment make up a 2. __D__. All the populations of organisms living together in environment make up a 3. __F__. This part of the environment and its physical factors make up an 4. __B__. Every population lives in a certain part of an ecosystem, known as its 5. __E__. Within this part of the ecosystem, each population has a certain role, or 6. __C__.

| G producers | I food chain | K decomposers |
| H energy pyramid | J food web | L consumers |

The sun provides the energy for almost every ecosystem on Earth. All life in an ecosystem depends on 7. __G__ to capture the energy of the sun, change it into living tissue, and pass it on to other organisms. All other organisms in an ecosystem community must eat to get the energy they need. So the animals in a community are 8. __L__. A 9. __I__ shows how consumers in an ecosystem are connected to one another according to what they eat. Plants are usually at the base. First-level consumers, or herbivores, eat the plants. Second-level consumers, or carnivores, eat the herbivores. 10. __K__, such as mushrooms and bacteria, break down the tissues of dead organisms. A 11. __J__ shows the relationships between many food chains within a single ecosystem. An 12. __H__ shows the amount of energy available to pass from one level of a food chain to the next.

AG 40 Assessment Guide   (page 1 of 5)   Unit B • Chapter 2

Name _____

__B__ 24. In a food chain, each level of consumer eats organisms—
   A from the level above it   C in the same niche
   B from the level below it   D in the same population

__F__ 25. What percentage of energy at any level of a food chain is passed on to the next higher level?
   F about 10 percent   H It depends on the population.
   G about 90 percent   J It depends on the community.

__B__ 26. Different organisms can share the same resource, such as a tree, because they have different—
   A populations   C communities
   B niches   D ecosystems

__H__ 27. A cleaner fish picks bits of food from between a shark's teeth. This relationship is an example of—
   F independence   H mutualism
   G competition   J camouflage

__D__ 28. Behaviors for building shelters, finding mates, and hunting are usually—
   A learned   C competitive
   B symbiotic   D instinctive

Use the following diagram to answer Questions 29–33. Write the letter of the organism that belongs at each level of the food chain.

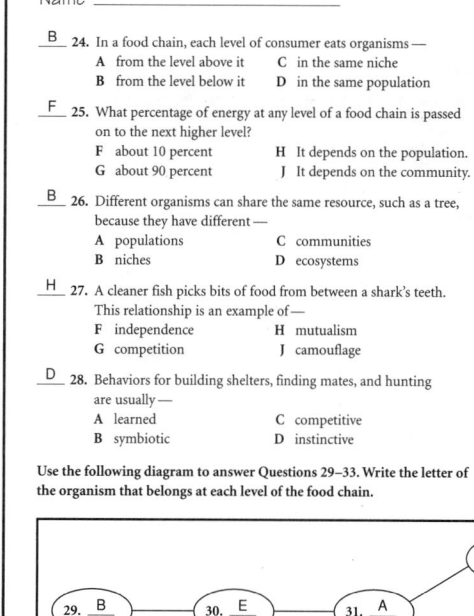

29. __B__   30. __E__   31. __A__   32. __C or D__   33. __D or C__

| A coyote | B green plant | C vulture | D mushroom | E rabbit |

AG 42 Assessment Guide   (page 3 of 5)   Unit B • Chapter 1

Answer Key

AG 171 Assessment Guide

Unit B • Chapter 3

Page 4 of 5 (Unit B • Chapter 1)

Name _____

Write the letter of the best choice.

__G__ 34. Which of the following is NOT a natural cause for a population decline?
- F drought
- G pesticides
- H floods
- J hurricanes

__A__ 35. Most declines in populations of organisms today are caused by —
- A human activity
- B natural disasters
- C disease
- D old age

Part III Critical Thinking   5 points each

Answer the following on a separate sheet of paper.

36. The environment determines an area's ecosystem. What might happen if an area has a dramatic decrease in rainfall?
   Possible answer: There would be fewer plants, and this decrease would affect the rest of the food/energy chain.

37. Giraffes, antelopes, and rhinos all eat from the same trees. What would happen if these animals were all the same size?
   Possible answer: They would all eat from the same parts of the trees, and there probably wouldn't be enough food for all of them.

38. What difference does it make if an organism becomes extinct?
   Possible answer: The extinction of an organism disrupts the balance of the whole ecosystem it was part of.

Part IV Process Skills Application   7 points each

39. How could you **gather data** about the number of red-tailed hawks that live in your state?
   Possible answer: Pick a small area to study, and observe the number of red-tailed hawks in that area at different times of the day and year. Then multiply by the number of areas of the same size.

Page 5 of 5 (Unit B • Chapter 1)

Name _____

40. What characteristics would you use to **classify** birds?
   Possible answers: what they eat and what eats them; what they do and which species are benefited or harmed by what they do; color, size, shape of beak, kind of feet

41. The larger the population in an area, the greater the competition for food. **Predict** what would happen if the population of a species in an area doubled.
   Possible answer: The doubled population will eventually return to a smaller size because its demands for food will be greater than the available food. If the species were threatened, doubling its size would not have that effect unless lack of habitat were the reason for the animal's threatened status.

42. Suppose an area that normally receives five inches of rain in May receives only one inch in May. **Draw a conclusion** about what will happen to the producers and first-level consumers in the area.
   Possible answer: The producers will not grow, and many of them will die. Many of the first-level consumers will also die, because they won't have food from the producers.

43. Domestic horses often become uneasy when they are away from other horses. From this fact, what can you **infer** about the behavior of wild horses?
   Possible answer: Wild horses live in herds.

Biomes

Part I Vocabulary   2 points each

Match each term in Column B with its meaning in Column A.

	Column A	Column B
__E__ 1.	Region where annual patterns of rainfall, temperature, and sunlight are similar throughout	A open-ocean zone
__A__ 2.	Area of deep water where most animal and plant organisms live at the surface	B biome
__F__ 3.	Area of calm water, constant temperature, and much algae growth	C estuary
__C__ 4.	Place where a freshwater river empties into the ocean	D intertidal zone
__B__ 5.	Large-scale ecosystem defined by the plants and animals adapted to live in its climate	E climate zone
__D__ 6.	Area where waves and tides reach the shore	F near-shore zone

Part II Science Concepts and Understanding   3 points each

Write the letter of the best choice.

__D__ 7. Desert biomes have all of the following EXCEPT —
- A hot and sunny days
- B usually cold night temperatures
- C very dry soil and air
- D animals active in the daytime

__H__ 8. The taiga has —
- F grasses with long, slender leaves
- G frozen soil with few plants
- H pine, fir, and spruce trees
- J oak, maple, and hickory trees

__C__ 9. The floor of the rain forest has little plant life because —
- A the vines and ferns choke off the other plants
- B the rain forest gets too much sunlight
- C very little sunlight gets through the canopy
- D toads and salamanders eat the plants on the forest floor

__G__ 10. Evergreens are adapted to life in the taiga because they —
- F shed needles that form a thick mat on the forest floor
- G have a waxy covering over their needles
- H grow taller than most deciduous trees
- J have roots that spread out near the surface

__A__ 11. What is the correct order of the ocean zones from shallowest to deepest?
- A intertidal zone, near-shore zone, open-ocean zone
- B near-shore zone, open-ocean zone, intertidal zone
- C near-shore zone, intertidal zone, open-ocean zone
- D intertidal zone, open-ocean zone, near-shore zone

__F__ 12. Freshwater ecosystems occur in —
- F swamps and marshes
- G oceans and seas
- H estuaries
- J the intertidal zone

__C__ 13. Permafrost is found in the ____ biome.
- A grassland
- B taiga
- C tundra
- D desert

Answer Key

Unit B • Chapter 4

Page 3 of 5 (Unit B • Chapter 3)

Name _____

__J__ 14. The biome with the greatest diversity of life is the —
  F taiga H deciduous forest
  G grassland J tropical rain forest

__B__ 15. Which is NOT true of estuaries?
  A Their waters are calm and still.
  B They have the fewest number of species of any biome.
  C They help prevent coastal flooding and erosion.
  D They are the most productive ecosystems on Earth.

__H__ 16. In an ocean ecosystem, the deeper the water the —
  F greater the number of animals
  G warmer the temperature
  H less the amount of sunlight
  J greater the number of plants

Part III Critical Thinking 9 points each

17. Why do large herbivores such as bison and elephants live in grasslands rather than in tropical rain forests?
Possible answer: They are better adapted to live in the grasslands. The foods they eat grow there. Their large bodies and type of feet (large or hooved) help them move around better in the grassland than in the tropical rain forest.

18. Why do plants of the tundra grow low to the ground and have a thick mat of shallow roots?
Possible answer: They are better protected from strong winds. The thick mat of shallow roots helps them take in water during a thaw. Longer roots would be of no use since the ground below the surface layer stays frozen.

Page 5 of 5 (Unit B • Chapter 3)

Name _____

22. Fill in the blanks in the chart below to compare the six biomes. 12 points

Biome	Plant Example	Animal Example	Rainfall (high, moderate, or low)
Tropical Rain Forest	orchids, ferns, tall trees, vines	snakes, frogs, birds, insects	very high
Deciduous Forest	maples, oaks, hickories	rabbits, skunks, deer, chipmunks	moderate
Grassland	grasses, grains	prairie dogs, badgers, mice, bison	low
Desert	cactus, mesquite, creosote	snakes, lizards	very low
Taiga	firs, spruce, pines	owls, hares, lynx, weasels, wolves	moderate to low
Tundra	mosses, lichens, dwarf willow	caribou, musk ox	low

Page 4 of 5 (Unit B • Chapter 3)

Name _____

19. Justin made a freshwater pond in his back yard and stocked it with goldfish. He might want to add some water lilies and cattails to make the pond beautiful. Give other reasons why Justin might add these plants.
Possible answer: Plants, such as water lilies and cattails, serve as hiding places for fish; they are sources of food for fish; and they provide oxygen as a by-product of photosynthesis.

20. At night, the temperature in the desert drops a lot, sometimes causing dew to form on some plants. Explain how dew helps preserve life in the desert.
Possible answer: Dew provides a source of water for small rodents, birds, and insects.

Part IV Process Skills Application

Observe these two hares.

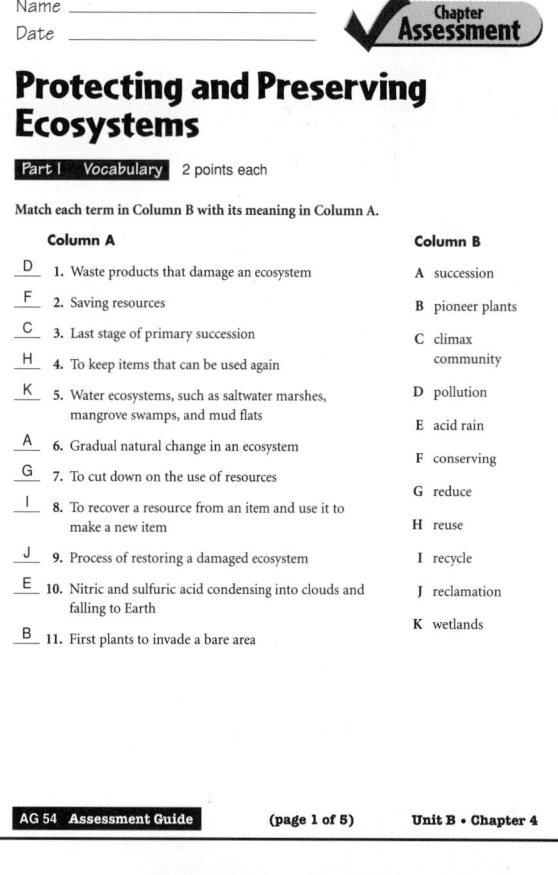

10 21. **Compare** the physical features of the two animals. What can you **infer** about how each hare is adapted to its environment?
The arctic hare has smaller ears to prevent heat loss. Its white coat helps aid in camouflage. The jackrabbit has big, wide ears to get rid of the heat. Its darker, mottled coat provides camouflage in the desert.

Page 1 of 5 (Unit B • Chapter 4) — Chapter Assessment

Name _____
Date _____

Protecting and Preserving Ecosystems

Part I Vocabulary 2 points each

Match each term in Column B with its meaning in Column A.

Column A

__D__ 1. Waste products that damage an ecosystem
__F__ 2. Saving resources
__C__ 3. Last stage of primary succession
__H__ 4. To keep items that can be used again
__K__ 5. Water ecosystems, such as saltwater marshes, mangrove swamps, and mud flats
__A__ 6. Gradual natural change in an ecosystem
__G__ 7. To cut down on the use of resources
__I__ 8. To recover a resource from an item and use it to make a new item
__J__ 9. Process of restoring a damaged ecosystem
__E__ 10. Nitric and sulfuric acid condensing into clouds and falling to Earth
__B__ 11. First plants to invade a bare area

Column B

A succession
B pioneer plants
C climax community
D pollution
E acid rain
F conserving
G reduce
H reuse
I recycle
J reclamation
K wetlands

Answer Key

Unit B • Chapter 4

Name _____

Part II Science Concepts and Understanding 2 points each

Write the letter of the best choice.

A 12. At which stage of primary succession do lichens start to grow on exposed rocks?
   A pioneer-plant stage   C grassy stage
   B mossy stage   D climax-community stage

J 13. During the second stage of primary succession, —
   F lichens grow on rocks   H alders and willows grow
   G wildfires often occur   J mosses take over

C 14. Secondary succession might happen after —
   A primary succession   C a forest fire
   B a harsh winter   D glaciers melt

H 15. Air pollution is caused by —
   F cutting trees   H burning fossil fuels
   G building roads   J strip mining

D 16. Which of the following is an example of reusing?
   A riding a bicycle   C recovering aluminum from cans
   B using solar heat   D cloth diapers

F 17. Which of the following human activities helps protect ecosystems?
   F using less water
   G using chemical fertilizers
   H strip mining
   J building shopping malls

B 18. Why are landfills NOT a perfect solution for disposing of solid wastes?
   A They use energy.   C They cause acid rain.
   B They use scarce land. D They pollute the air.

F 19. Why are wetlands important ecosystems?
   F They purify water.
   G They attract endangered animals.
   H They have been polluted.
   J They speed up succession.

Unit B • Chapter 4   (page 2 of 5)   Assessment Guide AG 55

Name _____

Use the letters of the terms in the Word Bank to label the stages of primary succession.

   A climax community   B pioneer-plant stage   C mossy stage   D grassy stage

29. B   30. C   31. D   32. A

Part III Critical Thinking 6 points each

33. If people did not change climax communities, would they stay the same forever? Why?
   No. One climax community will gradually give way to another. Fires and other natural events cause communities to change.

34. What are some ways people benefit from healthy ecosystems? Possible answers:
   They breathe the air, drink the water, and eat the food that grows in the soil; they have wilderness areas to admire and explore.

35. Suppose the people in Town A conserve resources and avoid burning fossil fuels. The people in Town B to the northwest burn lots of fossil fuels and dump wastes into the river. How might the people in Town A be affected by the actions of the people in Town B?
   Possible answer: They may have to breathe polluted air that moves in and drink polluted water that flows from Town B.

36. Compare the process of reclamation with that of secondary succession.
   Possible answer: Both are ways that damaged ecosystems return to their natural climax communities. Secondary succession occurs naturally. Reclamation is a process in which humans work to help ecosystems recover from changes caused by humans.

Unit B • Chapter 4   (page 4 of 5)   Assessment Guide AG 57

Name _____

C 20. Two examples of climax-community plants are —
   A lichens and mosses   C hemlock and spruce
   B grasses and wildflowers   D willows and aspens

J 21. Which of the following is NOT an example of reclamation?
   F constructing an artificial wetland
   G growing prairie grasses for lawns
   H cleaning up a polluted river
   J conserving electricity

A 22. What is the first step in the process of reclamation?
   A researching the problem   C building a small pond
   B attracting wildlife to the area D planting native plants

G 23. How can planting native plants help restore an ecosystem?
   F The plants provide food for people.
   G The plants attract wildlife to the area.
   H The plants add water to the habitat.
   J The plants attract builders to the area.

D 24. Which of the following does NOT describe wetlands?
   A They act as water filters.   C They are hard to restore.
   B They are homes for animals.   D They only contain fresh water.

F 25. How are forest fires helpful in an ecosystem?
   F They speed up secondary succession.
   G They draw nutrients from the soil.
   H They destroy unwanted plants and animals.
   J They add oxygen to the atmosphere.

D 26. The three Rs of conserving resources are —
   A reduce, reuse, and remind   C refuse, reduce, and release
   B reward, reuse, and recycle   D reduce, reuse, and recycle

G 27. The causes of acid rain include —
   F runoff from roads   H waste water from factories
   G exhaust from cars   J organic fertilizers

C 28. The fireweed is an example of —
   A an endangered plant   C a pioneer plant
   B a deciduous-forest plant   D a climax-community plant

AG 56 Assessment Guide   (page 3 of 5)   Unit B • Chapter 4

Name _____

Part IV Process Skills Application 4 points each

37. Design an experiment that will determine what kind of window covering will keep sunny classrooms the warmest in cool weather. What tools would you need to use? **Identify the variables** you might need to **control.** Possible answer: Place light-colored blinds or curtains in one room, dark-colored blinds or curtains in another room, and no blinds or curtains in a third room. Use thermometers to measure the temperature regularly, and make comparisons. The variables are the colors of the window coverings. The window with no covering is the control.

38. The following table shows how much water people use in various everyday activities. **Interpret** the data, and **infer** how people could conserve water.

Activity	Liters of Water Used
Drinking water	2 (per day)
Showering	19 (per minute)
Flushing toilet	23 (per flush)
Watering lawn	38 (per minute)
Bathing	135 (per day)
Leaking faucet	180–910 (per day)

Possible answer: People could conserve water by taking showers instead of baths, by modifying toilets so that less water is flushed, by designing landscapes to use native plants that require less water, and by fixing leaky faucets.

39. Describe how you could **make a model** of secondary succession.
   Possible answer: Build a model volcano out of clay, and cover it with mud. Plant seeds for flowers or grasses in the mud. Water the mud to allow the seeds to grow. Over time these plants could be replaced by larger plants and trees.

AG 58 Assessment Guide   (page 5 of 5)   Unit B • Chapter 4

Unit B

Systems and Interactions in Nature

Write the letter of the best choice. 3 points each

__C__ 1. How does nitrogen move through an ecosystem?
  A plants → soil → animals
  B lightning → soil → animals
  C soil → plants → animals
  D animals → plants → soil

__G__ 2. What process releases oxygen to the air?
  F respiration H evaporation
  G photosynthesis J condensation

__A__ 3. Which is the correct path of water in the water cycle?
  A evaporation → condensation → precipitation
  B precipitation → condensation → evaporation
  C condensation → evaporation → precipitation
  D precipitation → condensation → transpiration

__J__ 4. Plants return water to the environment through —
  F photosynthesis
  G condensation
  H evaporation
  J transpiration

__B__ 5. Why is only 1 percent of Earth's fresh water usable?
  A Groundwater cannot be used.
  B Most is frozen in glaciers.
  C Fresh water evaporates instantly.
  D Most is found in plants.

__J__ 6. An ecosystem is made up of —
  F the living things in a community
  G air, water, and land
  H species of plants and animals
  J a community and its physical environment

__D__ 7. Two different consumers exist in the same environment and eat the same food. One hunts at night and the other hunts during the day. These animals have different —
  A habitats C ecosystems
  B communities D niches

__H__ 8. What does NOT determine the types of plants in an ecosystem?
  F temperature range
  G soil conditions
  H number of animals
  J amount of precipitation

__D__ 9. Which shows a possible food chain?
  A sun → consumer → producer → decomposer
  B herbivore → plant → decomposer → carnivore
  C sun → mushroom → grass → snake → grasshopper
  D plant → herbivore → snake → third-level consumer

__H__ 10. How does available energy change as it is passed from one level to the next in a food chain?
  F Each level receives more energy than the level before.
  G The same amount of energy is passed from one level to the next.
  H About 10 percent of the energy is passed from one level to the next.
  J No energy is passed from one level to the next.

__A__ 11. Which two organisms would you expect to compete with each other?
  A hyenas and cheetahs
  B deer and fish
  C fish and trees
  D flowers and rabbits

__G__ 12. Which two organisms have a symbiotic relationship?
  F cheetahs and zebras
  G bees and flowers
  H raccoons and sea turtles
  J warblers and insects

__C__ 13. A behavior that an organism is born with is —
  A a learned behavior
  B a competition
  C an instinct
  D a symbiotic behavior

__J__ 14. Which is NOT a result of human development in an ecosystem?
  F endangered species
  G competition for food
  H destruction of animal habitat
  J an increase in a population

__B__ 15. What happens when a natural event kills the producers in a food chain?
  A The consumer population increases.
  B The consumer population decreases.
  C The producer population increases.
  D There is no effect.

__G__ 16. If a species becomes endangered, it —
  F will definitely disappear
  G may become extinct
  H is increasing in population
  J has lost its instincts

__C__ 17. A biome includes _____, but a climate zone does not.
  A temperature C animals
  B rainfall D amount of sunlight

__F__ 18. Why are there few plants on the floor of the rain forest?
  F not enough sunlight
  G too many herbivores
  H lack of water
  J too little space

__D__ 19. Which plant is NOT matched with its biome?
  A oak tree – deciduous forest
  B mesquite – desert
  C grass – grasslands
  D palm tree – tundra

__F__ 20. Which is NOT a saltwater ecosystem?
  F lake zone H intertidal zone
  G near-shore zone J open-ocean zone

__D__ 21. Areas where fresh and salt water mix at the mouth of a river are called —
  A springs C vents
  B ports D estuaries

__G__ 22. Which is an example of primary succession?
  F land uncovered by a melting glacier
  G sprouting and growth of pioneer plants
  H land covered by a volcanic eruption
  J an earthquake damaging land

__B__ 23. Secondary succession occurs after —
  A an increase in native species
  B an ecosystem has been heavily damaged
  C a short growing season
  D a long, cold winter

__J__ 24. Which are two types of waste produced by human activity?
  F energy and acid rain
  G energy and air pollution
  H oxygen and air pollution
  J acid rain and air pollution

__A__ 25. A change from which an ecosystem cannot recover is called a —
  A catastrophic change
  B primary change
  C secondary succession
  D new beginning

__H__ 26. The process of restoring damaged ecosystems is called —
  F recycling H reclamation
  G rural development J rebirth

__B__ 27. Which is an example of conserving our resources?
  A throwing away newspapers
  B reusing old clothes
  C running a half-full dishwasher
  D using disposable paper plates

Answer in complete sentences.

6 28. Describe the carbon–oxygen cycle.
Possible answer: Plants take in carbon dioxide from the air or water. Plants use energy from sunlight to turn the carbon into food and release oxygen into the air. The plants store the carbon. As animals eat the plants, they obtain the carbon. The animals release carbon dioxide into the environment through a process called respiration.

6 29. Do you think Jerome, Alabama, should fill in its remaining wetlands with more housing developments? Explain your answer.
Possible answer: No. Most of the wetlands in the United States are already gone, and we need to save what is left. They are important ecosystems because lots of marine organisms make the wetlands their home. Wetlands also provide a natural purification process for water.

7 30. When you are using resources wisely, what are the three Rs to remember, and how can you put them to use?
Possible answer: The three Rs are recycle, reuse, and reduce. I can recycle my used cans and newspapers. To reuse, I can give my old clothes and toys to a needy family. To reduce electricity and water use, I can run the washing machine or dishwasher only when I have a full load of clothes or dishes.

Answer Key

Unit C • Chapter 1

Name _____
Date _____

Changes to Earth's Surface

Part I Vocabulary 1 point each

Match the terms in Column B with the meanings in Column A.

Column A

- __D__ 1. Remains or traces of past life found in the crust
- __A__ 2. Theory of how continents move over Earth's surface
- __O__ 3. Shaking of ground from energy release in the crust
- __F__ 4. Hot, soft rock from the lower mantle
- __N__ 5. Physical feature on Earth's surface
- __C__ 6. Place where pieces of the crust move
- __M__ 7. "Supercontinent" on Earth millions of years ago
- __J__ 8. Opening in the crust through which lava flows
- __I__ 9. Rigid block of crust and upper-mantle rock
- __G__ 10. Downhill shifting of rock and soil because of gravity
- __P__ 11. Process in which soil, sand, and sediment are formed
- __E__ 12. Process of moving sediment from one place to another
- __H__ 13. Process of dropping sediment in a new location
- __L__ 14. Outer, very thin layer of Earth
- __K__ 15. Center and hottest layer of Earth
- __B__ 16. Middle layer of Earth

Column B

- A continental drift
- B mantle
- C fault
- D fossils
- E erosion
- F magma
- G mass movement
- H deposition
- I plate
- J volcano
- K core
- L crust
- M Pangea
- N landform
- O earthquake
- P weathering

Name _____

Write the letter of the best choice.

- __B__ 23. Why would footprints made on the moon last for hundreds of years?
  - A There is no weathering on the moon.
  - B There is no wind or water to erode the footprints.
  - C The footprints on the moon are very deep because of the Apollo astronauts' shoes.
  - D The Apollo astronauts on the moon made shoe deposits with space-age materials.
- __J__ 24. If the center of Earth is its hottest part, why is it solid?
  - F because the core is made of metal
  - G because that is where rocks come from, and rocks are solid
  - H because the hotter things are, the more solid they are
  - J because of the great pressure at the center of Earth
- __A__ 25. What does it mean to say that Earth's plates "float"?
  - A The plates float on the soft rock of the lower mantle, which has currents like water.
  - B The plates float on the oceans, which is why there is water underground.
  - C The plates never become liquid rock or sink, so they float.
  - D The plates only sometimes become liquid rock, so they float.
- __H__ 26. What does it mean to say that "the Atlantic Ocean is getting wider, pushing Europe and North America apart"?
  - F The ocean is eroding more of the beaches on the coasts of North America and Europe.
  - G The ocean deposits heavy sediment on both coasts, pushing them apart.
  - H The North American and European plates are moving away from each other.
  - J The North American and European plates are moving closer to each other.

Name _____

Part II Science Concepts and Understanding 3 points each

For Questions 17–19, describe how water is weathering rock in each of the pictures.

17. Acid rain is dissolving rock.
18. Water tumbles rocks onto one another, breaking them into pieces.
19. Water freezes and expands, breaking rock into pieces.

Use the following pictures to answer Questions 20–22.

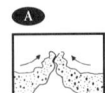 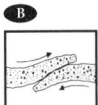 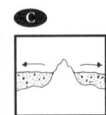 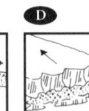 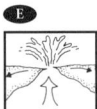

20. Which picture or pictures show how mountains are formed?
    A, B, C, and E
21. In what other way can a mountain form that is **NOT** pictured above? Name a famous mountain range of this type.
    The pressure at the boundaries of a plate pushes a block of rock upward.
    Possible answer: the Grand Tetons
22. Which picture shows how most of the highest mountains are formed? Name a famous mountain range of this type.
    A. Possible answer: the Himalayas

Name _____

Part III Critical Thinking 8 points each

27. How do fossils help scientists learn about plants and animals of the past?
    Possible answer: Fossils are records of organisms that died long ago, and the Earth may no longer have any types of these organisms left alive.

28. Would you expect many earthquakes to occur along the Ring of Fire? Why or why not?
    Possible answer: There would be many earthquakes expected at the Ring of Fire, because it is located along the boundaries of a plate.

29. What would the surface of Earth eventually look like if Earth's plates stopped moving? Why?
    Possible answer: There would be no more new mountains, and eventually everything would be rounded or flat because of weathering and erosion except for canyons, which would remain.

30. How is it possible that rock from some of the highest mountains has fossils?
    Students should realize that the rock, which once must have been under the sea, was pushed up by plate pressures into a mountain.

31. In 1963 a new island formed off the coast of Iceland. This island, named Surtsey, is part of the Mid-Atlantic Ridge. What forces do you think are building Surtsey? Why?
    Possible answer: Volcanic pressures are creating Surtsey, because the Mid-Atlantic Ridge is formed by two plates moving apart and magma coming through the gap between them.

Answer Key

Unit C • Chapter 2

Name _____

Part IV Process Skills Application

Look at the picture below. For Question 32, name a place where you *observe* that water weathering has occurred. For Question 33, name a place where you *observe* that wind weathering has occurred.

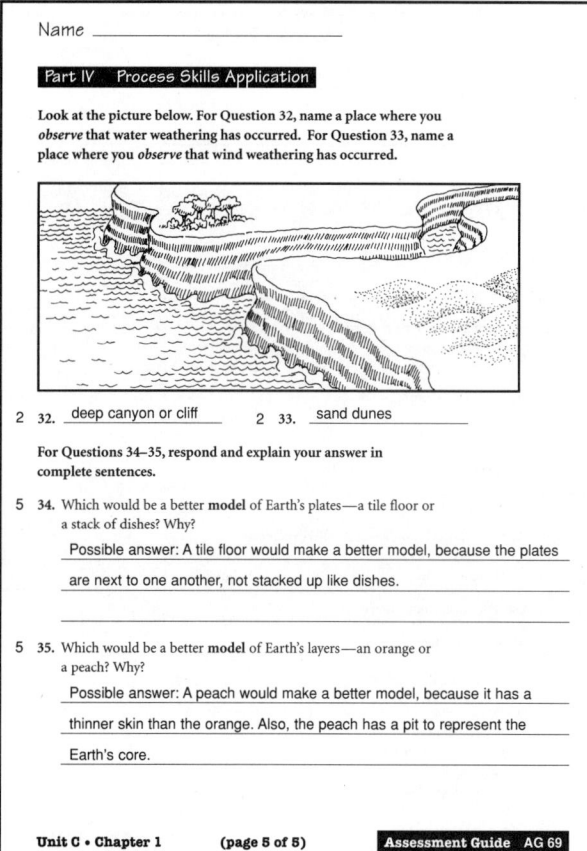

2 32. ___deep canyon or cliff___   2 33. ___sand dunes___

For Questions 34–35, respond and explain your answer in complete sentences.

5 34. Which would be a better **model** of Earth's plates—a tile floor or a stack of dishes? Why?
  ___Possible answer: A tile floor would make a better model, because the plates are next to one another, not stacked up like dishes.___

5 35. Which would be a better **model** of Earth's layers—an orange or a peach? Why?
  ___Possible answer: A peach would make a better model, because it has a thinner skin than the orange. Also, the peach has a pit to represent the Earth's core.___

Unit C • Chapter 1   (page 5 of 5)   Assessment Guide AG 69

Name _____

Part II Science Concepts and Understanding   3 points each

For Questions 10–13, use the following chart. Choose the best answer.

MOHS' HARDNESS SCALE 1 is softest. 10 is hardest.									
1	2	3	4	5	6	7	8	9	10
Talc	Gypsum	Calcite	Fluorite	Apatite	Orthoclase	Quartz	Topaz	Corundum	Diamond

__C__ 10. Which of the following minerals is the hardest?
  A gypsum   C topaz
  B talc   D calcite

__J__ 11. Which of the following minerals can fluorite scratch?
  F quartz   H orthoclase
  G apatite   J calcite

__B__ 12. Which of the following minerals can scratch corundum?
  A gypsum   C quartz
  B diamond   D topaz

__J__ 13. Scientists sometimes use a copper penny with a hardness of 3 or a glass with a hardness of 6 to test a mineral's hardness. Which of the following minerals could be scratched by a glass but **NOT** by a penny?
  F quartz   H orthoclase
  G gypsum   J apatite

For Questions 14–16, choose the best answer.

__C__ 14. You find a rock with pieces of seashells in it. Which kind of rock is it?
  A metamorphic   C sedimentary
  B volcanic   D igneous

Unit C • Chapter 2   (page 2 of 4)   Assessment Guide AG 73

Name _____
Date _____

✓ **Chapter Assessment**

Rocks and Minerals

Part I Vocabulary   2 points each

Use the letters of the terms in the Word Bank to complete the sentences.

A mineral	D streak	G rock cycle
B rock	E igneous rock	H metamorphic rock
C sedimentary rock	F hardness	I luster

__E__ 1. Rock that forms when melted rock hardens is called ___.

__I__ 2. A mineral's ___ describes how its surface looks when light reflects from it.

__G__ 3. Earth's ___ is the pattern of slow changes in rocks from one kind to another.

__C__ 4. ___ forms when rock pieces deposited over time are squeezed and stuck together.

__D__ 5. When you rub a mineral against a white tile, its ___ is the color of the powder left behind.

__B__ 6. Material made up of one or more minerals is called ___.

__H__ 7. A rock that has been changed by high heat and great pressure is ___.

__A__ 8. A natural solid that has its particles arranged in a crystal pattern is called a ___.

__F__ 9. A mineral's ___ is its ability to resist being scratched.

AG 72 Assessment Guide   (page 1 of 4)   Unit C • Chapter 2

Name _____

__G__ 15. Which of the following is **NOT** a characteristic scientists use to classify minerals?
  F hardness   H luster
  G volume   J streak

__C__ 16. Halite is another term for —
  A water   C table salt
  B pepper   D copper

Part III Critical Thinking

9 17. Why is a piece of pumice lighter than a piece of obsidian of equal size?
  ___Answers may include that pumice has tiny holes in it that are caused by gases escaping from lava as it cools. This makes it lighter than a same-sized piece of obsidian.___

10 18. How is a rock different from a mineral?
  ___Answers may include that a mineral is a solid material with a repeating crystal pattern. Rocks can be made up of one or more minerals.___

10 19. Why aren't you likely to find a fossil in metamorphic rock or igneous rock?
  ___Answers may include that the pressure and heat required to form metamorphic or igneous rock would destroy any fossils that might be contained in the rock.___

Part IV Process Skills Application   8 points each

20. Which would be a better **model** of how an igneous rock changes into a sedimentary rock—an eraser rubbed on paper, or crushed graham crackers that are mixed with melted butter and pressed into a pie pan to make a crust? Explain your answer.
  ___Graham crackers; explanations will vary but should include that sedimentary rocks are formed when other rocks are broken up and then pressed, as happens when graham crackers are broken up to make a graham cracker crust.___

AG 74 Assessment Guide   (page 3 of 4)   Unit C • Chapter 2

Answer Key   AG 177 Assessment Guide

Unit C • Chapter 3

Name _____

21. Which would be a better **model** of how metamorphic rocks form — chocolate chip cookie dough that is flattened and then baked into cookies, or chocolate chips and milk melted together in a pan and then cooled to make fudge? Explain your answer.

The cookie dough is a better model. Possible explanation: Metamorphic rocks form under pressure and heat. The cookie dough was squeezed and then baked. The fudge is more like an igneous rock. The chocolate melted completely and mixed with another material. The result was a completely new material.

Use the following *classification* chart for Questions 22–23.

Mineral	Color	Color of Streak	Hardness
Talc	light green	white	1
Fluorite	light purple	white	4
Feldspar	white, salmon pink	white	5
Quartz	clear, milky white, rose, violet, smoky gray	none	7

__A__ **22.** A mineral sample has a white streak and is so soft that it can be scratched by your fingernail. Which mineral is it?
 A talc C fluorite
 B quartz D feldspar

__H__ **23.** A mineral sample is purple, has a white streak, and cannot be scratched by a penny. Which mineral is it?
 F talc H fluorite
 G quartz J feldspar

Unit C • Chapter 2   (page 4 of 4)   Assessment Guide AG 75

Name _____

Part II Science Concepts and Understanding   2 points each

Use the following diagram to answer Questions 16–19.

__B__ **16.** What is happening at Point I?
 A condensation C evaporation
 B precipitation D humidity

__J__ **17.** What is happening at Point II?
 F humidity H precipitation
 G evaporation J condensation

__A__ **18.** What is happening at Point III?
 A evaporation C condensation
 B humidity D precipitation

__G__ **19.** What process is shown in the diagram above?
 F condensation H cloud formation
 G water cycle J humidity

Write the letter of the best choice.

__A__ **20.** Which is a type of cloud?
 A stratus C novas
 B precipitation D condensed

__G__ **21.** What is NOT observed or measured by weather forecasters?
 F temperature
 G atmosphere height
 H humidity
 J wind speed and direction

Unit C • Chapter 3   (page 2 of 5)   Assessment Guide AG 79

Name _____
Date _____

Weather and Climate

Part I Vocabulary 2 points each

Write the letter of the correct term in each blank below.

A climate	D greenhouse effect	F microclimate
B El Niño	E local winds	G prevailing winds
C global warming		

The 1. __A__ is the average of weather conditions in an area through all seasons over a period of time. It remains fairly stable because of 2. __G__ that blow constantly from the same direction. A short-term climate change is the 3. __B__ effect.
The climate changes all the time. Even a 4. __F__, the climate of a very small area, may change. 5. __E__ can change because a new building or parking lot is built in an area. But a large change in climate usually takes a long time.
6. __C__, an abnormal rise in Earth's average temperature, can happen because too much carbon dioxide absorbs some of the heat given off by the Earth, causing a 7. __D__.

H air pressure	J condensation	L humidity	N air masses
I atmosphere	K evaporation	M precipitation	O fronts

Almost all weather occurs in the lowest layer of air, or the 8. __I__. The sun heats the oceans, causing 9. __K__ of water. The invisible water vapor cools and turns back into liquid water in a process called 10. __J__. When the 11. __L__ is high enough, the droplets fall as 12. __M__. Usually, rain or snow can be predicted if the surrounding 13. __H__ drops. Most weather changes occur at 14. __O__, the boundaries between large bodies of air called 15. __N__.

AG 78 Assessment Guide   (page 1 of 5)   Unit C • Chapter 3

Name _____

Use the following picture to answer Questions 22–25.

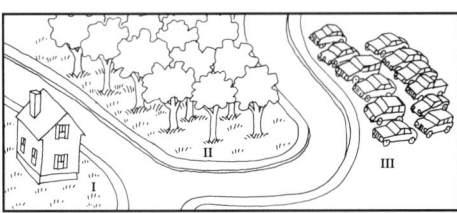

__B__ **22.** How would the temperature and humidity probably change if you were to walk from Area I to Area II?
 A It would get warmer, with more humidity.
 B It would get cooler, with more humidity.
 C It would get warmer, with less humidity.
 D It would get cooler, with less humidity.

__H__ **23.** How would the temperature and humidity probably change if you were to walk from Area II to Area III?
 F It would get warmer, with more humidity.
 G It would get cooler, with more humidity.
 H It would get warmer, with less humidity.
 J It would get cooler, with less humidity.

__B__ **24.** In which area would you expect the humidity to be the highest?
 A Area III
 B Area II
 C Area I
 D They will all have the same level of humidity.

__F__ **25.** What are Areas I, II, and III called?
 F microclimates
 G temperate zones
 H stratospheres
 J climate zones

AG 80 Assessment Guide   (page 3 of 5)   Unit C • Chapter 3

Unit C • Chapter 4

Page 1 (Unit C • Chapter 3, page 4 of 5)

Name _____

Look at each picture below. Write *toward the land* or *toward the sea* to describe which way the wind is likely to be blowing.

26. toward the land
27. toward the sea

Part III   Critical Thinking

9 28. Most weather forecasts are for large areas. Why is it sometimes more difficult to predict local weather conditions?
   Possible answer: Local weather is determined by many factors, including bodies of water, buildings, and pavements. Also, it is difficult to measure all the weather factors in the various small locales.

9 29. How do fronts affect weather changes?
   Possible answer: At a front, rising warm air cools and forms clouds. Precipitation usually follows.

10 30. How can human activities affect local and global climates?
   Possible answer: Human activities such as building cities and burning fossil fuels can cause temperature to increase, causing a heat island. Increasing carbon dioxide also causes temperature to increase. Because of prevailing winds heated air and pollutants easily move over the globe, affecting the entire planet.

Unit C • Chapter 3   (page 4 of 5)   Assessment Guide AG 81

Exploring the Oceans

Name _____
Date _____

Chapter Assessment

Part I   Vocabulary   1 point each

Match each term in Column B with its meaning in Column A.

Column A		Column B
F	1. Wall of rocks built out into the ocean	A tide
G	2. Up-and-down movement of surface water	B salinity
A	3. Repeated rise and fall in the level of the ocean	C current
C	4. Stream of water that flows like a river through the ocean	D shore
L	5. Self-contained underwater breathing apparatus	E desalination
D	6. Area where ocean and land meet	F jetty
J	7. Small underwater vehicle	G wave
H	8. Rocky point along a shore	H headland
K	9. Pool of sea water found along a rocky shoreline	I sonar
E	10. Removal of salt from sea water	J submersible
I	11. Sound waves that can be used to map the ocean floor	K tide pool
M	12. Weight of water pressing on an object	L scuba
B	13. Percent of salt in ocean water	M water pressure

Unit C • Chapter 4   (page 1 of 5)   Assessment Guide AG 85

Page 3 (Unit C • Chapter 3, page 5 of 5)

Name _____

Part IV   Process Skills Application   3 points each

Use the following table to answer Questions 31–36.

City's Five-Day Temperature and Rainfall Readings

Using your *observations*, describe the weather.

31. From Monday to Tuesday:
    Temperature rose; no rain.

32. From Tuesday to Wednesday:
    Temperature fell; some rain on Wednesday.

33. From Wednesday to Thursday:
    Temperature remained the same; more rain on Thursday than on Wednesday.

34. From Thursday to Friday:
    Rain ended Thursday; temperature rose on Friday.

35. Based on the information above, can you **predict** what is going to happen on Saturday? Why or why not?
    No, because the temperature and rain gauge only measure current conditions.

36. If it is raining in the city on a summer day, what can you **infer** about the temperature?
    The temperature will be lower than if there were no rain.

AG 82 Assessment Guide   (page 5 of 5)   Unit C • Chapter 3

Page 4 (Unit C • Chapter 4, page 2 of 5)

Name _____

Part II   Science Concepts and Understanding   3 points each

Write the letter of the best choice.

C 14. Waves form because—
   A Earth spins on its axis
   B currents flow through the ocean
   C wind blows over the surface of the water
   D Earth's gravity pulls the water up and down

F 15. Earth's rotation causes ocean currents—
   F to bend to the right in the Northern Hemisphere
   G to bend to the right in the Southern Hemisphere
   H to form larger tides
   J to spread out over the equator

D 16. Differences in ___ cause deep-ocean currents.
   A air temperature
   B wind speed
   C current direction
   D water temperature

F 17. Tides are caused by—
   F Earth's rotation and the gravitational pull of the moon and sun
   G the effect of wind on both hemispheres
   H uneven heating of Earth's surface
   J deep-ocean currents

D 18. Scientists discovered the presence of vents along the mid-Atlantic ridge by using the submersible—
   A *Scuba*
   B *Titanic*
   C *Trieste*
   D *Alvin*

H 19. A rip current—
   F moves along the surface of the ocean
   G carries huge amounts of beach materials
   H flows away from the beach
   J varies with high and low tides

AG 86 Assessment Guide   (page 2 of 5)   Unit C • Chapter 4

Answer Key   AG 179 Assessment Guide

Unit C

Name _____

A 20. A headland may be all that remains when —
  A soft rock erodes
  B arches erode
  C soft rock and hard rock become layered
  D hard rock is layered

H 21. Sonar is used to —
  F scrape samples from the ocean floor
  G collect objects at sea level
  H measure the depth of the ocean
  J help people breathe under water

D 22. When a submarine explores the ocean bottom, what type of currents affect it?
  A surface currents
  B tidal currents
  C ebb currents
  D deep-ocean currents

F 23. Why does a tsunami pass unnoticed under ships but destroy everything when it reaches the shore?
  F Increased friction with the ocean bottom decreases the speed of the wave, causing it to grow.
  G The tsunami speeds up and gets larger when it reaches the shore.
  H The tsunami splits into many waves that join into one large wave when they reach the shore.
  J Tsunami waves continue to combine and grow until they reach the shore.

B 24. The salinity of ocean water comes from —
  A the gravitational pull of the moon
  B minerals weathered from Earth's crust
  C seaweed and other ocean plants
  D water pressure on the ocean's floor

F 25. How does water in a wave move?
  F in a circle
  G back and forth
  H down to the bottom of the sea
  J up from the bottom of the sea

Unit C • Chapter 4   (page 3 of 5)   Assessment Guide AG 87

Name _____

Part IV   Process Skills Application

Observe the following pictures to answer Question 34.

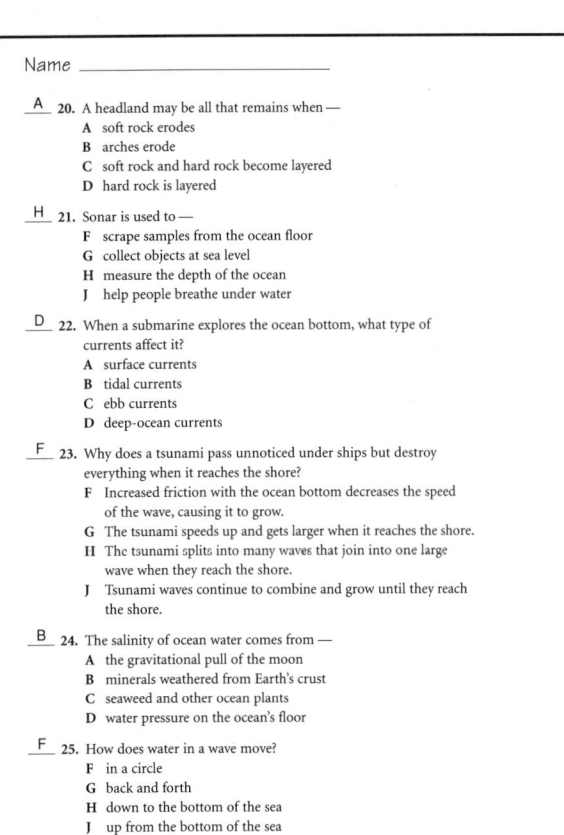

3 34. **Compare** Picture A with Picture B.
  Possible answer: Picture A shows a natural beach. Picture B shows a beach with a jetty. While the jetty helps build up sand on one side, it takes away sand from the other.

3 35. Which is a better **model** of sonar—an echo or a reflection in a mirror? Why?
  Possible answer: An echo is a better model; it uses sound instead of light, and the surface it hits does not have to be smooth to reflect sound as a mirror does to reflect light.

5 36. Rainwater flows along the sides of the street, carrying leaves and twigs and depositing them where the flow turns a corner. Is this a good **model** for longshore currents that carry beach materials? Why or why not?
  Possible answer: Yes; longshore currents drop their sediments to form beaches where the water changes direction, just as the flow of rainwater deposits leaves and twigs where it turns a corner.

Unit C • Chapter 4   (page 5 of 5)   Assessment Guide AG 89

Name _____

B 26. The deeper you go in an ocean, the ____ the water pressure becomes.
  A less   C deeper
  B greater   D shallower

H 27. The removal of salt from ocean water is called —
  F saline removal   H desalination
  G estuarial   J sodium chloride

B 28. Resources such as ____ can be found in the ocean.
  A petroleum   C coal
  B salt   D natural gas

J 29. Because of erosion, a rocky beach may become —
  F an estuary   H a valley
  G a mountain   J a sandy beach

Part III   Critical Thinking   7 points each

Answer Questions 29–32 on a separate sheet of paper.

30. Even though Cape Hatteras has had three jetties built to protect a lighthouse, the lighthouse is threatened by increased erosion. How might the erosion problem be fixed?
  Possible answer: The jetties have not helped prevent erosion, so the lighthouse may have to be moved.

31. Suppose a boater sails a large boat almost onto shore during high tide. Explain what will happen if the boater tries to leave during low tide.
  Possible answer: The boat will be stuck on the shore because during low tide the water will be farther from the shore.

32. Are tides higher when the moon is full? Why or why not?   Possible answer: Whether or not the moon is full does not have an effect on the tide. The tides are higher when the moon is in a straight line with the sun and Earth. The moon may or may not be full at those times.

33. If a bottle is dropped into the ocean near England, where might the bottle wash ashore? Why?
  Possible answer: The bottle might wash ashore along the European coast or cross the Atlantic Ocean to North America.

AG 88 Assessment Guide   (page 4 of 5)   Unit C • Chapter 4

Name _____
Date _____

Unit Assessment

Processes That Change the Earth

Write the letter of the best choice. 3 points each

B 1. Breaking rock into silt and other tiny pieces is known as —
  A erosion
  B weathering
  C deposition
  D mass movement

J 2. Which of the following is **NOT** an example of changing landforms?
  F wind creating sand dunes
  G floodplains at the end of rivers
  H terminal moraines from glaciers
  J the sun warming desert sands

A 3. Which would most likely cause the highest mountain to form?
  A two continental plates colliding
  B a continental and an oceanic plate colliding
  C magma bubbling up between plates that are pulling apart
  D the sudden release of energy as plates scrape past each other

G 4. The difference between magma and lava is —
  F lava is always hotter than magma
  G lava is magma that reaches the surface of Earth
  H lava is inside a volcano and magma is outside
  J magma is found only under oceanic plates

A 5. When the plates in Earth's crust grind past each other, the result is —
  A earthquakes   C volcanoes
  B mudslides   D mountains

J 6. The position of a rock layer in the Grand Canyon, as compared to those above and below it, can tell us —
  F which direction is north
  G whether or not there is coal nearby
  H how the Grand Canyon was formed
  J the age of the layers in relation to the other layers

AG 92 Assessment Guide   (page 1 of 4)   Unit C

Unit D • Chapter 1

Name _____

__A__ 7. If similar fossils are found in North America and in Europe, which conclusion could be drawn?
 A The two land masses were once joined together.
 B At one time there were no oceans on Earth.
 C The fossils formed at the same time.
 D Ancient animals could swim long distances.

__G__ 8. Which of the following best describes a mineral?
 F a compound made from living matter
 G a solid material arranged in a repeating pattern
 H the remains of organisms found in sedimentary rock
 J hot, soft rock from Earth's mantle

__C__ 9. On Mohs' hardness scale, quartz has a hardness of 7 and glass has a hardness of 6. If they are rubbed together —
 A the quartz and glass would scratch each other
 B neither rock would get scratched
 C the quartz would scratch the glass
 D the glass would scratch the quartz

__G__ 10. Scientists use a streak plate to —
 F measure the hardness of a mineral
 G observe the true color of a mineral
 H categorize the luster of a mineral
 J measure the clarity of a mineral

__A__ 11. Which item includes a use for copper?
 A a stereo   C a pencil
 B a bicycle   D a pair of scissors

__J__ 12. Rocks that are formed when magma hardens are known as —
 F frozen rocks   H sedimentary rocks
 G solid rocks   J igneous rocks

__D__ 13. Shale is a —
 A fossilized rock
 B igneous rock
 C metamorphic rock
 D sedimentary rock

__G__ 14. Marble is often used in —
 F chalkboards   H roofs
 G statues   J paper

__B__ 15. What is needed to change a sedimentary rock into a metamorphic rock?
 A erosion
 B heat and pressure
 C compaction and cementing
 D melting

Unit C   (page 2 of 4)   Assessment Guide AG 93

Name _____

__G__ 28. What does desalination remove from ocean water?
 F sand   H water
 G salt   J oil

Answer in complete sentences.

5 33. Explain the theory of "continental drift," starting with Pangea.
Continental drift is the theory of how Earth's continents move on its surface. Originally there was only one continent, Pangea. This continent slowly split apart into two different continents, Gondwana and Laurasia. These two continents slowly broke apart into the continents that are on Earth today.

5 34. You find a rock in your back yard. Explain how you could determine the hardness of this unknown rock, using rocks that you have already identified.
Possible answer: You would compare a rock of known hardness (for example, quartz) to your unknown rock by rubbing them together. If the quartz scratches the unknown rock, then the quartz is harder. If the opposite occurs, then the unknown rock is harder. You would repeat the process with other identified rocks until you narrow down the unknown rock's hardness.

6 35. The shoreline of Olympic National Park in Washington has many headlands, sea caves, and sea arches. Explain how these occur and change with time.
Possible answer: Headlands are created by uneven erosion of the land by the waves. Softer rock erodes faster and leaves points of harder rock called headlands. When waves continue to erode away headlands, sea caves can form. Sea arches are formed when two caves are eroded so much that they join and form a large opening in a headland.

Unit C   (page 4 of 4)   Assessment Guide AG 95

Name _____

__J__ 16. Which one does **NOT** help to change rocks in the rock cycle?
 F wind   H volcanoes
 G rivers   J sunlight

__C__ 17. Most of Earth's weather occurs in the —
 A substratosphere
 B hemisphere
 C troposphere
 D stratosphere

__F__ 18. How does warm air compare to cold air?
 F Warm air has low air pressure.
 G Warm air has less humidity.
 H Warm air weighs more.
 J Warm air is drier.

__B__ 19. If a meteorologist predicts that the barometric pressure is going to drop, what will most likely happen?
 A It will be sunny and clear.
 B The weather will be rainy.
 C An earthquake will occur.
 D There will be a drought.

__H__ 20. Clouds form when —
 F water evaporates
 G air pressure increases
 H water vapor condenses
 J humidity decreases

__B__ 21. Which type of wind will affect South America as well as Africa?
 A local wind
 B prevailing wind
 C stratospheric wind
 D breeze wind

__F__ 22. Because of the prevailing westerly winds in the United States, most air masses tend to move from —
 F west to east
 G north to south
 H east to west
 J south to north

__C__ 23. What changes when you walk from a city street to a park with a pond?
 A El Niño   C microclimate
 B global winds   D climate zone

__J__ 24. If humans continue to burn fossil fuels at the current rate, how will Earth's temperature be affected?
 F no change at all
 G a significant decrease
 H a slight decrease
 J a significant increase

__D__ 25. Which of the following is a type of current?
 A shore   C hemispheric
 B jetty   D longshore

__H__ 26. A boat about 15 miles offshore is above the —
 F continental shelf
 G abyssal plain
 H continental slope
 J continental plain

__B__ 27. Most waves are caused by —
 A ocean water moving forward
 B wind blowing over the water
 C extremely high air pressure
 D differences in water temperature

AG 94 Assessment Guide   (page 3 of 4)   Unit C

Name _____
Date _____

Chapter Assessment

Earth, Moon, and Beyond

Part I   Vocabulary   1 point each

Use the letters of the terms in the Word Bank to complete the sentences.

A axis	D revolves	G space probes	J asteroids	M solstice
B eclipse	E rotates	H telescope	K planets	
C orbit	F satellite	I comets	L equinox	

Early robotic 1. __G__ that were sent into deep space could not report how it felt to be in space. They could only provide data and pictures. At first, even a simple 2. __H__ could provide a better view of space objects than they could.

The moon 3. __D__ in a closed path around Earth and is Earth's only natural 4. __F__. Its path around Earth is its 5. __C__. Earth 6. __E__, or turns, on an imaginary line called an 7. __A__. It is daytime for locations that face toward the sun, and it is nighttime for locations that face away from the sun. At times, an 8. __B__ occurs when Earth or the moon passes into the other's shadow.

Earth is one of nine 9. __K__ that orbit the sun. Other objects in the solar system include thousands of rocks called 10. __J__ and balls of ice and rock called 11. __I__. Each point in Earth's orbit at which the daylight hours are at their greatest or fewest is called a 12. __M__. Each point at which they are equal is the 13. __L__.

AG 96 Assessment Guide   (page 1 of 5)   Unit D • Chapter 1

Answer Key

AG 181 Assessment Guide

Part II Science Concepts and Understanding 3 points each

Write the letter of the best choice.

__D__ 14. Earth and the moon are alike in that both —
  A have liquid water
  B have satellites
  C have an atmosphere
  D are made of rock

__J__ 15. The three main types of landforms that make up the moon's surface are —
  F craters, equators, and gyrators
  G volcanoes, highlands, and eclipses
  H marias, santas, and domes
  J highlands, craters, and marias

__C__ 16. The moon landings were part of what program of space exploration?
  A Galileo   C Apollo
  B Mercury   D Newton

__G__ 17. The first artificial satellite launched into space was —
  F Viking   H Hubble
  G Sputnik   J Apollo

__A__ 18. Choose the order in which the following things were used to study space.
  A telescope, satellite, space probe, space shuttle
  B space probe, telescope, satellite, space shuttle
  C space probe, satellite, space shuttle, telescope
  D telescope, space probe, satellite, space shuttle

__J__ 19. The first Americans were sent into space in what program?
  F Apollo   H Voyager
  G Viking   J Mercury

Unit D • Chapter 1   (page 2 of 5)   Assessment Guide AG97

__B__ 20. The first scientist to use a telescope to observe the sky was —
  A Armstrong
  B Galileo
  C Copernicus
  D Glenn

__G__ 21. Timekeeping on Earth is based on Earth's —
  F hemispheres
  G time zones
  H satellites
  J distance from the sun

Use the following picture to answer Questions 22–23.

__D__ 22. What does the symbol ↻ represent in the diagram above?
  A a revolution
  B an eclipse
  C an orbit
  D a rotation

__H__ 23. What paths do the dotted lines represent in the diagram above?
  F revolutions
  G eclipses
  H orbits
  J rotations

AG98 Assessment Guide   (page 3 of 5)   Unit D • Chapter 1

__D__ 24. Which of the following shows the correct order for phases of the moon?

Use the following diagrams to answer Questions 25–26. What is happening in each picture?

25. __a lunar eclipse__   26. __a solar eclipse__

Part III Critical Thinking 8 points each

Answer the following on a separate sheet of paper.

27. Does a total solar eclipse block all of the sun from the Earth? Explain.
  Possible answer: Yes. In a solar eclipse, the moon is directly in front of the sun, completely covering it except for a small area around the edges.
28. Compare the advantages and disadvantages of crewed space exploration and space probes. Possible answer: Space probes, which are robots, can go where humans cannot go and do not need food or water. But humans can think and make decisions.
29. Describe the relationships of the Earth-moon-sun motions.
  Possible answer: The Earth and the moon are part of the sun's planetary system. Together they revolve around the sun. Similarly, the moon revolves around the Earth.

Unit D • Chapter 1   (page 4 of 5)   Assessment Guide AG99

Part IV Process Skills Application 8 points each

30. What can you **infer** from studying the depths and diameters of craters on the moon?
  Possible answer: The moon has been struck by objects of different sizes, creating craters whose depths and diameters vary.

Use the following pictures to answer Questions 31–32.

31. If you tie a string to a rock and spin the string and rock in a circle, you are **modeling** the orbit of Earth (the rock) around the sun (your hand). **Infer** what would happen if the string were only half as long and still being turned with the same force. What would the shorter string **model**?
  Possible answer: The rock would orbit the hand much faster. The shorter string would model a shorter distance between the Earth and the sun.

32. Use **time and space relationships** to **compare** the two pictures with the moon's orbit around Earth and Earth's orbit around the sun.
  Possible answer: The moon orbits Earth much faster than Earth orbits the sun because the moon is much closer. Therefore, the picture on the right represents the moon's orbiting Earth, and the picture on the left represents Earth's orbiting the sun.

AG100 Assessment Guide   (page 5 of 5)   Unit D • Chapter 1

AG 182 Assessment Guide   **Answer Key**

Unit D • Chapter 2

The Sun and Other Stars

Part I Vocabulary   1 point each

Match each term in Column B with its meaning in Column A.

Column A	Column B
__I__ 1. Dark areas on the surface of the sun	A corona
__G__ 2. Burst of energy from the sun's atmosphere	B galaxy
__E__ 3. Type of most stars	C light-year
__C__ 4. Distance light travels in one year	D magnitude
__J__ 5. Everything that exists	E main-sequence
__H__ 6. Particles thrown into space by the sun	F photosphere
__B__ 7. Group of stars, gas, and dust	G solar flare
__D__ 8. Brightness of a star	H solar wind
__F__ 9. Surface of the sun	I sunspots
__A__ 10. Atmosphere of the sun	J universe

Part II Science Concepts and Understanding   2 points each

Write the letter of the best choice.

__B__ 11. Solar energy is produced by—
  A hot gas   B fusion   C electricity   D waves

__F__ 12. The sun is the original source of energy for fossil fuels because —
  F organisms that died long ago depended on the sun for energy
  G heat from the sun caused dead organisms to turn into fossils
  H the sun dried out fossils and turned them into fuel
  J the sun caused Earth to form, and pressure from Earth turned fossils into fossil fuel

__D__ 13. Energy from the sun travels in—
  A aurora borealis   C particles of helium
  B particles of hydrogen   D waves

Use the following picture to answer Questions 14–16.

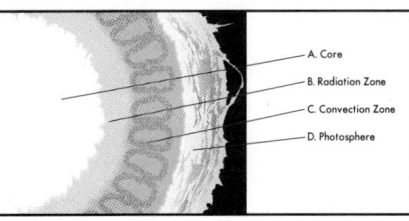

__D__ 14. In which layer do sunspots occur?

__A__ 15. Which layer is the hottest part of the sun?

__C__ 16. In which layer are cooler particles pulled down by gravity?

Write the letter of the best choice.

__H__ 17. The absolute magnitude of a star depends on—
  F its absolute brightness   H the amount of light it produces
  G its closeness to Earth   J whether you use a telescope

__B__ 18. What evidence is there that the sun rotates?
  A Solar wind causes magnetic storms.
  B Sunspots move across the sun, disappear, and reappear on the other side.
  C Granules, which are the tops of gas columns, rise through the convection layer.
  D Cycles of sunspots occur every 11 years.

__J__ 19. If you know the mass of a star, you know—
  F how bright it is   H the surface temperature
  G how much hydrogen it has   J nothing except its mass

__A__ 20. Which of these energy waves are NOT released by the sun?
  A microwaves   C X rays
  B infrared waves   D radio waves

Use the diagram below to answer 21–24 in the table.

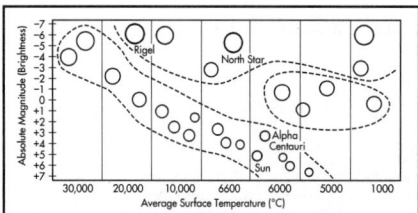

Star	Absolute Magnitude	Temperature (°C)
North Star	−5	23. 6600
Rigel	21. −6	20,000
Sun	+5	24. 6000
Alpha Centauri	22. +4	6000

Number the statements below from 1 to 4 to describe the sequence of change for a star like our sun.

__4__ 25. The star shrinks and becomes a white dwarf.

__3__ 26. The star uses up most of its fuel and grows to become a red giant.

__1__ 27. A swirling cloud of dust, a nebula, becomes a small, cool star.

__2__ 28. A protostar grows in mass and its temperature rises until it begins to glow.

If the statement is true, write *true*. If the statement is false, change the underlined term to make it true.

__Apparent__ 29. Absolute magnitude is how bright the star appears from Earth.

__Nothing__ 30. A galaxy is bigger than the universe.

__True__ 31. The Local Group is bigger than the Milky Way.

__brighter__ 32. Granules are darker than sunspots.

__spiral galaxy__ 33. The sun is located in an elliptical galaxy.

Write the letter of the best choice.

__G__ 34. Which of these is NOT a type of galaxy?
  F barred spiral   G circular   H elliptical   J irregular

__D__ 35. Astronomers hypothesize that a star forms in a cloud of dust and gas called a—
  A Local Group   B universe   C galaxy   D nebula

Part III Critical Thinking   5 points each

36. The sun makes one complete revolution around the center of the Milky Way Galaxy about every 250 million years. Telescopes often see objects more than 250 million light-years away. Why, then, can't we see the light from the sun through a telescope? We cannot see the light from the sun from across the galaxy because light travels faster than we do, and light from where the sun was would already have passed by.

37. Why is a star said to be "dead" when it becomes a white dwarf?
Possible answer: because it has lost most of its fuel and has become very small and dim

38. Why are older stars located at the center of a spiral galaxy, while younger stars make up the arms of a spiral galaxy?
Possible answer: because gravity pulls stars into the center of the galaxy, and younger stars haven't been around long enough to be pulled in

Answer Key

Unit D

Name _____

39. Why do scientists think that studying the sun helps us learn about other stars?
   Possible answer: because the sun is a main-sequence star, and most stars are main-sequence stars

Part IV Process Skills Application 4 points each

40. The solar wind disturbs compasses. What materials would you use to **model** this disturbance? Explain what you would do.
   Possible answer: a magnet and a compass; bring the magnet near the compass

41. Suppose a large solar flare has just occurred. **Hypothesize** about the presence of one or more sunspots in the area of the solar flare.
   Possible answer: There are many sunspots or a large sunspot near the area of the solar flare.

42. Earth's atmosphere deflects many harmful energy waves from the sun. **Draw conclusions** about why astronauts on a mission need protection from this energy.
   Possible answer: because astronauts are outside the protection of Earth's atmosphere

43. Sunspots appear to move across the sun's surface from west to east. What can you **infer** about the sun from this observation?
   Possible answer: The sun rotates from west to east.

44. A massive, hot blue star was formed about the same time as our sun. **Predict** which star will last longer. What information did you use to make your prediction?
   Possible answer: The sun will last longer because a star that is more massive uses up hydrogen faster than the sun.

Unit D • Chapter 2   (page 5 of 5)   Assessment Guide AG 107

Name _____

_F_ 10. The future plans of space exploration start with the completion of a —
   F space station   H Mars base
   G moon base   J warp drive

_A_ 11. The sun's energy causes which of the following on Earth?
   A thunderstorms
   B the oceans' tides
   C greenhouse gases
   D air pollution

_H_ 12. (2.1) Sunspots occur on what layer of the sun?
   F radiation zone
   G corona
   H photosphere
   J core

_A_ 13. The temperature of a star can be detected by its —
   A color   C orbit
   B distance D rotation

_H_ 14. Which of the following sequences is the correct order for the first five stages of a star?
   F nebula, red giant, protostar, main sequence, expanding star
   G red giant, nebula, main sequence, expanding star, protostar
   H nebula, protostar, main sequence, expanding star, red giant
   J protostar, nebula, main sequence, expanding star, red giant

_D_ 15. The largest group of objects in space is —
   A a solar system
   B a galaxy
   C the Milky Way Galaxy
   D the universe

_H_ 16. Which of the following is NOT a type of galaxy?
   F irregular
   G barred
   H regular
   J spiral

_A_ 17. The Milky Way Galaxy is —
   A a spiral galaxy
   B a barred galaxy
   C an elliptical galaxy
   D an irregular galaxy

_H_ 18. If you want to locate a galactic cluster in the night sky, you should look for a —
   F twinkling yellow star
   G red supergiant star
   H faint blur of stars
   J group of bright stars

Unit D   (page 2 of 4)   Assessment Guide AG 111

Name _____
Date _____

The Solar System and Beyond
Write the letter of the best choice. 4 points each

_C_ 1. How does the moon move in relation to Earth?
   A The moon revolves around Earth in a circle-shaped orbit.
   B Earth revolves around the moon in an ellipse-shaped orbit.
   C The moon revolves around Earth in an ellipse-shaped orbit.
   D The moon revolves around the sun, but not around Earth.

_F_ 2. Earth passes into the shadow of the moon during —
   F a solar eclipse
   G a lunar eclipse
   H nighttime only
   J a waxing crescent

_D_ 3. What exists on Earth but NOT on the moon?
   A aluminum   C craters
   B rocks   D air

_G_ 4. The moon appears bright in the night sky because it —
   F gives off its own light
   G reflects light from the sun
   H reflects light from Earth
   J absorbs light from the stars

_B_ 5. If it is 11 A.M. in New York, what time is it in California?
   A 5 A.M.   C 11 A.M.
   B 8 A.M.   D 2 P.M.

_F_ 6. The date is September 21, and there is an equal time of day and night. Which of the following has occurred?
   F autumn equinox
   G spring equinox
   H autumn solstice
   J spring solstice

_C_ 7. Earth has seasons because it —
   A revolves around the moon
   B rotates around the sun
   C is tilted on its axis
   D rotates on its axis

_G_ 8. Chunks of rock, perhaps left over from the formation of planets, are —
   F comets   H moons
   G asteroids J stars

_D_ 9. Which was used first by scientists to explore outer space?
   A satellites   C space probes
   B spacesuits   D telescopes

AG 110 Assessment Guide   (page 1 of 4)   Unit D

Name _____

_B_ 19. About 95 percent of the stars scientists have observed are organized into a band called the —
   A barred galaxy
   B main sequence
   C solar system
   D Milky Way

_F_ 20. What is true about the brightness of stars?
   F The closer a star is, the brighter it appears.
   G Brighter stars have hotter surface temperatures.
   H Red stars are the hottest and brightest stars.
   J The sun is the brightest star in the universe.

_C_ 21. The absolute magnitude of a star depends on —
   A its absolute brightness
   B its closeness to Earth
   C the amount of light it produces
   D whether you use a telescope

_J_ 22. Which of these energy waves are NOT released by the sun?
   F X rays
   G radio waves
   H infrared waves
   J microwaves

AG 112 Assessment Guide   (page 3 of 4)   Unit D

AG 184 Assessment Guide   Answer Key

Unit E • Chapter 1

Name _____

Answer in complete sentences. 4 points each

23. In terms of energy, how are we dependent on the sun?
    Answers may include: We get our energy from eating plants or animals, animals get their energy from eating other animals or plants, and plants get their energy from the sun. Or, without the sun, we would have no heat or light and everything on Earth would freeze.

24. Two stars have the same brightness when viewed from Earth. Is it correct to say the stars are the same distance from Earth and have the same temperature? Explain.
    Possible answer: The stars' apparent magnitude is the same, but their absolute magnitude may not be. Both magnitude and distance affect a star's brightness. As for temperature, color is a clue to the surface temperature of the star. Blue stars have the hottest surface temperature, and red stars have the coolest temperature.

25. What is the difference between a solar eclipse and a lunar eclipse?
    A solar eclipse occurs when Earth passes through the moon's shadow. A lunar eclipse occurs when the moon passes through Earth's shadow.

Unit D (page 4 of 4) Assessment Guide AG 113

Name _____

Part II Science Concepts and Understanding 3 points each

Write the letter of the best choice.

_D_ 15. Which of the following is **NOT** a physical property?
  A color   B density   C solubility   D reactivity

_F_ 16. When iron rusts, it no longer conducts electricity. This is because it —
  F changed chemically   H is in water
  G changed physically   J lost its luster

_D_ 17. The density of an object is a —
  A combustible property   C chemical property
  B reactive property   D physical property

_G_ 18. Weight is measured on a scale. Mass is measured on a —
  F thermometer   H barometer
  G balance   J scale

_B_ 19. Changing the shape and amount of a substance does **NOT** change its —
  A volume   B density   C mass   D appearance

_J_ 20. In which of the pictures below is a substance undergoing a chemical change?
  F I   G II   H III   J IV

I

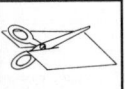
III

II

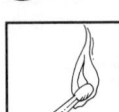
IV

Unit E • Chapter 1   (page 2 of 5)   Assessment Guide AG 115

Name _____
Date _____

Matter and Its Properties

Part I Vocabulary 2 points each

Use the letters of the terms in the Word Banks to complete the sentences.

A gas	C liquid	E mass	G matter
B solid	D volume	F weight	H solubility

All material that takes up space is called 1. _G_. The amount of material in an object is called the object's 2. _E_. An object's 3. _F_ is the pull of gravity on the object.

All material takes the form of a solid, a liquid, or a gas. A 4. _C_ has a definite volume but no definite shape. A 5. _A_ does not have a definite volume or a definite shape. A 6. _B_ has both definite volume and shape. You can measure the amount of space a solid object takes up, or the 7. _D_ of a solid object, by placing the object in a graduated cylinder with water and measuring how much water is displaced. Sometimes the ability to be dissolved, or 8. _H_, can be used to identify a substance.

I condensation	K density	M evaporation
J physical properties	L reactivity	N combustibility

A liquid can change into a gas. This process is called 9. _M_. A gas can also turn into a liquid. This reverse process is called 10. _I_.

Other 11. _J_ of substances, like color, size, and hardness, can be found without changing the substance into something else. You can divide the mass of an object by its volume to find the object's 12. _K_.

Chemical changes can turn substances into other substances. The ability of a substance to go through a chemical change is called 13. _L_. The ability of a substance to burn is called 14. _N_.

AG 114 Assessment Guide   (page 1 of 5)   Unit E • Chapter 1

Name _____

_B_ 21. A person's _____ is different on a high mountain than it is at sea level.
  A mass   C chemical property
  B weight   D density

_H_ 22. A solution is a type of —
  F balance   H mixture
  G matter   J combustibility

_D_ 23. Which of the following does **NOT** signal a chemical change?
  A color change
  B production of light and heat
  C production of a gas
  D change in state

_F_ 24. Making skim milk is an example of —
  F using physical properties to separate a mixture
  G using chemical properties to separate a mixture
  H solubility
  J combustibility

Use the following pictures to answer Question 25.

_A_ 25. What do the pictures show about the solubility of these substances?
  A Sugar is soluble in water, but pepper is not.
  B Pepper is soluble in water, but sugar is not.
  C Sugar and pepper have the same solubility.
  D If stirred, the pepper would have the same solubility as sugar.

AG 116 Assessment Guide   (page 3 of 5)   Unit E • Chapter 1

Answer Key

Unit E • Chapter 1

Name _____

H 26. Two similar-looking substances are burned. One produces a red flame, and the other produces a yellow flame. This is an example of—
  F a combustibility test   H a flame test
  G an indicator test   J a reactivity test

A 27. A pure substance always has ____ density when measured under ____ conditions.
  A the same; the same   C the same; different
  B a different; different   D a different; the same

Part III Critical Thinking   5 points each

28. How does the volume of liquid water change when it turns to water vapor? Explain.
  Possible answer: Its volume increases because the molecules are moving faster and spreading out.

29. Can water be used to separate salt from sugar? Why or why not?
  Possible answer: No, because both salt and sugar are soluble in water.

30. Describe what would happen to a cold empty glass if it was suddenly placed in a hot, humid room. Explain your answer.
  Possible answer: Water would condense on the surface of the glass. The water vapor in the warmer air changes to a liquid when it contacts the cooler glass.

Unit E • Chapter 1 (page 4 of 5)   Assessment Guide AG 117

Name _____

Part IV Process Skills Application   6 points each

31. Suppose you had 5 g of paper. You burned it and found that its new mass was 3 g. **Infer** where the 2 g of mass went.
  Student responses may include: The 2 g of mass went into the air.

32. Suppose two substances are combined. You observe bubbles forming from the mixture. **Draw a conclusion** about what is happening.
  A chemical reaction is taking place.

33. How do you **measure** density?
  by dividing the measured mass by the measured volume

AG 118 Assessment Guide   (page 5 of 5)   Unit E • Chapter 1

Unit E • Chapter 2

Name _____
Date _____

Chapter Assessment

Atoms and Elements

Part I Vocabulary   1 point each

Match each term in Column B with its meaning in Column A.

Column A		Column B
G 1. Center of an atom		A atom
D 2. Substance made up of only one kind of atom		B compound
I 3. Subatomic particle with a positive charge		C electron
A 4. Smallest unit of an element with all the properties of that element		D element
F 5. Subatomic particle with no charge		E molecule
H 6. Arrangement of elements by similar properties		F neutron
B 7. Substance made up of the atoms of two or more elements		G nucleus
E 8. Two or more atoms joined together		H Periodic Table
C 9. Subatomic particle with a negative charge		I proton

Part II Science Concepts and Understanding   2 points each

Write the letter of the best choice.

D 10. Atoms are held together by the attraction between—
  A protons and neutrons
  B protons and the nucleus
  C electrons and neutrons
  D electrons and protons

Unit E • Chapter 2 (page 1 of 5)   Assessment Guide AG 121

Name _____

H 11. The atomic number of an element is the number of ____ in its nucleus.
  F electrons   H protons
  G neutrons   J atoms

C 12. In the Periodic Table, elements are arranged by atomic number and—
  A color   C similar properties
  B size   D atomic mass

G 13. Which is **NOT** true of metals?
  F They conduct electricity.   H They are ductile.
  G They are good insulators.   J They conduct heat.

A 14. What is the formula for a molecule with 1 carbon atom, 2 hydrogen atoms, and 3 oxygen atoms?
  A H_2CO_3 C HC_2O_3
  B H_3CO_2 D H_3C_2O

Use the diagram on the right to answer Questions 15–17.

G 15. In this model, the I represents—
  F an atom   H a neutron
  G a proton   J an electron

D 16. The II represents—
  A an atom   C a neutron
  B a proton   D an electron

J 17. The III represents—
  F a nucleus   H a neutron path
  G a subatomic particle   J an energy level

Hydrogen Atom

Use the following formula to answer Questions 18–19.

$$MgCO_3$$

3 18. How many atoms of oxygen are in the chemical formula?

5 19. How many total atoms are in the chemical formula?

AG 122 Assessment Guide   (page 2 of 5)   Unit E • Chapter 2

AG 186 Assessment Guide

Answer Key

Unit E

Page 3 of 5

Use the part shown of the Periodic Table to answer Questions 20–22.

C 20. All elements listed in Column 18 of the table have the same physical state, so they are all —
  A liquids B metals C gases D neutrons

G 21. All elements listed in Columns 10–12 are —
  F liquids H nonmetals
  G metalloids J neutrons

D 22. What are the atomic number and the chemical symbol for silver?
  A 14, Si B 16, S C 52, Te D 47, Ag

Write the letter of the best choice.

J 23. If an element has electrons bound tightly to their atoms and conducts hardly any electricity, it can be used in —
  F lusters
  G transfers
  H ductiles
  J insulators

Page 4 of 5

A 24. Which of the following is true of all compounds?
  A They are made of atoms of two or more elements.
  B They are found in all atoms in nature.
  C They can be mixed with molecules to form liquids.
  D They react when combined with acids.

25. Write a paragraph using each of the following words in the correct context. 10 points — 2 for each correct usage

| alloy | conductor | ductile | insulator | malleable |

Paragraphs should relate all terms to metals or the properties of metals. An alloy is a mixture of metals. Examples are bronze, steel, and brass. A conductor is a material that can transfer electricity. Most metals are good conductors. Nonmetals such as glass, plastics, and rubber do not conduct electricity and so are called insulators. A metal is ductile if it can be drawn into wire, as can copper and aluminum. A malleable metal can be hammered or rolled into a thin sheet. Aluminum is a malleable metal.

Part III Critical Thinking 9 points each

26. Are protons from two different elements alike? Explain why or why not.
Possible answer: Yes. Protons are subatomic, so they don't have properties of the element.

27. If you added a proton, a neutron, and an electron to an atom, explain why the atom would not still be the same element.
Possible answer: An additional proton, neutron, and electron give it different properties.

Page 5 of 5

28. Would you want a plastic, a metal, or a metalloid handle for a metal pot? Why?
Possible answer: A plastic handle would be best; it does not conduct heat as well as the other two materials.

Part IV Process Skills Application

Use the following table to answer Questions 29–31.

Element Number	Symbol	Name	Melting Point	Boiling Point
1	H	Hydrogen	−259°C	−253°C
2	He	Helium	−272°C	−269°C
3	Li	Lithium	181°C	1342°C
4	Be	Beryllium	1287°C	2472°C
5	B	Boron	2027°C	4002°C
6	C	Carbon	3827°C	4197°C

12 29. Normal room temperature is 25°C. If the elements listed in the table are at room temperature, **infer** which elements are solids.
lithium, beryllium, boron, and carbon

6 30. **Observe** the boiling points of elements 1 and 2. **Infer** what state they would be in at room temperature.
gas

6 31. **Predict** the state of lithium at 50°C.
solid

Building Blocks of Matter

Write the letter of the best choice. 4 points each

B 1. What do all of the following have in common? water, wood, cement, animals, plants, glass
  A They are all found in nature.
  B They are all made of matter.
  C They are all made of minerals.
  D They are all living things.

J 2. You observe that a ball is red. What type of property is the red color?
  F elemental
  G chemical
  H organizational
  J physical

A 3. What do we call the measurement of the gravitational pull on an object?
  A weight C density
  B mass D volume

G 4. If an object has a mass of 100 kg and a volume of 2 cubic meters, what is its density?
  F 200 kg/m³ H 100 kg/m³
  G 50 kg/m³ J 10 kg/m³

B 5. You have two blocks of aluminum. One has a volume twice that of the other. Which measurement is identical for both blocks?
  A mass C volume
  B density D weight

J 6. Which is a characteristic of solids?
  F A solid does not have a definite shape.
  G A solid floats on water.
  H A solid takes the shape of its container.
  J A solid has a definite shape.

A 7. When water changes from a gas into a liquid, it —
  A condenses C boils
  B evaporates D melts

F 8. The melting point of table salt is 801°C, so its boiling point is —
  F greater than 801°C
  G less than 801°C
  H also 801°C
  J less than 500°C

Unit F • Chapter 1

Answer Key

Name _____

___B___ 9. Which is an example of a chemical change?
  A water boiling
  B a nail rusting
  C iron melting
  D glass shattering

___H___ 10. What occurs when two or more elements come together and make a new substance?
  F a physical change
  G a biological change
  H a chemical change
  J an elemental change

___B___ 11. Chlorine's ability to combine with elements chemically is known as its —
  A combustibility
  B reactivity
  C physical activity
  D mechanical ability

___J___ 12. Which has the chemical property of combustibility?
  F salt   H aluminum
  G iron   J charcoal

___A___ 13. In a chemical reaction, the mass of the products will be ____ the mass of the reactants.
  A equal to
  B less than
  C greater than
  D much greater than

___G___ 14. A subatomic particle with a positive charge is —
  F a neutron   H an electron
  G a proton   J an atom

___D___ 15. Which item would be considered an element?
  A sugar
  B water
  C table salt
  D aluminum foil

___G___ 16. Which of the following is NOT a property of a metal?
  F luster   H malleability
  G size   J ductility

___C___ 17. An atom's nucleus is made up of —
  A protons and electrons
  B neutrons and electrons
  C protons and neutrons
  D neutrons only

___F___ 18. What determines what kind of element an atom is?
  F the number of protons
  G the number of atoms
  H the number of neutrons
  J the number of molecules

Unit E   (page 2 of 4)   Assessment Guide AG 129

Name _____

Answer in complete sentences. 6 points each

23. Do all substances have a solid, liquid, and gas phase? Explain.
  Possible answer: No, some substances will skip the liquid phase. For example, dry ice sublimates, or changes state from a solid directly to a gas.

24. You are given a solid cube of an unknown substance. Describe at least three measurements you would take and which physical properties you could use to help identify the substance.
  Possible answer: You can measure the dimensions using a ruler and find the volume. Using a balance, you can find the mass of the cube. The density formula will give you the density of the object based on its volume and mass.

Unit E   (page 4 of 4)   Assessment Guide AG 131

Name _____

___B___ 19. What makes a compound different from an element?
  A A compound has only one type of element in it.
  B A compound has more than one type of element in it.
  C A compound always has more atoms.
  D A compound always weighs more than an element.

___G___ 20. The modern periodic table has elements arranged —
  F in order of decreasing atomic weight
  G in order of increasing atomic number
  H alphabetically by element name
  J alphabetically by chemical symbol

___A___ 21. Which type of grouping is used on the periodic table?
  A nonmetal/metal/metalloid
  B solid/liquid/gas
  C dark/light colors
  D heavy/light weight

___H___ 22. Which of the following is a compound?
  F gold
  G helium
  H water
  J carbon

AG 130 Assessment Guide   (page 3 of 4)   Unit E

Name _____
Date _____

Chapter Assessment

Forces

Part I Vocabulary 2 points each

Match each term in Column B with its meaning in Column A.

Column A		Column B
___E___ 1. Push or pull that causes an object to move, stop, or change direction		A work
___A___ 2. Use of force to move an object through a distance		B friction
___D___ 3. Force that pulls all objects toward each other		C magnetism
___F___ 4. A thing that makes work seem easier by changing the size or direction of a force		D gravitation
___G___ 5. Forces equal in size and opposite in direction		E force
___B___ 6. Force that opposes motion when two surfaces rub against each other		F machine
___C___ 7. Force of pushing or pulling between magnetic poles		G balanced forces
___H___ 8. Opposing forces of which one force is greater than the other		H unbalanced forces
___J___ 9. Value of combined forces on an object		I power
___I___ 10. Amount of work done for each unit of time		J net force

AG 132 Assessment Guide   (page 1 of 5)   Unit F • Chapter 1

Name _____

Part II   Science Concepts and Understanding   4 points each

Write the letter of the best choice.

___A___ 11. Which of the following is NOT a force?
- A newton
- B gravity
- C friction
- D magnetism

___G___ 12. What force causes a teardrop to roll down someone's cheek?
- F friction
- G gravity
- H magnetism
- J water

___D___ 13. What force slows a skateboard when a skateboarder puts a foot down to brake?
- A motion
- B magnetism
- C gravity
- D friction

___H___ 14. What do magnets have that acts on objects without touching them?
- F a power
- G a machine
- H a force
- J a current

___A___ 15. If two arm wrestlers exert a force on each other's hands and the hands don't move, the forces must be—
- A balanced
- B unbalanced
- C weak
- D strong

___G___ 16. If a refrigerator magnet can't hold a piece of paper against a refrigerator, the forces acting on the magnet must be—
- F balanced
- G unbalanced
- H weak
- J strong

___C___ 17. Two people try to push a 2000-newton crate, but it doesn't move. They have done—
- A 4000 joules of work
- B 1000 joules of work
- C zero joules of work
- D balanced work

___G___ 18. When you lift a 2-newton book 1 meter off of your desk, you do—
- F 1 joule of work
- G 2 joules of work
- H 3 joules of work
- J 4 joules of work

Unit F • Chapter 1   (page 2 of 5)   Assessment Guide AG 133

Name _____

___C___ 19. Which of the following can change the size or direction of a force?
- A friction
- B a magnet
- C a machine
- D speed

___F___ 20. A shovel is a compound machine made up of—
- F a lever and a wedge
- G a pulley and a screw
- H a wedge and a pulley
- J a screw and a wedge

Part III   Critical Thinking   6 points each

21. Suppose you are playing a game of catch with a friend. What forces act on the ball when it is in the air?

    Possible answer: When the ball is in the air, the forces of gravity and friction are acting on it.

22. Suppose a shoe on the top shelf of your closet falls to the floor when you open the closet door. How do you know a force has acted on the shoe?

    Possible answer: The motion of an object changes only when a force has acted on it. In this case, the shoe changed from sitting on the shelf to falling to the floor, so some force must have acted on it.

23. Which requires more work—running around the block or walking around the block? Which requires more power? Explain your answers.

    Possible answer: Walking and running around the block require an equal amount of work because they involve moving an equal amount of weight (your body) an equal distance. Running requires more power because you do the same amount of work in less time.

AG 134 Assessment Guide   (page 3 of 5)   **Unit F • Chapter 1**

Name _____

Part IV   Process Skills Application   4 points each

The following table shows data gathered when a dog chases three cats.

	Force Needed (Weight of Object)	Distance	Work (Force × Distance)	Time	Power (Work ÷ Time)
Cat 1	40 newtons	10 m	400 joules	4 sec	100 watts
Cat 2	55 newtons	10 m	550 joules	5 sec	110 watts
Cat 3	45 newtons	10 m	450 joules	5 sec	90 watts
Dog	100 newtons	10 m	1000 joules	10 sec	100 watts

___D___ 24. **Interpret the data** to determine which animal does the most work.
- A Cat 1
- B Cat 2
- C Cat 3
- D Dog

___G___ 25. **Compare** the animals to find which one uses the most power.
- F Cat 1
- G Cat 2
- H Cat 3
- J Dog

Use the following graph to answer Questions 26–27.

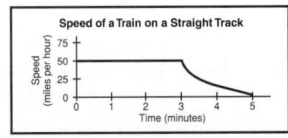

Speed of a Train on a Straight Track

26. **Interpret the data** to determine when the train's brakes started exerting force on the train's wheels. Explain your answer.

    At 3 minutes the speed began to decrease, so the data indicates that this was when the brakes started exerting force on the wheels.

27. What **conclusion** can you **draw** about the forces on the train during the time its speed stayed the same?

    Before braking, the forces on the train were balanced because the speed of the train was constant on a straight track.

Unit F • Chapter 1   (page 4 of 5)   Assessment Guide AG 135

Name _____

The following picture shows two plans for investigating the force of friction. Study the plans before answering Questions 28–29.   3 points each

How many blocks must you stack under the end of the board before the book begins to move?

Plan A — Trial 1, Trial 2 (Sandpaper)
Plan B — Trial 1, Trial 2 (Sandpaper)

28. Which of the two plans is a better **plan for investigating** the force of friction? Why?

    Plan A, because it uses the same book in each trial. The only thing that varies is the type of surface on the board. In Plan B the surface and the weight of the book change, so it is impossible to tell which variable caused any difference.

29. Study the better plan, and **draw a conclusion** about whether Trial 1 or Trial 2 will take more blocks to make the book move. **Hypothesize** why.

    Trial 2 will take more blocks to make the book move than Trial 1. The friction (resistance to movement) of the sandpaper is greater than that of the smooth board.

AG 136 Assessment Guide   (page 5 of 5)   **Unit F • Chapter 1**

Answer Key

AG 189 Assessment Guide

Unit F • Chapter 2

Motion

Part 1 Vocabulary   1 point each

Use the letters of the terms in the Word Banks to complete the sentences.

A velocity	C position	E speed
B momentum	D acceleration	

To measure the movement of an object, one must first locate the 1. __C__ of that object. The 2. __E__ of an object is the distance it travels in a given period of time. The term used to describe the speed of an object in a certain direction is 3. __A__. A change in the direction or speed of an object is called 4. __D__. A truck that is moving at a high rate of speed is difficult to stop because of its 5. __B__, which is a product of its velocity and mass.

F action force	I law of universal gravitation
G orbit	J reaction force
H inertia	

The first law of motion states that an object that is not moving will remain at rest because of 6. __H__. The force that you exert on an object at rest is called an 7. __F__. That object exerts a force on you, called a 8. __J__. An object in motion will travel in a straight line unless another force acts on it. An object in an 9. __G__ travels around another object as a result of inertia and gravity working together. According to the 10. __I__, all objects are attracted to all other objects.

Part II Science Concepts and Understanding   3 points each

Write the letter of the best choice.

__C__ 11. The first law of motion says that an object at rest will remain at rest unless —
    A it continues in a straight line
    B a nearby star acts on it
    C an outside force acts on it
    D it is placed on a flat surface

__G__ 12. According to the third law of motion, for every action there is —
    F a force sending it backward
    G an equal and opposite reaction
    H a greater force pushing on it
    J a movement in all directions

__C__ 13. When you observe an object, how do you know if it is moving?
    A Its mass and velocity change.
    B Its frame of reference changes.
    C Its position changes.
    D Its momentum changes.

__H__ 14. Suzette keeps her schoolbooks in a basket on the handlebars of her bicycle. When she rides, why do the books seem not to be moving?
    F Her eyes must be playing tricks on her.
    G Books cannot move by themselves.
    H From her frame of reference, the books are stationary.
    J From her frame of reference, the books are accelerating.

__D__ 15. If one car moves ahead of another car that is traveling in the same direction, do the cars have the same velocity?
    A No, they are traveling in different directions.
    B Yes, they are traveling in the same direction.
    C Yes, the direction and speed of the cars are the same.
    D No, the cars are traveling at different speeds.

__F__ 16. Do two skaters traveling in different directions at the same speed have the same velocity?
    F no, because the direction is different
    G no, because the skaters are different
    H yes, because the speed is the same
    J yes, because the acceleration is the same

__B__ 17. A train traveling on a curved track at a constant speed is accelerating because —
    A the train travels faster around a curved track
    B the direction of the train is constantly changing
    C the train's size will eventually slow it down
    D the clockwise direction of the train is constant

__J__ 18. The brakes on an adult bicycle must be stronger than the brakes on a children's bicycle because —
    F a child's mass causes more momentum
    G an adult's mass causes less momentum
    H an adult rider is farther from the ground
    J an adult rider will have more momentum

__C__ 19. What do the laws of motion explain?
    A how *frame of reference* influences movement
    B the relationship between the four basic elements
    C the movement of objects on Earth and in space
    D why all moving objects eventually stop moving

__G__ 20. Inertia explains why —
    F friction can be overcome for all objects
    G people in a car move forward in their seats when the car stops quickly
    H gravitational forces are stronger on Earth than on the moon or other satellites
    J the ground pushes against your feet when you run

__A__ 21. If an equal force acts on each of the following objects, which will have the greatest acceleration?
    A a golf ball   C a football
    B a soccer ball   D a baseball

__J__ 22. When a baseball player strikes a ball with a bat, the ball exerts a force on the bat. What is this an example of?
    F universal law of gravitation
    G frame of reference
    H the second law of motion
    J the third law of motion

__D__ 23. *Conservation of momentum* explains how —
    A a spacecraft can travel in space for thousands of years
    B a ball thrown into the air always falls back toward Earth
    C trucks slow down when they are traveling uphill
    D a pole can be knocked down when a moving car hits it

Use the following drawing to answer Questions 24–25.

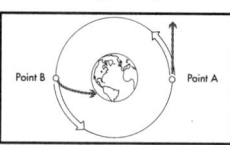

24. Draw an arrow to show what would happen to the path of the moon if it and Earth suddenly lost their gravitational attraction at Point A.

25. Draw an arrow to show what would happen to the path of the moon if its inertia suddenly decreased at Point B.

Part III Critical Thinking   7 points each

26. At the airport, Sam and Jose are trying to get to their gate on time. They are walking at the same speed. Sam takes the moving sidewalk, but Jose chooses to walk alongside. How can you tell that Sam is in motion even though he is standing still on the sidewalk?
Sam's position changes. First, he is located at the entrance of the moving sidewalk. Then he is at different positions along the sidewalk, until he finally gets off.

AG 190 Assessment Guide   **Answer Key**

Unit F • Chapter 3

Name _____

27. A clown is performing in front of a crowd. He is pretending to walk, but he is not actually changing his position in front of the crowd. Why can't we measure his speed?

Speed is a measure of distance and time. If the clown stays in one place, his distance will be equal to zero.

28. If Earth pulls on a puppy with a force of 2 newtons, what amount of force does the puppy exert on Earth? Explain why.

The puppy will also exert a force of 2 newtons because all forces exist in balanced pairs.

Part IV Process Skills Application 8 points each

29. The following observations were made of two cars traveling at various speeds and directions.

Car A: 30 mph, 45 mph, 20 mph, north, south, east
Car B: 50 mph, 30 mph, 15 mph, west, south, northeast

From the information above, **record** in the following table the **data** that will show both cars having the same velocity.

	Speed	Direction
Car A	30 mph	south
Car B	30 mph	south

30. What do you **hypothesize** would happen if you tried to make a shopping cart go around a corner by itself? Explain your answer.

The cart will not make the turn because it will continue in a straight line.

31. Suppose that you are a toymaker who **experiments** to find ways to limit the speed of battery-powered toy cars. **Identify** the **variables** that must be **controlled** in the experiments.

You will need to control the weight of the materials and the amount of energy provided by the battery.

Unit F • Chapter 2   (page 5 of 5)   Assessment Guide AG 143

Name _____

Use the letters of the terms in the Word Bank to complete the sentences.

A conduction	C convection	E radiation
B heat	D temperature	

The direct transfer of thermal energy between objects that touch is called 17. **A**. The mixing of a gas or liquid causes the transfer of thermal energy by 18. **C**. 19. **E** occurs when electromagnetic waves transfer thermal energy. 20. **B** is the transfer of thermal energy. The average kinetic energy of the molecules in an object is called 21. **D**.

Part II Science Concepts and Understanding 2 points each

Write the letter of the best choice.

A 22. What happens when you unscrew a light bulb in a series circuit?
  A All the lights go out.   C You get a shock.
  B All the lights stay on.   D The lights on each side go out.

G 23. Which of the following is an advantage that an electromagnet has over a regular magnet?
  F It attracts more types of materials.   H Opposites are attracted to each other.
  G It can be turned on and off.   J It requires an electrician.

C 24. If you grab the hot handle of a pot on a stove, you will experience —
  A radiation   C conduction
  B convection   D insulation

H 25. Which of the following is true of people who are farsighted?
  F They do not need glasses to read fine print.
  G They use concave lenses to correct their vision.
  H They use convex lenses to correct their vision.
  J They use conduction to correct their vision.

A 26. Which of the following is NOT an example of a release of chemical energy?
  A bouncing a ball   C burning wood
  B using batteries   D digesting food

Unit F • Chapter 3   (page 2 of 5)   Assessment Guide AG 147

Name _____
Date _____

Chapter Assessment

Forms of Energy

Part I Vocabulary 2 points each

Match each term in Column B with its meaning in Column A.

Column A

C 1. Iron bar with a coil wrapped around it that becomes a magnet when electric current flows through it
F 2. The result of a gain or loss of electrons
B 3. Loudness of a sound
I 4. Attraction or repulsion of electric charges
E 5. Piece of clear material that bends, or refracts, light rays
D 6. Energy of motion
G 7. Energy an object has because of its location or its condition
L 8. Flow of electrons
N 9. Bending of light rays
O 10. Material that allows electrons to travel easily
H 11. Path along which electrons flow
M 12. Material that doesn't carry electrons
K 13. Light bouncing off an object
J 14. Speed with which sound waves move
P 15. Material that slows the flow of electrons
A 16. Ability to cause change in matter

Column B

A energy
B volume
C electromagnet
D kinetic energy
E lens
F electric charge
G potential energy
H electric circuit
I electric force
J pitch
K reflection
L electric current
M insulator
N refraction
O conductor
P resistor

AG 146 Assessment Guide   (page 1 of 5)   Unit F • Chapter 3

Name _____

H 27. Which of the following describes how sound travels in space?
  F Sound is more intense.   H Sound cannot travel.
  G Sound travels farther.   J Sound bounces off of Earth.

C 28. Radiators in homes transfer heat by —
  A conduction   C radiation
  B convection   D insulation

F 29. Electric force is like gravitational force because —
  F both forces depend on distance
  G electric force increases when objects are far apart
  H electrons move in the same direction
  J electrons don't move in any direction

C 30. How do our bodies maintain a constant body temperature?
  A They convert thermal energy into mechanical energy.
  B They convert mechanical energy into potential energy.
  C They convert chemical energy into thermal energy.
  D They convert kinetic energy into potential energy.

G 31. Most of Earth's energy comes from —
  F Earth's center   H plants
  G the sun   J the oceans

A 32. Elastic potential energy can be found in —
  A stretched rubber bands   C concrete floors
  B bowling balls   D rocks

G 33. What happens when you twirl a jump rope?
  F You give it thermal energy.   H You give it potential energy.
  G You give it kinetic energy.   J You give it chemical energy.

D 34. Which of the following does NOT possess kinetic energy?
  A a pitcher winding up for a pitch   C a baseball moving toward center field
  B a swinging baseball bat   D a ball caught in a catcher's mitt

F 35. Which of the following is NOT an example of energy changing matter?
  F a baseball player that is about to hit a ball
  G a wooden baseball bat striking a baseball
  H heat from striking a ball warming the air
  J a batter running from home plate to first base

AG 148 Assessment Guide   (page 3 of 5)   Unit F • Chapter 3

Answer Key

Unit F • Chapter 4

Page 4 of 5 (Unit F • Chapter 3)

Name _____

__C__ 36. The law of conservation of energy states —
  A that energy cannot be transformed from one form to another
  B that transformation of energy happens only at low temperatures
  C that energy can be changed, but it cannot be created or destroyed
  D that energy can be changed only one time during one activity

__G__ 37. Which of the following best describes potential energy?
  F It cannot change form more than once.
  G It can be found in many forms.
  H It can be transformed by gravity only.
  J It includes electric energy.

__C__ 38. Electrons flowing through a light-bulb filament produce —
  A heat and sound   C light and heat
  B light and movement D movement and heat

Part III Critical Thinking

4 39. Compare the way a blue whale's song can travel hundreds of kilometers underwater to the way a human voice travels through air.

  Possible answer: Denser material carries sound energy farther and faster.
  Water is more dense than air. Therefore the blue whale's song travels great
  distances. The human voice travels through air. Therefore it is slower and
  does not travel as far.

5 40. Explain how a yo-yo transfers potential energy to kinetic energy and back again as it moves up and down its string.   Possible answer: As the yo-yo
  drops, it transfers potential gravitational energy (along with the potential
  energy of the spinner's arm) to kinetic energy in the form of spinning motion.
  When the toy is stopped by the string pulling on it, the kinetic energy is
  temporarily changed back to potential energy. As the yo-yo continues to spin,
  it uses kinetic energy to wind itself up the string to the top, where potential
  energy is restored.

5 41. When a cup of hot chocolate cools, is energy lost? Why or why not?
  Possible answer: Energy cannot be created or destroyed. The energy is not
  "lost." Rather, it is transferred from the liquid to the surrounding cup and air.

How People Use Energy

Part I Vocabulary 2 points each

Use the letters of the terms in the Word Bank to complete the sentences.

A tidal energy	D chemical bonds	G solar energy
B fusion energy	E nuclear energy	H biomass
C hydroelectric energy	F geothermal energy	

The energy of sunlight is 1. __G__, which can be changed into electricity and other forms of energy. In living things, this energy from sunlight is stored in 2. __D__ that join atoms of carbon to each other and to atoms of other elements in living things. Electricity generated from the force of falling water is 3. __C__. One form of this kind of energy, 4. __A__, depends on the difference in water height between high tide and low tide. 5. __H__, or organic matter such as garbage, can be burned for energy. Another source of energy, 6. __F__, comes from heat inside Earth. Yet another source, 7. __E__, comes from splitting nuclei of atoms. One source of energy that may be available in the future is 8. __B__.

Part II Science Concepts and Understanding 3 points each

Write the letter of the best choice.

__C__ 9. Which of the following happens when we burn fossil fuels?
  A Turbines turn to generate electricity.
  B Atoms break down to create hydrogen.
  C Molecules break apart and release heat.
  D We produce hydroelectric energy.

__J__ 10. Gasoline and diesel fuels are —
  F a primary source of electricity in the United States
  G energy sources found only outside the United States
  H renewable energy sources
  J energy sources for transportation

Page 5 of 5 (Unit F • Chapter 3)

Part IV Process Skills Application 5 points each

42. Study the following diagram. **Predict** what would happen to the angle of reflection if you increased the angle of incidence, and explain why. **Design an experiment** to test your prediction. Be sure to **identify and control variables.**

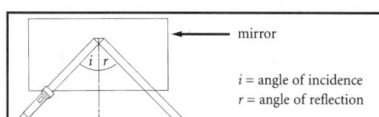

  i = angle of incidence
  r = angle of reflection

  An increase in the angle of incidence increases the angle of reflection. To test
  this hypothesis, set the flashlight at different angles, increasing the angle each
  time and recording the angle of incidence and angle of reflection for each.

43. Kim used a spring scale and a variety of rubber bands (same length, different widths) to measure the amount of force it took to stretch each band 30 centimeters. Use the following table to **compare the data** and **draw a conclusion** about the relationship between band width and the amount of force used. **Predict** how much force it would take to stretch a 3-centimeter-wide band 30 centimeters. When the bands are stretched, do they have potential or kinetic energy?

Rubber Band Width	Force Required
0.5 cm	0.25 newton
2 cm	1 newton
1 cm	0.5 newton
1.5 cm	0.75 newton
2.5 cm	1.25 newton
3 cm	

  The width of the band directly relates to the amount of force it takes to
  stretch it 30 centimeters. It would take 1.5 newtons of force to stretch the
  3-centimeter band 30 centimeters. When the bands are stretched, they
  represent elastic potential energy.

Page 2 of 5 (Unit F • Chapter 4)

__B__ 11. Fossil fuels can easily be —
  A renewed within a few years
  B burned for a variety of uses
  C used to reduce pollution
  D removed from the ground

__F__ 12. How do dams help produce hydroelectric energy?
  F They increase the water pressure.
  G They attract fish and other wildlife.
  H They decrease the depth of trapped water.
  J They help to control flooding.

__D__ 13. Which of the following is a disadvantage of wind turbines?
  A They don't generate electricity.
  B They create too much wind in the area.
  C They are unpopular with farmers.
  D They don't produce a constant flow of energy.

__F__ 14. The energy in fossil fuels that is turned into thermal energy when it burns is —
  F chemical energy
  G light
  H electric energy
  J heat

__B__ 15. The main source of energy for transportation is —
  A propane
  B petroleum
  C electricity
  D natural gas

__F__ 16. How do fossil fuels add to global warming?
  F They release carbon dioxide.
  G They release oxygen.
  H They make crude oil.
  J They cause nuclear fusion.

Answer Key

Unit F

(page 3 of 5) — Assessment Guide AG 155

D 17. The blades of a generator's turbine would **NOT** be spun by —
 A water
 B steam
 C wind
 D electricity

H 18. Which of the following releases the least amount of heat per kilogram when burned?
 F hard coal
 G gasoline
 H hardwood
 J propane gas

B 19. Burning garbage to make steam and then electricity is an inexpensive use of —
 A oil products
 B biomass
 C farm products
 D natural resources

H 20. Which of the following is a disadvantage of nuclear energy?
 F It requires too many engineers.
 G It uses too many nonrenewable resources.
 H It produces dangerous waste products.
 J It requires large amounts of fuel.

D 21. What do solar cells use to generate electricity?
 A steam, turbines, and electric generators
 B moving water, dams, and power lines
 C the movement of Earth around the sun
 D the freeing of electrons by sunlight

G 22. Geothermal energy occurs when underground water is near —
 F burning natural gas
 G magma
 H volcanoes
 J nuclear plants

(page 4 of 5) — AG 156 Assessment Guide

A 23. In what form do living organisms and fossil fuels store solar energy?
 A chemical energy   C kinetic energy
 B potential energy   D wasted energy

Use the letters of the terms in the Word Bank below to label the following diagram. 2 points each

| A electric generator | B dam | C turbine | D falling water | E power lines |

24. **B**   25. **D**   26. **C**   27. **A**   28. **E**

Part III Critical Thinking — 5 points each

29. How could attaching a greenhouse to a building help heat the building?
Possible answer: If the greenhouse were situated on the sunniest side, it could absorb heat during the day, trap it, and distribute it with fans or forced-air pipes to the rest of the house at night.

30. How could computer control of a wind turbine make the turbine more efficient?
Possible answer: A computer could point the blades into the wind and adjust the angle of the blades to keep the turbine turning at the maximum speed.

31. Why do you think there are fewer nuclear power plants being built today?
Possible answer: Builders of power plants have not been able to cost-effectively solve the problem of hazardous waste disposal.

(page 5 of 5) — Assessment Guide AG 157

Part IV Process Skills Application

4 32. **Compare** the data in the graphs below. What do you **observe** about the data?

Possible answer: The United States has the most reactors in use but reactors supply only about 20 percent of the energy used in this country.

5 33. Complete the table below to **communicate** the data shown in the two graphs above.

WORLD'S NUCLEAR POWER

Country	Reactors in Use	Approximate Percent of Country's Energy Supplied by Reactors
France	59	78
Japan	54	45
Russia	29	14
United States	107	20

5 34. **Plan a simple investigation** to determine the best spot in your yard or neighborhood to build a small windmill. Describe factors you would consider in picking the best spot. Then **devise an experiment** to determine the size of blades you should use. What **variables** should you **identify and control** as you conduct your experiment? Possible answer: The best location would be in an open area that gets the wind and that isn't in the way of family or neighborhood activities. The number of blades, shape of blades, material in blades, weather conditions, and height of blades should be identified and controlled.

(page 1 of 4) — AG 160 Assessment Guide

Motion and Energy

Unit Assessment

Write the letter of the best choice. 4 points each

B 1. If the north-seeking pole of one magnet is held close to the north-seeking pole of another magnet, the magnets will —
 A attract each other
 B repel each other
 C attract and then repel each other
 D neither attract nor repel each other

H 2. The force of gravitation is the strongest between —
 F small and large object far apart
 G a small and large object close together
 H two large objects close together
 J two small objects close together

C 3. If you push on a box and it does not move, the forces between you and the box are —
 A unequal forces
 B magnetic forces
 C balanced forces
 D unbalanced forces

J 4. If you push a cart with 50 lb of force to the left, and someone else pushes with 100 lb of force to the right, the net force is —
 F zero
 G 150 lb to the right
 H 50 lb to the left
 J 50 lb to the right

C 5. Which two simple machines make up a pair of scissors?
 A a wedge and an inclined plane
 B a lever and a pulley
 C a wedge and a lever
 D a lever and an inclined plane

J 6. If you lift a box weighing 50 newtons to a height of 2 meters, how much work have you done?
 F 25 joules   H 52 joules
 G 50 joules   J 100 joules

B 7. If it took you 2 seconds to lift a box weighing 100 newtons to a height of 3 meters, how much power did you use?
 A 50 watts   C 200 watts
 B 150 watts   D 300 watts

Answer Key — AG 193 Assessment Guide

Name _____

_H_ 8. Which has more momentum, a 300-kilogram motorbike or a 100-kilogram bicycle traveling at the same velocity?
  F both
  G the bicycle
  H the motorbike
  J neither one

_B_ 9. If an object's velocity is increasing, then —
  A its momentum is not changing
  B it is experiencing acceleration
  C its speed is decreasing
  D it is not moving

_J_ 10. Which of the following is an example of the conservation of momentum?
  F lightning striking a tree
  G throwing a dart at a dartboard
  H a surfer picking up speed while riding a wave
  J a complete transfer of speed between two balls

_C_ 11. If you push a chair with your hand, the force from your hand is called —
  A inertia   C action force
  B manual labor D reaction force

_F_ 12. If an object is moving in an orbit —
  F a force is acting on it
  G no forces are acting on it
  H it is moving in a straight line
  J it is rotating on an axis

_B_ 13. A car resting at the top of a hill has —
  A kinetic energy
  B potential energy
  C magnetic energy
  D thermal energy

_J_ 14. The stretched rubber of a blown-up balloon is an example of —
  F mechanical energy
  G thermal potential energy
  H gravitational energy
  J elastic potential energy

_B_ 15. Electric energy is created by the transfer of —
  A protons   C neutrons
  B electrons D atoms

_J_ 16. In order for current to flow around a circuit, the circuit must be —
  F coiled   H open
  G insulated J closed

_D_ 17. When a ray of light passes from one material to another and bends, it is being —
  A absorbed   C reflected
  B destroyed D refracted

_G_ 18. What can light waves travel through that sound waves cannot?
  F air   H water
  G space   J soil

Unit F   (page 2 of 4)   Assessment Guide AG 161

Name _____

Answer in complete sentences.

4 25. Can a car be driven at a constant speed and have a changing velocity? Explain.
  Possible answer: An object's velocity is its speed and its direction.
  An object can change its direction while keeping the same speed,
  therefore changing its velocity.

4 26. You are riding a roller coaster. Explain the forms of energy you have at the top of the first hill, at the bottom of the first hill, and somewhere in the middle of the hill.
  Possible answer: At the top of the hill I have a lot of (gravitational)
  potential energy, at the bottom I have a lot of kinetic energy, and somewhere
  in between the potential energy is transforming into kinetic energy.

5 27. Explain one disadvantage of using fossil fuels as a primary source of energy.
  Answer may include: Fossil fuels are a nonrenewable resource. We cannot
  use them forever. Burning them creates pollution and greenhouse gases.
  Resources are limited to specific areas on the planet and will run
  out eventually.

Unit F   (page 4 of 4)   Assessment Guide AG 163

Name _____

_A_ 19. Which word means the transfer of thermal energy from one substance to another?
  A heat   C potential
  B temperature D kinetic

_H_ 20. The transfer of thermal energy by electromagnetic radiation is —
  F conduction H radiation
  G convection J absorption

_D_ 21. Chemical energy is stored in fuels in the form of —
  A radiation   C electrons
  B thermal energy D chemical bonds

_G_ 22. Which of the following is an example of using fossil fuels?
  F drinking spring water
  G cooking on a gas stove
  H digging fossils with a shovel
  J eating olive oil on a salad

_A_ 23. A hydroelectric power plant converts the _____ into electricity.
  A kinetic energy of water
  B thermal energy of water
  C ionic energy of water
  D electromagnetic energy

_J_ 24. Which of the following is a disadvantage to using solar power?
  F The energy is directly converted into electricity.
  G Not much energy is produced by the sun.
  H There are many pollutants and byproducts.
  J Large solar collectors and cells are expensive.

AG 162 Assessment Guide   (page 3 of 4)   Unit F

AG 194 Assessment Guide   **Answer Key**